The Creed

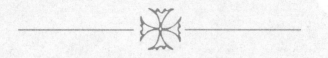

The Creed

WHAT CHRISTIANS BELIEVE
AND WHY IT MATTERS

LUKE TIMOTHY JOHNSON

IMAGE

DOUBLEDAY

New York   London   Toronto   Sydney   Auckland

AN IMAGE BOOK
PUBLISHED BY DOUBLEDAY
a division of Random House, Inc.

A hardcover edition of this book was published by Doubleday in 2003.

IMAGE, DOUBLEDAY, and the portrayal of a deer drinking from a stream are
registered trademarks of Random House, Inc.

The Library of Congress has cataloged the hardcover edition as follows:
Johnson, Luke Timothy.
The creed : what Christians believe and why it matters / Luke Timothy Johnson.
p.   cm.
1. Nicene Creed. 2. Catholic Church—Creeds—History and criticism. I. Title.
BT999.J64 2003
238'.142—dc21
2003043409

ISBN 0-385-50248-6

PRINTED IN THE UNITED STATES OF AMERICA

September 2004

First Image Books Edition

9   10   8

Contents

Preface

Like a lot of Roman Catholics my age (nearly sixty), I memorized the creed as a child and have recited it—first in Latin, then in English—every Sunday at Mass. I have been slower to appreciate what it is and what it does.

As a young theologian in the heady days following the Second Vatican Council, I understood the historical role of the Rule of Faith as an instrument of self-definition in early Christianity, but I had little appreciation for the present-day role of the creed. Indeed, I shared the common preference for an existential understanding of "faith as response" to God over "faith as belief" in God.

More experience of life, broader reading, and a growing awareness of the deeply confused state of contemporary Christianity have led me to the writing of this book and to the rejection of my earlier prejudice.

I hold as strongly as ever that faith in God is an existential response of the whole person characterized by trust, obedience, and loyalty. But I now have come to appreciate how critical the role of belief is in structuring that response.

And I hold as strongly as ever that the church is the gathering of those committed by faith to such a radical response to God. But I have grown in my appreciation of how important it is for the church to have a communal sense of identity, and how hard that is to come by without something like a creed.

The creed is remarkable for its concise rendering of the Christian story and the structure of the Christian vision of reality. It is an instrument that can at once define the community of faith and challenge alternative stories and visions of reality.

I never thought I would say this, but I have come to think that the creed may be the essential instrument needed for the church to regain a sense of its own integrity and to recover a healthier reading of its Scripture. This book offers the thinking that has led to that conclusion.

My thanks to the members of St. Charles Borromeo Parish in Bloomington, Indiana, who patiently endured an early version of these thoughts some fifteen years ago, and to my fellow parishioners at Sacred Heart Church in Atlanta, who received a more recent version with generous attention. Their eagerness to learn what they were saying every Sunday, and our joint discovery of how little we appreciated what we were saying when we said it, encouraged the writing of this book, which goes far beyond my adult education classes but owes much to them. I am grateful as well for the intellectual stimulation (I should say challenge) offered by my brother, Patrick Johnson, to whom this book is dedicated in the full knowledge that he will not be convinced by anything in it. As always, I thank my friends Barry Jay Seltser and Steven Kraftchick and Mary Jo Weaver for companionship along the narrow and winding path of inquiring faith. I am particularly grateful to Andrew Corbin of Doubleday for his patience in seeing this project through, and for providing much-needed editing. Last of all—and first of all—my thanks to Joy for all her years of love and support. She is the best of partners in faith.

Luke Timothy Johnson
December 29, 2002

The Creed

Introduction

Many Christians know that deadly moment at a party when their friends realize they actually believe something everyone has merrily been belittling. They recall their stammered reassurances, their tortured reinterpretations, their relief when the conversation moves on, their self-contempt. They may never have heard of Nietzsche, may not be able to define Modernity, and may think of the Enlightenment as a chapter in a first-year college textbook. But their embarrassment at being seen as believers reveals them to be Christians whose view of the world has been shaped less by the Christian creed than by its cultured despisers.

At least since the middle of the nineteenth century, being part of the intelligentsia has meant despising creeds in general and Christianity's creed in particular. Nietzsche speaks for many when he distinguishes those who inquire from those who believe. Intelligence requires us "to reason in a way diametrically opposed to the traditional one: wherever we find strength of faith too prominent, we are led to infer a lack of demonstrability, even something improbable, in the matter to be believed" (*Genealogy of Morals* 24).

For Modernity, belief in a creed is a sign of intellectual failure. Creeds involve faith, and faith makes statements about reality that can't be tested. Everyone knows that statements can be true only when they don't really say anything about the world or when they have been empirically tested. Creeds are therefore structures of fantasy. One cannot be both a believer and a critical thinker. Creeds also express convictions held by a group of people, and for intellectual elitists, the many is always a herd, and a herd will always believe what it is told. A creed negates the need for individuals to seek truth as a quest for authenticity. To be authentic, people must own each statement they make passionately and personally, and must accept nothing on the basis of outside authority. Better to stay silent than to speak a single word that is not a personal testimony.

For intellectuals in the West, it is the *Christian* creed that most offends. Nietzsche is again refreshingly direct: "In the Christian world of ideas there is nothing that has the least contact with reality—and it is in the instinctive hatred of reality that we have recognized the only motivating force at the root of Christianity" (*The Antichrist* 39). Christians are pitiable not only because they live by faith rather than by evidence, but because the faith they declare has so thoroughly been demolished by the evidence. This is the conviction lying behind all the raised eyebrows, averted glances, and embarrassed silences when the cultured cognoscenti find a committed Christian in their midst.

Isn't it obvious, these gestures suggest, that science has disproved each and every Christian claim? Adherence to them can be attributed only to an ineradicable (and probably insincere) social conservatism, invincible ignorance, or stupidity—and we thought you were one of us! If the Christian creed has been shown to be false, and even its adherents know that it is false, their willing submission to its herd mentality must come from intellectual laziness or psychological weakness.

AN EMPTY PROJECT?

Anyone setting out, as I am, to provide a positive reading of the Christian creed needs to be aware how inane, literally empty, such a project must seem to those who consider themselves Christianity's cultured despisers. To them, my effort must seem at best an irrelevant entertainment. At worst it must seem a willful exercise in bad faith, a far-from-innocent manipulation of people's hopes and fears by one who, by the very admission of knowing and appreciating alternative views, shows himself (they think) less than a true believer.

I could spend a great deal of time trying to justify my project in such eyes. I could suggest that faith in the face of doubt and uncertainty is as genuine as the skepticism the mind of Modernity approves—that it is one expression of that personal and passionate quest for authenticity it values. I could point out that life in the world is not possible without some form of creed, and that even the hardest of physical sciences now admit that they cannot demonstrate their basic premises but must accept them on faith.

And I could offer that there are more ways of knowing reality than the simple one ("Can it be empirically verified?") Modernity imposes, so that the truth of creeds *can* be tested by other criteria. But such arguments would not only consume the entire book, they would not have much effect, for cultured despisers are not likely to read this book and even less likely to be persuaded by an author who, after all, claims the Christian creed as his own.

Nevertheless, we should hold such cultured despisers constantly in mind as we consider the creed, for two reasons. The first is that the world shaped by Modernity is the world in which most Christians live, and the premises of Modernity are the premises running that world. Christians need to be aware just how little what they say they believe agrees with the world as understood by science and technology, commerce, law, politics, or the arts—or with the world as understood by many of their neighbors.

A second reason is that many Christians who recite the creed each week share the worldview of Modernity, but do not realize it. Thus, they sometimes reinterpret the creed along lines more palatable to that part of themselves that lives within Modernity. Making alternative views of reality conscious enables us to more clearly grasp what it is (we say) we believe and how it matters (or ought to matter).

The creed is also a source of controversy among Christians. A significant number of Christians reject any form of the creed. For some, especially in the Anabaptist and Free Church traditions, the creed is too much an instrument of ecclesiastical tradition and power, too much associated with the development of Christianity into Catholicism, too much shaped by philosophy and too little by Scripture. Such Christians, who view the Bible as an exclusive authority that individuals can understand by themselves, consider the creed to be an instrument of coercion rather than a glad confession of faith, a monument to the church's power rather than a movement of the Holy Spirit. For other Christians, a fixed structure of belief is less desirable than a good heart and an open mind. Creeds, they think, close minds and harden hearts.

A perfect marriage between Bible-based Christianity and the spirit of Modernity is found in those who reject the creed in the name of "the historical Jesus." The Jesus Seminar says, "The Christ of creed and dogma, who had been firmly in place in the

Middle Ages, can no longer command the assent of those who have seen the heavens through Galileo's telescope." The church "appears to smother Jesus," and its instrument is "the smothering cloud of historic creeds." The figure of Jesus in the creed is "a mythical or heavenly figure, whose connection with the sage from Nazareth is limited to his suffering and death under Pontius Pilate. Nothing between his birth and death appears to be essential to his mission or the life of the church" (*The Five Gospels*, 2, 7–8). The founder of the Jesus Seminar, Robert Funk, states emphatically that the creed "left a blank where Jesus should have come" (*Honest to Jesus*, 43, 303).

UNAPPEASED CRITICS

These critics will be as little impressed by my effort to provide a positive appreciation of the creed as the cultured despisers, and will be as little warmed by being shown that some of their criticisms are shared by Christianity's more radical disparagers. They will not be swayed by the gentle observation that the human Jesus, as a Jew of the first century, undoubtedly joined his community in the creedal expression of the *Shema* ("Hear O Israel, the Lord your God is One," Deut 6:4; see Matt 22:33–40), or by the quiet reminder that within the earliest church, the formation of brief creeds undoubtedly preceded the writing of epistles and Gospels and their eventual inclusion in Scripture (see 1 Cor 12:3). They will not accept the idea that the creed does not replace but rather stands in creative tension and living conversation with the other elements of Christian identity and tradition.

Those who set Scripture and creed in opposition to each other will not be appeased by the suggestion that the creed is, among other things, a guide for a reading of Scripture that accords with the experience of God in Jesus. Nor will those who identify a structured statement of belief with theological coercion readily acknowledge that in fact they rely on such statements implicitly even as they dismiss them explicitly, and that an open and public statement of shared conviction may be a less virulent form of theological tyranny than is sometimes exercised in the name of scriptural witness.

Yet it is important to keep such divergent views of the creed constantly before us. The critics remind us that there are real dangers in adhering to a creed. It can be accepted uncritically and unthinkingly. It can abet intellectual laziness. It can be used as a theological cudgel. It can replace the reading of Scripture and legitimate the embrace of a divine Christ that obscures his humanity.

A CONTROVERSIAL CREED

There are still other Christians for whom the creed is not controversial, mainly because they have not much given it serious thought, even if they say it every Sunday. Many Christians recite the creed as a regular part of their community's worship with little sense of its controversial roots, history, or position in the larger world. Some sleepwalk through the words they memorized as children, bothered not at all by the outrageous ideas to which they are declaring their commitment.

Others find elements in the creed personally offensive but deal with the scandal by freelance editing, passing over in silence or altering the statements they disagree with. Still others try to pay attention but find the creed simply unintelligible. Its language is far removed from the ordinary world in which they spend their days. They stumble through it as an act of piety because the church tells them to.

These are the people for whom I am writing. My aim is to make the creed controversial for those Christians who say it but do not understand it and therefore do not grasp what a radical and offensive act they perform when they declare these words every week in a public assembly. In other words, I want to make the creed more controversial rather than less—controversial for the right reasons rather than the wrong reasons.

I think that the Christian creed enunciates a powerful and provocative understanding of the world, one that ought to scandalize a world that runs on the accepted truths of Modernity. There is something in the creed to offend virtually every contemporary sensibility. At the same time, it communicates a compelling vision of the world's destiny and humanity's role that challenges the accustomed idolatries and the weary platitudes of current worldly wisdom. Christians who say these words should know what they are doing when they say them and what they are saying when they mean them. This is the precondition to their celebrating a specifically Christian conception of reality, and the presupposition for their challenging the dominant conceptions of the world where they should be challenged.

There is some point, then, to engaging the questions of why the creed is said at all, why it is said in the liturgy, and what it means in its parts and as a whole. A responsible answer to such questions requires some study of history and language, to find what its terms might have meant to the ancients who first used them. But it requires even more the study of theology, for the essential question we have to answer is not what the creed once meant, but what it declares about the world in which we now live, and how we might affirm it with sincerity and intellectual integrity.

Chapter One

ORIGINS AND
DEVELOPMENT

Before considering its individual elements, we do well to think about the existence of the Christian creed as such. Where does it come from? What does it do? Why do we still have it? By no means is it obvious, after all, that people should gather themselves into intentional communities with elaborate statements of what the members believe. The word "creed" comes from its opening word in Latin, *credo* ("I believe") or *credimus* ("we believe"). Not all religions even have creeds. Belief as such is not nearly so central to most other religions as it is to Christianity.

Many religions put more emphasis on orthopraxy (right practice) than on orthodoxy (right opinion or belief). Judaism and Islam each have created sophisticated systems of law to guide behavior, but have allowed an astonishing freedom of conviction and intellectual expression. Both have been able to get along with comparatively short statements of belief. Buddhism and Hinduism concentrate on the practices of ritual and transformation rather than on uniformity of belief. And tribal religions express their view of reality through a variety of myths, not a "rule of faith" for their members. What is it about Christianity that placed such peculiar emphasis on belief, and, given that emphasis, led to an ever more elaborate and official statement of beliefs in a creed?

In what follows, I want to show that the creed is not a late and violent imposition upon the simple gospel story—as some of its critics charge—but rather a natural development of Christianity best understood in light of the specific character of the Christian religion and the crises it faced from the start. I will try to show that the Christian creed began as a variation of Judaism's *Shema Israel*. We will see from Israel's experience that a creed takes its significance within a context of competing loyalties, the proper understanding of a communal narrative of experience, and serves both to identify the proper object of loyalty and to define the group that shows such loyalty. But the experience of Jesus as the resurrected one led his followers to a fundamental alteration in the narrative that they shared with their fellow Jews. With other Jews, they confessed one God, and so distinguished themselves from the polytheism of the Greco-Roman world. But they distinguished themselves from other Jews by professing Jesus as Christ, Lord, and Son of God, terms that later found their way into the creed.

This profession was rooted in deep religious experience. Indeed, in the early baptismal rites we see the close connection between the confession and first Christians' experience. I will then try to show that the creed became more explicit and elaborate in response to three challenges. The first challenge was to define the experience of Jesus within and over against the shared story of Israel. The second challenge was to clarify the complex understanding of God that was embedded in the resurrection experience. The third challenge was to correct misunderstandings of the newly emergent "Christian narrative" that was, at heart, a "story about Jesus."

I. ORIGINS

The Book of Deuteronomy contains an ancient rudimentary confession of belief known as the *Shema* (from its first word, "Hear"): "Hear O Israel, the Lord our God is one Lord. And you shall love the Lord your God with all your heart and all your soul and all your might" (Deut 6:4). The statement has three features of special interest. First, it is a call for communal, and not simply individual, commitment. Second, in the context of surrounding polytheistic cultures, it is exclusive: The Lord (the proper name of Israel's God, Yahweh) is both the "one" God and the only God toward whom Israel owes allegiance. Finally, it is a personal commitment: Israelites are to "love" the Lord God with their whole heart and whole soul and whole might. In other words, the *Shema* both defines the one to whom loyalty is given and defines Israel among all the nations by its unique loyalty to this deity.

The *Shema Israel* stands within the community's shared narrative of how God has been at work in the people. A compressed version of that story is spoken by the Lord to introduce the Ten Commandments: "I am the Lord your God, who brought you out of the land of Egypt, out of the house of slavery," from which follows the conclusion, "You shall have no other Gods before me" (Exod 20:2–3). The people respond with faith and obedience to the one who first showed love and fidelity to them. The creedal statement "The Lord our God is one Lord" does not replace their experience and story, but is its most compressed expression.

The Christian creed takes its origin in just this need to express a people's experience and story, and to distinguish their specific allegiance in the context of competing claims. It is, like the *Shema*, a call for communal, personal, and exclusive commitment. Christianity began within Judaism, and the *Shema* remained the basic framework for Christian belief as indicated by the clear allusions to it in the Gospels (e.g., Mark 12:29–31), Paul (Rom 3:29; 1 Cor 8:4–6), and James (2:19).

But the specific character of the Christian experience of Jesus made it necessary to alter the *Shema* and, with it, the story of God and God's people. Thus, the origins of the creed are easily detectable within the pages of the New Testament. Christianity was born not because followers of Jesus considered him to be the Messiah during his lifetime, but because many of them experienced him after his crucifixion and death as more powerfully alive than before, as sharing, indeed, the very life of God, a life that he in turn made available to them through the gift of the Holy Spirit.

The resurrection of Jesus was not regarded as a simple continuation of his mortal body through resuscitation—a historical event—but as a new form of existence as the "life-giving Spirit" (1 Cor 15:45) who could touch and transform all other human bodies. It ended one world and began another: "If anyone is in Christ, there is a new creation" (2 Cor 5:16; Gal 6:15). By virtue of his resurrection, then, Jesus is much more than a Jewish messiah; he is a new Adam (1 Cor 15:45; Rom 5:12–21), the firstborn of a new humanity (Rom 8:29; Col 3:11).

A careful reading of the entire New Testament suggests that the resurrection experience involved both Jesus and his followers, took place not only on the single day later known as Easter but continuously, and consisted of the presence of the risen Jesus among his followers through the Holy Spirit. Corresponding to the experiential dimension of possession of the Holy Spirit in the community was the conviction that "Jesus is Lord," that is, he now shares the life of God and is the source of the Spirit by which they now live (see 1 Cor 12:3).

The claims made about Jesus were extraordinary. A new sect gathered in his name, not because he was an effective political leader or a persuasive teacher, but because—despite his shameful and violent death by crucifixion—they experienced him as the source of a life that transformed the very structures of human existence. We can get some sense of this as we consider three of the designations for Jesus in the New Testament that find their way into the creed. By these designations—Christ, Lord, and Son of God—Jesus' followers distinguished themselves from other Jews.

JESUS IS THE CHRIST

Christianity takes its name from the claim that Jesus is the Christ (*Christos*), the anointed one or Messiah (see Acts 11:26). In first-century Judaism, calling Jesus "the Christ" (Mark 8:29; Matt 16:16; Luke 9:20) would have distinguished these "messianists" from other Jewish groups, but not because they challenged basic Jewish convictions. Many Jews believed in the coming of a messiah, after all. This leader or that could be considered a messiah without in the least threatening the unity of the people gathered by the *Shema Israel* (see Acts 5:34–40). Even if Jesus turned out to be a failed messiah—one who did not restore the fortunes of the Jews—neither he nor his followers would on this account have ruptured relations with Judaism.

If proclaiming Jesus as the Messiah did not by itself challenge Jewish convictions, proclaiming him to be the Messiah because of his resurrection did. This is what Peter does in Acts 2:36: "Let the entire house of Israel know with certainty that God has made him both Lord and Messiah, this Jesus whom you crucified." Many of Peter's contemporaries expected a future resurrection, and there is no reason why the Messiah should not also be among those who rise in the new age (Luke 20:27–40; Acts 23:6–9). But the claim that Jesus was already resurrected challenged Jewish convictions for two reasons. They believed the resurrection would inaugurate the age to come, the time of God's (and God's people's) triumph on earth, but Jesus alone was raised. The lack of any visible present victory for God's saints in this world is therefore evidence against the claim being made for Jesus' resurrection by his followers.

Even more important, Jews believed the resurrection would be the triumph of the *righteous*, but Jesus' life did not correspond to the prescribed pattern of righteousness in first-century Judaism. He did not observe the Sabbath (Mark 2:23–28; Luke 14:1–6), he reinterpreted Torah (the Jewish Law) without respect to the tradition (Matt 5:21–48), he neglected the temple tax (Matt 17:24–27), and he associated with tax collectors and sinners—people who deserved to be called "unrighteous" (Luke 7:34–8:3; 15:1–2). And decisively, the way he died—the legalized form of lynching known as crucifixion—was, according to the specific wording of Torah, a death cursed by God (Deut 21:23; see Gal 3:13).

In much of the New Testament, "Christ" appears so frequently as a title for Jesus that it has virtually become part of his proper name, "Jesus Christ" or "Christ Jesus." But with two important exceptions, language about Jesus as Christ plays little role in the earliest Christian efforts to express the experience of the resurrected Jesus.

The most noteworthy exception is Paul's statement in 1 Corinthians of "the good news that I proclaimed among you, which you received, in which you stand, and through which you are being saved, if you are holding on to the very word that I proclaimed to you as good news, unless you have believed in vain. For I handed on to you among things of first importance what I also received" (1 Cor 15:1–3a). Paul is concerned that his readers "stand within" and "hold firmly" this good news, as the condition of their being "saved by it." Getting the story wrong in its essentials amounts to "believing in vain." Paul summarizes the good news in the form of a narrative sequence:

> That Christ died in behalf of our sins according to the Scriptures. And that he was buried. And that he was raised on the third day according to the Scriptures. And that he appeared to Cephas, and then to the twelve, and then he appeared to more than five hundred brothers at the same time. Some from among them remain until now, but some have died. And then he appeared to James, and then to all the apostles. Last of all he appeared also to me, as to one born out of season. (1 Cor 15:3b–8)

Christos ("Christ") is the subject of this entire sequence. This passage is especially important because it will help form the heart of the eventual Christian creed.

The other exception is the use of the term in the first and second letters of John. Some believers do not have the proper profession of Jesus. Unfortunately, the precise nature of their error is not clear. 1 John 2:22 describes a straightforward denial that Jesus is the Christ, complicated by an implied denial of both "son" and "father." The implication is that getting Jesus wrong is also getting God wrong. 1 John 4:2 seems to describe a misapprehension of Jesus' humanity. It is less important that we grasp exactly what the ancient dispute was than that we recognize how, even within the pages of the New Testament, there is a concern for protecting the integrity of the experience of Jesus in all its fullness in the face of controversy generated precisely by diverse understandings of that experience.

JESUS IS LORD

This confession is most closely associated with his followers' experience of Jesus' resurrection (1 Cor 12:3; Rom 10:9; Phil 2:11). It is *this* conviction—that Jesus is Lord—rather than the confession that Jesus was Christ, that decisively separated early Christians from their fellow Jews. They were applying to Jesus, a failed messiah and cursed criminal, the very *name* that in Judaism had been reserved exclusively to the God of Israel!

The frequent use of Psalm 110:1 in connection with the resurrection indicates an understanding of the resurrection as an exaltation by which Jesus enters into a share of God's presence and dominion: "The Lord said to my lord, 'Sit at my right hand until I make your enemies a footstool for your feet' " (Matt 22:44; Mark 12:36; Luke 20:42; Acts 2:34; 1 Cor 15:25; Heb 1:3, 13). The close connection between the title "Lord" and language about the Holy Spirit points to the conviction that the risen one is present powerfully among his followers: "No one speaking in the Spirit says 'Jesus be cursed,' and no one can say, 'Jesus is Lord' except by the Holy Spirit" (1 Cor 12:3).

The complexity of this experience-conviction is suggested by Paul's statement in 2 Corinthians 3:17–18:

Now the Lord is the Spirit. And where the Spirit of the Lord is, there is freedom. And we all with unveiled face, gazing on the glory of the Lord, are being transformed from glory to glory into the same image, just as from the Lord-Spirit.

The close coordination in status and activity among God, Lord, and Spirit is suggested by Paul's final words in this same letter, "The grace of the Lord Jesus Christ and the love of God and the fellowship of the Holy Spirit be with you all" (2 Cor 13:14). The later creeds will seek to make clearer the relations that, at the experiential level, have no need of explication: this is all God's work among them.

The perception that the risen Jesus had become "life-giving Spirit" (1 Cor 15:45) and ruled as "Lord" meant that Jesus shared the life, the ruling power, and the life-giving functions of God. His designation as Lord also indicated his capacity to return to judge the living and the dead (Acts 17:31; 1 Thess 4:14; Rom 14:7–9). Here was a much more provocative claim than that Jesus was a messiah or even a resurrected messiah. Calling Jesus "Lord" after his death could only mean that divine status was being claimed for a human being. In Jewish eyes, this amounted to "having two powers in heaven," or committing the unforgivable sin of polytheism. It meant that Christians were breaking decisively with the *Shema Israel.*

The first sign of stretching the *Shema* to the breaking point is Paul's statement in 1 Corinthians 8:5–6. He begins with a clear reference to the *Shema*: "We know that no idol in the world exists and that 'there is no God but one' " (1 Cor 8:5), and he continues, "Even though there may be so-called gods in heaven or on earth—as in fact there are many gods and many lords—yet for us there is one God, the Father, from whom are all things and for whom we exist" (1 Cor 8:6). Up to this point, Paul is utterly consistent with Judaism, for which God was the Father of the people, the source of all things and the goal of all human striving. Paul and his readers stand with Jews against the idolatry of the pagans. Then Paul adds the conviction that identified Christians and separated them from Judaism: "and one Lord, Jesus Christ, through whom are all things and through whom we exist" (1 Cor 8:6). Paul's language is both dense and precise.

The care Paul takes in this statement anticipates the more elaborate efforts to clarify the relationship of God and Jesus that we will see in the creed's development. First, he recognizes that belief is subjective. In a pluralistic world of many beliefs, a commitment to one God and to one Lord is "for us," that is, "as far as we are concerned." Second, he maintains the supremacy of the Father as the one God, the creator and the goal of all creation. Third, he delicately locates the status of Jesus and his function as a combination of equality and subordination to God. For us, Paul says, there is one God *and* one Lord, but he separates "God" and "Lord" in a way that other Jews never would, assigning the name "God" to the Father and "Lord" to Jesus Christ. The simple "and," however, ascribes divinity to both, in contrast to the "many gods and many lords" of the Greco-Roman world.

The subordinate functions of Jesus as Lord are suggested by Paul's subtle use of prepositions. All things are "out of" and "for whom" God the Father, and "all things are through" the Lord Jesus—indicating a role in the creation of the world—while "we are through him," indicating that the Christians as a people are brought into existence through the death and resurrection of Jesus.

JESUS IS SON OF GOD

This title also emphasizes Jesus' share in God's life. By itself, the designation "Son of God" need not imply divinity. Scripture can use it to describe a human being who, by office or character, has a special relationship with God.

In the case of Jesus, the designation takes on special weight because of the resurrection, although the only time "Son of God" occurs in an explicit statement of belief is in Matthew's version of Peter's confession, "You are the Christ, the son of the living God" (Matt 16:16). Thus, in Acts 13:33, Paul applies the words of Psalm 2:7 to Jesus' resurrection: "You are my son; this day I have begotten you" (see also Heb 1:5). Paul makes the same link in the opening of his letter to the Romans, where he speaks of "the gospel concerning his son, who was descended from David according to the flesh and designated Son of God in power according to the spirit of holiness by his resurrection from the dead, Jesus Christ our Lord" (Rom 1:3–4).

With the designation of Jesus as Son of God, as with the confession of him as Lord, we catch glimpses of the early Christian experience of baptism. It is highly probable that already in the first generation, Christians made a profession of faith in the context of baptism that articulated the implications of their entering into the story of Jesus. He is God's Son, and in the Holy Spirit, they also become children of the same father by adoption. The title "Son of God" when applied to Jesus points to the new relation that believers have not only with the resurrected one but also with God, through the agency of the Holy Spirit. These reports agree with the explicit baptismal formula found in Matthew 28:19, "Go therefore and make disciples of all nations, baptizing them in the name of the Father and of the Son and of the Holy Spirit."

In his letter to the Galatian churches, Paul tells his readers, "in Christ Jesus you are all children of God through faith. For all of you who were baptized into Christ have clothed yourselves with Christ. There is no longer Jew or Greek, there is no longer slave or free, there is no longer male and female, for all of you are one in Christ Jesus" (Gal 3:26–28).

This baptismal experience of his readers is the context for the statement that follows shortly, "When the fullness of time had come, God sent his Son, born of a woman, born under the law, in order to redeem those who were under the law, so that we might receive adoption as children. And because you are children, God had sent the Spirit of his Son into our hearts, crying, 'Abba! Father!' So you are no longer a slave but a child, and if a child, then also an heir, through God" (Gal 4:4–7).

Here is a story into which the experience of the readers fits. By their ritual initiation into the messianic community through baptism, they are "in Christ," and thereby carry forward the story that God began in Jesus. In this case, Paul tells the story in terms of the redemption of heirs held under bondage by a Son who is sent forth by God to release (or redeem) them. In baptism, they have received the Holy Spirit of the Son, which gives them the status of adopted children (Greek: "sons").

They signal this adoption through the Holy Spirit by crying out (quite possibly during the ritual itself) *abba*. This Aramaic term (see also 1 Cor 16:22) used in worship must have been used by the first generation of Palestinian believers, and possibly goes back to Jesus himself (see Mark 14:36). Paul immediately provides the Greek equivalent, "Father." Given Paul's language elsewhere about "drinking the one Spirit"—also in connection with baptism (1 Cor 12:13)—there can be little doubt that he is here expatiating on the Galatians' ritual experience.

The ritual of baptism, in short, drew early believers into the complex set of relations that I have called the resurrection experience. Jesus is the Son who was sent by God as redeemer, and he is also the Son who provides them the Spirit. Because they have his Spirit, they are adopted sons, and can address God directly as "my father."

Paul combines the same set of convictions and experiences in Romans 8:14–29. Basing his statement on his readers' experience of baptism (6:1–23) and gift of the Holy Spirit (8:9–13), he declares, "For all who are led by the spirit of God are children of God. For you did not receive a spirit of slavery to fall back into fear, but you have received a spirit of adoption. When we cry, 'Abba! Father!' it is that very Spirit bearing witness with our spirit that we are children of God, and if children, then heirs, heirs of God and joint heirs of Christ" (8:14–17). He adds in Romans 8:29 that "those whom [God] foreknew he also predestined to be conformed to the image of his son, that he might be the firstborn of many children [Greek: 'sons']."

Because the origins of the Christian creed are easily detectable within the pages of the New Testament, the later development of the creed that I trace next should not be regarded as an invention of the post-apostolic church. Rather, the creed develops implications of the experience, the convictions, and the language present in Christianity from its birth. The experience of Jesus demanded a new telling of the biblical story, and the proper understanding of that story needed to be defined and defended.

II. SECOND- AND THIRD-CENTURY DEVELOPMENTS

In the second century CE, it is possible to catch glimpses of short professions of faith, which, even in their diverse expressions, show a steady movement toward an increasingly standard creed. Both their diversity and their agreement are important. The points of agreement tend to be the same elements of Jesus' story that we have already detected in the writings of the New Testament. The diversity reflects local concerns and rhetorical circumstances, and shows that although the early Christians felt the impulse to develop a creed, they were not concerned with uniformity of expression.

We don't have everything written by the Christians of the second century. I will survey five creedal formulas drawn from the writings we do have. They illustrate in various ways some of the impulses driving Christians to develop the creed.

Ignatius the bishop of Antioch is our first example. While journeying across Asia Minor on his way to a martyr's death in Rome (ca. 115), he wrote a series of letters to churches in Asia Minor and Rome. His pastoral concern was stimulated at least in part by what he perceived as dissension and deviance in these churches. Ignatius fervently championed what he regarded as the proper understanding of the faith. He especially targeted those known as Docetists, people who denied that Jesus shared fully and physically in the human condition.

In his *Letter to the Trallians* 9:1–2, Ignatius exhorts his readers, "Be deaf, therefore, whenever anyone speaks to you apart from Jesus Christ, who is of the stock of David, who is of Mary, who was truly born, ate and drank, was truly persecuted under Pontius Pilate, was truly crucified and died in the sight of the beings of heaven, of earth and the underworld, who was also truly raised from the dead . . ." His providing historical details from the Jesus story (naming David, Mary, and Pontius Pilate) and his emphasizing on Jesus' "truly" being born, eating and drinking, being persecuted, and dying show his concern that Jesus be known to have shared fully in the human condition.

A second example is the apocryphal writing the *Epistula Apostolorum* (ca. 150?). It also arises in the context of conflict over the proper understanding of Jesus among Christians, and also opposes those who deny the full humanity of Jesus. Declaring itself to be written by the apostles to the churches throughout the world, it contains dialogues between the risen Jesus and his followers. Of special interest to us is the very short statement of faith, five short phrases cited as an interpretation of the five loaves in Jesus' miraculous feeding: "They are a picture of our faith concerning the great Christianity; and that is in the Father, the ruler of the entire world, and in Jesus Christ our Savior, and in the Holy Spirit, the Paraclete, and in the Holy Church, and in the forgiveness of sins."

We find here not only separate phrases devoted to the Father, Son, and Spirit, but also a separate function attributed to each: the Father is ruler, the Son is savior, the Holy Spirit is Paraclete (the Greek word *paraklētos* means advocate or comforter). And for the first time, we find creedal statements concerning the church and the forgiveness of sins. Each of them will appear in more developed creeds. This brief but thoroughly "orthodox" statement of belief is particularly interesting because it is found within a composition that contains fairly extravagant and nonstandard speculations.

A third example is found in Justin Martyr's *First Apology* 61. The great apologist (martyred around 165) is defending the Christian movement to the Roman emperor, and this passage describes the manner of Christian baptism as it was practiced in the middle of the second century. Those who "are persuaded and believe that what we teach and say is true, and undertake to live accordingly" receive baptism "In the name of God, the Father and Lord of the universe, and of our Savior Jesus Christ, and of the Holy Spirit." Then, as the person who has repented is led to the bath, "there is pronounced over him who chooses to be born again, and has repented of his sins, the name of God the Father and Lord of the universe." In the actual washing, the other names are invoked: "And in the name of Jesus Christ, who was crucified under Pontius Pilate, and in the name of the Holy Spirit, who through the prophets foretold all things about Jesus, he who is illumined is washed."

The passage is important for two reasons. First, it shows how confession accompanied baptism. Second, it gives more evidence for the natural expansion of the elements of the confession. God is now "Father and Lord of the universe." Jesus is "Savior" and the one "who was crucified under Pontius Pilate." And the Holy Spirit is now the one who "through the prophets foretold all things about Jesus."

Our fourth example of early forms of the creed comes from an account of the trial of Justin and his companions before the Roman prefect. Like other examples of the *Acts of the Martyrs*, it takes the form of an examination of the defendants by the Roman authority. We see Justin bearing witness in a setting eerily like that of baptism. He will soon face the ultimate initiation into Christ that is martyrdom. It is preceded—and enabled—by his public profession of faith, this time not before a welcoming band of brothers, but before the gaze of a hostile inquisitor.

The prefect asks Justin what kinds of doctrines he professes, and Justin responds: "That according to which we worship the God of the Christians, whom we reckon to be one from the beginning, the maker and fashioner of the whole creation, visible and invisible; and the Lord Jesus Christ, the Son of God, who had also been preached beforehand by the prophets as about to be present with the race of men, the herald of salvation and teacher of good disciples."

Justin's profession of faith is powerful and poignant. The language he uses in his final confession is best understood in light of his historical situation, especially the debate with Judaism and the conflict with dualism. The expression "the God of the Christians" reflects the debate with Judaism. Justin wrote another book called the *Dialogue with Trypho*. It is a long debate between Justin and a Jewish leader named Trypho at the time of the final destruction of Jerusalem in 135 CE. The debate shows how separate a religion Christianity had by that time become.

The disputation revolves mainly around the proper reading of the prophets. The question to be answered is whether or not they foretold Jesus. We are not surprised therefore to see the emphasis Justin placed, as he faced martyrdom, on the prophetic utterances that were "preached beforehand" concerning Jesus. The "God of the Christians" is "one from the beginning" who also spoke through the prophets. The implication of this way of putting things is that the story of the creator God is properly continued in the story of Jesus.

The expression "maker and fashioner of the whole creation, visible and invisible" reflects the conflict with the dualistic heresies that were emerging in Christianity by the middle of the second century. One of the earliest and most influential of such heresies was Marcion's. He insisted on a radical break with Judaism. For Marcion, matter was evil, spirit good. There were also two Gods. The evil God of the Old Testament formed the material world in which humans find themselves imprisoned. Jesus, in contrast, represents a spiritual God who liberates humans from the bonds of material existence.

Justin knew and rejected the radical dualism of Marcion. His expansion of the confession concerning the creator God makes sense in light of this conflict. The one God is "maker and fashioner of the whole creation, visible and invisible." There are not two Gods, one the creator of evil materiality and the other associated with spirit. There is but one God who creates all.

The fifth and final example of a simple creed is found in Hippolytus of Rome's short treatise against the heresy of Noetus, probably written between 200 and 236. Noetus taught that Christ was so much to be identified with God the Father that we can say that "the father himself was born, suffered, and died." This doctrine is usually called "patripassionism" (i.e., the father suffers). When he claimed that his teaching actually glorified Christ, the elders of the church of Smyrna who had summoned him replied, "We too know in truth one God. We know Christ. We know that the son suffered even as he suffered, and died even as he died, and rose again on the third day, and is at the right hand of the Father, and cometh to judge the living and the dead. And these things we have learned we allege."

For obvious reasons, the part of the creed dealing with Christ is elaborated here in the form of a narrative. By declaring that the resurrected Jesus is now at the right hand of the Father and will come to judge the living and the dead, the Smyrnean presbyters distinguish the status and function of Father and Son both in the present and in the future. The effect is to suggest the same distinction in the earlier part of the narrative concerning the incarnation and passion.

These five fragmentary creedal expressions are fascinatingly diverse in form and function, even as they share a certain identifiable narrative. Specific elements are expanded or contracted in response to circumstances. We see in Justin that Christian initiation continues to involve a profession of faith, and in the context of persecution, profession can also declare a religious identity distinct both from paganism and Judaism. In Ignatius of Antioch, the *Epistula Apostolorum*, and the presbyters of Smyrna, we find elements expanded to respond to deviant understandings of the shared Christian story. Ignatius and the *Epistula* stress the reality of the narrative against those who think it merely a matter of appearance, whereas the presbyters of Smyrna stress the distinction between Father and Son against someone who blended them.

Toward the end of the second and into the third century, there is a more definite and concerted push toward a norm by which to measure "orthodoxy" (right teaching) and "heterodoxy" (false teaching). Two interrelated factors accelerate the process. The first and primary factor is that Christianity was increasingly an ecumenical or worldwide church with a desire to establish more coherence among its many local communities. The second is the increased sharpness of the challenge posed by dualistic versions of Christianity. Marcion is only one among a cluster of influential teachers often classified as "Gnostics" (the term derives from *gnōsis*, the Greek word for knowledge), who understood Christianity in terms of a saving knowledge and an escape from matter. The Gnostic challenge was real, widespread, and serious. The push toward a norm, in short, occurred as the natural result of expansion, but was intensified by deep internal divisions concerning the very nature of salvation.

I will survey three theologians whose work illustrates this push toward a norm by which to determine "orthodoxy" and "heterodoxy." In the work of Irenaeus, Tertullian, and Origen, we see how the creed expanded to meet the challenges to the Christian story and identity. A prime example of the orthodox response to the challenge of Gnosticism is Irenaeus of Lyons (120–202). He wrote *Against Heresies* around 180 CE to rebut Marcion and a variety of other Gnostic teachers. He begins his massive work by reciting a version of "the faith" that the church received from the apostles and their disciples. He insists that, though this orthodoxy was scattered throughout the world, the church believes "this faith and this preaching" as though "she had but one soul, and one and the same heart, and she proclaims them and teaches them, and hands them down, with perfect harmony, as though she had only one mouth."

His lengthy version of "this faith" resembles the creedal fragments that I have already cited, but adds the phrase "became incarnate for our salvation," which is critical as a response to the Gnostic position that God would not enter material reality and that people are saved by escaping their material existence.

Irenaeus also greatly expands the part of the common tradition dealing with the future: Jesus' manifestation, the general resurrection, the judgment, and the future life of believers (*Against Heresies* I, 10, 1).

The North African teacher Tertullian (145–220) refers in several of his works to a Rule of Faith (*Regula Fidei*) by which genuine believers live and against which the heresies of false teachers can be measured (see *On Prescription Against Heretics* 12, 19; *Against Marcion* 3, 1; 4, 5; *Against Praxeas* 2). Like Irenaeus, he emphasizes the fact that this Rule derived from the apostles and was handed down faithfully in the church (*Marcion* 4, 5). But the Rule of Faith also serves as a measure for Christian behavior that is "immovable and irreformable" (*On the Veiling of Virgins* 1).

Although Tertullian provides at least two versions of this Rule, they do not agree in their wording. For Tertullian, the Rule of Faith's antiquity and stability are compatible with flexibility in formulation. The shortest version is that given in *Veiling of Virgins*: "believing in one only God omnipotent, the creator of the universe, and His Son Jesus Christ, born of the virgin Mary, crucified under Pontius Pilate, raised again the third day from the dead, received in the heavens, sitting now at the right hand of the Father, destined to come to judge the living and the dead through the resurrection of the flesh as well (as of the spirit)." As we shall see below, this brief recital bears many points of resemblance to the so-called Apostles' Creed.

Origen of Alexandria (185–254) is the greatest of Christianity's early biblical interpreters, apologists, and theologians. He is most famous for *On First Principles*, a pioneering work of systematic theology. The name Origen is often associated with philosophical speculation—indeed, developments of some of his

positions, called "Origenism," were later condemned as hereti-
cal—but he was himself deeply committed to the life and the
practice of the church. For Origen, the Rule of Faith is the basis
and guide for theology.

Without using that term, he nevertheless deliberately begins
First Principles with a long statement concerning the elements of
belief that are shared and disputed among Christians. He notes
that Christians disagree with each other even "on subjects of
highest importance, as, for example, regarding God, or the Lord
Jesus Christ, or the Holy Spirit." Nevertheless, he says, since "the
teaching of the church, transmitted in orderly succession from
the apostles, and remaining in the churches to the present day, is
still preserved, that alone is to be accepted as truth which differs
in no respect from ecclesiastical and apostolical tradition" (Preface, 2).

His concern to distinguish between what must be believed
and what legitimately can be pursued as a matter of investigation
into the truth leads him to move through the "teaching of the
apostles" from what is most essential to what is most open to investigation. Thus, he states first what the church believes about
the "one God who created and arranged all things . . . the Father
of our Lord Jesus Christ," then he recites the basic narrative concerning Jesus, emphasizing, as did Ignatius of Antioch, that these
things really happened, and finally says that the apostles related
"that the Holy Spirit was associated in honor and dignity with the
father and the son," while leaving some questions concerning the
Holy Spirit unclear (Preface, 4).

Only after affirming his own allegiance to these basic beliefs
shared by the church does he move into the more disputed points
of doctrine concerning the soul, the devil, and angels, the origin
and future of the world, and the Scriptures. In Origen's opinion,

the apostolic teaching does not take up these matters with any consistency. The theologian is therefore free to investigate them.

III. ROMAN SYMBOL AND APOSTLES' CREED

Out of the process and pieces that we have examined, there eventually developed the standard form of profession of faith in the West that has come to be called the Apostles' Creed, which is still part of the prayer life of many Western Christians. Many Protestant Christians use this form of the creed in worship. Many Catholics use it in their life of prayer (for example, in the Rosary).

The earliest set form of this creed we have is found in the *Apostolic Tradition* of Hippolytus (ca. 215 CE). It takes the form of questions and answers. The context was undoubtedly that of baptism in the city of Rome. Here is the version given by Hippolytus:

> Do you believe in God, the Father Almighty?
> Do you believe in Christ Jesus, Son of God,
> Who was born (*natus*) by the Holy Spirit out of Mary the Virgin, and was crucified under Pontius Pilate and died and was buried, and rose on the third day alive from among the dead, and ascended into heaven, and sits at the right hand of the Father, to come to judge the living and the dead?
> Do you believe in the Holy Spirit, and the Holy Church, and the resurrection of the flesh?

The person to be baptized, we can safely assume, responded "yes" or "I do believe" (*pisteuō*). The creed is fuller and more complex than the one given by Justin Martyr. But we recognize the same basic narrative line that has run through all of the Christian expressions of faith concerning Christ.

Another version of this creed appears in a letter written to Pope Julius I by Marcellus, the bishop of Ancyra (ca. 340). His version differs from that given by Hippolytus mainly in the term he uses for the birth of Jesus ("begotten") and in his addition at the end of phrases dealing with the forgiveness of sins and life eternal. Marcellus had apparently been charged with heresy and presumably uses this formula to prove his orthodoxy in the expectation that it would be recognized by Rome as legitimate.

With minor variations, this Roman Symbol (as it is often designated) appears in the fourth and fifth century in several places at once: at the very end of a manuscript of the New Testament (Codex E); in an explanation of the creed by Ambrose, the bishop of Milan (339–397); in Sermons 213 and 215 by Augustine the bishop of Hippo in North Africa (354–430); and in Sermons 57–62 by Peter Chrysologus, bishop of Ravenna (400–450). These multiple appearances reveal the move toward standardization in the Western church.

The most noteworthy appearance is in the *Commentary on the Apostles' Creed* composed by Rufinus of Aquileia (ca. 404). Rufinus points out several instances where the version of his church differs from that used in Rome. So far as we can tell, Rufinus is the first to relate the tradition that this is the "Apostles' Creed," although the notion that the basic structure of belief was handed on intact from the apostles, we have seen, was common among teachers before him. Of greatest interest in Rufinus's version is the introduction of the clause "descended into hell": Jesus was "crucified under Pontius Pilate and buried, he descended into hell (*descendit ad inferna*), rose from the dead on the third day. . . ." The statement is apparently based on 1 Peter 3:18–20 and Acts 2:27.

Local variations in the Western creed appear for several centuries. The final, standard version of the Apostles' Creed, which owed so much to the Roman Symbol and was in turn finally accepted by Rome as its own, is attested in the seventh century:

I believe in God the Father almighty, creator of heaven and earth. And in Jesus Christ, his only son, our Lord, who was conceived by the Holy Spirit, born of the Virgin Mary, suffered under Pontius Pilate, was crucified, died, and was buried. He descended to hell, on the third day rose again from the dead, ascended to heaven, sits at the right hand of God the Father almighty, thence he will come to judge the living and the dead.

I believe in the Holy Spirit, the holy catholic church, the communion of saints, the forgiveness of sins, the resurrection of the body, and life everlasting. Amen.

NICENE CREED

There is less evidence allowing us to trace the development of the creed in Greek-speaking Christianity in the Eastern part of the empire. Examples of local creedal formulations are found in writings of the significant fourth-century teachers Eusebius of Caesarea (*Letter to His Diocese*, 325), Cyril of Jerusalem (*Catacheses* VI–XVII, ca. 348), Epiphanius of Salamis (*Ancoratus*, 374), and Theodore of Mopsuestia (*Catecheses* I–X, ca. 381–392). The most important form of the creed, however, was that produced by the first ecumenical council at Nicea in 325, which was intended to stand as a measure of orthodoxy for the entire Christian community.

The Council of Nicea was summoned by the emperor Constantine in an effort to unify the newly Christian empire that had been severely divided by the teaching of a presbyter in Alexandria named Arius (256–336). In defense of God's absolute uniqueness and transcendence, Arius argued that God's essence (*ousia*) could not be shared, for such sharing in nature would imply a division in God. The Word of God cannot therefore be fully God, but must be a creature that the Father formed, and as a creature, then the Word had a beginning and was subject to change.

The Word is called "Son of God," then, only as an honorary title, because of his participation in grace. He is God in name only. Arius used Scripture to support his position, but his approach to Christ was fundamentally philosophical and logical. Those who opposed Arius, above all the great bishop of Alexandria, Athanasius (295–373), defended the divinity of the Word above all because of their conviction that in Christ, it really was God who was saving humanity. They responded by describing the Son with a philosophical term, declaring him "one in essence" (*homoousios*) with God.

The theological controversy threatened the stability both of Christianity and of the empire whose glue Constantine wished it to be (see Eusebius, *Life of Constantine* 62–64). His summoning of a council of bishops from all over the empire to settle doctrine for the entire church may have been motivated by piety, but it was also very much motivated by politics.

The creed formulated at Nicea was an innovation on at least three counts. First, it clearly brought the church into a position of cooperation—it could even be argued co-optation—with the state. Second, it imposed a universal creed to take precedence over treasured local versions. Third, it used philosophical language within a profession of faith that was supposed to articulate the

Christian story in the language of Scripture. For these three reasons many Christians regard the Nicene Creed (and its developed version we use today) as an instrument of politics more than piety, of coercion more than freedom, of philosophy more than gospel.

Three responses can be made to these objections. First, the version of the creed enunciated at Nicea had very much in common with the creeds that had developed in a natural and organic way over time. Second, the schisms within Christianity had reached such a point that some unifying instrument was needed—the church was now catholic, after all, in the sense of being universal. It was more than a federation of local congregations, and needed a measure that could apply to all. Third, the traditional belief had been challenged in philosophical terms, and required a philosophical defense—though even now, philosophical language was placed within the context of traditional scriptural language.

The 318 bishops gathered at Nicea worked for months, and on 19 June 325 issued a creed in Greek with this wording:

> We believe in one God, the Father almighty, maker of all things visible and invisible;
>
> And in one Lord Jesus Christ, the Son of God,
>
> Begotten [*gennēthenta*] of the Father as only-begotten, that is, out of the being [*ousia*] of the Father, God from God, Light from Light, True God from True God, begotten not made [*gennēthenta ou poiēthenta*], one in being [*homoousios*] with the Father, through whom all things are made, things in heaven and things on earth, who, for us humans and for our salvation came down and became flesh [*sarkothenta*], becoming human [*enanthrōpēsanta*], he suffered, and he rose on the third

day, and having gone into the heavens, is coming to judge
the living and the dead.

And in the Holy Spirit.

Those who say, "There was a time when he was not"
and "before he was begotten he was not" and that he was
made from what was not, or that he was of another being
or substance or a creature . . . let the universal church consider them anathema.

The final lines reveal the thoroughly official and defensive character of the original Nicene Creed. Knowing that any formulation
could endlessly be debated and refined, the bishops tried to close
the loopholes by identifying precisely the kinds of affirmations it
was seeking to repel. Indeed, according to one of the participants,
Athanasius, the creed itself became increasingly complex as the
fifteen bishops from the Arian side sought such loopholes during
the time of discussion (*On the Nicene Synod*).

We can note briefly three significant aspects of this creed. In
contrast to many creeds before this, which began "I believe," and
thus emphasized the personal commitment of faith, the formulation "*we* believe" is deliberately communal, seeking to establish
shared boundaries of conviction. In addition, the distended character of the part of the creed dealing with the Son (with one line
given to the Father and a very small line devoted to the Spirit)
once more reveals the Nicene Creed as a *definitio*, an instrument
of definition in response to that particular part of the common
faith that was under challenge. Finally, the declaration "for us
humans and for our salvation" shows that it is really the integrity
of the Christian experience that is at question. For the orthodox,
if God was not really incarnate, then humans are not really saved.

By no means did the Nicene Creed stem the Arian

controversy, which became even more divisive over the following fifty years. The orthodox party rallied around Athanasius and the *homoousios* ("one in being") formulation for Christ. The "radical Arians," led by Eunomius, the bishop of Cyzicus, pushed even harder for a rational "explanation" of the relationship between God and the Word, reaching the conclusion that the Son is "un-like" (*anomoios*) the Father and is a creature. And if the Son is a creature, the Holy Spirit is also a creature.

Such radical teaching drew the great Cappadocian teachers (Basil, Gregory of Nyssa, Gregory Nazianzen) into the fray on the side of orthodoxy. Gregory of Nyssa summed up the conflict in this fashion: "The whole controversy, then, between the church and the Anomeans [the radical Arians] turns on this: are we to re-gard the Son and the Spirit as belonging to created or uncreated existence?" (*Against Eunomius*, I, 19, 56). In other words, is God truly experienced by humans in Jesus and in grace, or is it all merely a matter of psychological projection or psychic manipula-tion?

CONSTANTINOPOLITAN CREED

After a long period of instability in the empire, the Chris-tian emperor Theodosius I restored order and gave intense attention to the unification of the church under the banner of orthodoxy. In May of 381, he called a synod in Constantinople. One hundred and fifty bishops attended, all from the Eastern part of the empire, and all orthodox in persuasion. They approved a creed that substantially agrees with the Nicene Creed, but differs from it in two significant ways.

The most obvious is that it elaborated the dignity and role of the Holy Spirit in response to the radical Arians, but did so using scriptural rather than philosophical language. This creed also more nearly approached the narrative style of earlier creedal traditions, especially in the section dealing with the Son. As a result, the so-called Nicene-Constantinopolitan Creed is richer and fuller than the original Nicene Creed, and is better suited to liturgical recitation.

Here, then, at long last, is the text of the creed as it is recited in the liturgy in churches around the world today, and which is the basis for my commentary in this book:

We believe [*pisteuomen*] in one God, the Father all mighty [*pantokratora*], maker [*poiētēn*] of heaven and earth, of all things visible and invisible;

And in one Lord Jesus Christ, the only-begotten Son of God, Begotten from the Father before all time, Light from Light, True God from True God, begotten not made [*gennēthenta ou poiēthenta*], of the same substance [*homoousion*] as the Father, through whom all things were made;

who for us men and for our salvation came down from heaven and was incarnate [*sarkothenta*] by the Holy Spirit and the Virgin Mary, and became human [*enanthrōpēsanta*]. He was crucified for us under Pontius Pilate, and suffered, and was buried, and rose on the third day, according to the scriptures, and ascended to heaven, and sits on the right hand of the Father, and will come again with glory to judge the living and the dead. His kingdom shall have no end.

And in the Holy Spirit, the Lord and Giver of life, who proceeds from the Father, who together with the Father and Son is worshiped and glorified, who spoke through the prophets; and in one, holy, catholic, and apostolic church. We confess [*homologoumen*] one baptism for the forgiveness of sins. We look forward [*prosdokomen*] to the resurrection of the dead and the life of the world to come. Amen.

I have supplied the Greek for some of the key and disputed phrases, which will be taken up in my discussion of the various elements. I have also supplied the Greek for the three verbs, which distinguish between "we believe" (*pisteuomen*) for the most essential declarations, "we confess" (*homologoumen*) for baptism, and "we expect" (*prosdokomen*) for the future life.

In the West, a lingering concern for Arianism led to the modification of the declaration concerning the Holy Spirit. The Council of Toledo in 589 added the phrase *filioque* ("and the Son") to the phrase *qui ex patre procedit*, so that it now says that the Holy Spirit "proceeds from the Father and the Son." This innovation was one of the reasons for the estrangement between Latin-speaking and Greek-speaking Christians in the succeeding centuries.

CONCLUSION

The Nicene-Constantinopolitan Creed seems dramatically different from the Christians' first simple exclamation, "Jesus is Lord." Its complexity and philosophical formulation can easily be viewed as a betrayal of the gospel story. Yet, as we have traced its development from the New Testament to the end of the fourth century, we have seen the same impulses at work within changing circumstances.

The creed does not appear suddenly in history as an imposition from on high. It has been there from the first moments of self-definition, from the first impulse to articulate experience, from the first effort to defend against distortion, from the first attempt to summarize the story by which this new thing in the world claimed at once to be the people of the one God, yet touched more profoundly and intimately by God than humans had ever before imagined, in the flesh of Jesus, in the Spirit of the risen Lord.

Chapter Two

WHAT THE CREED IS
AND WHAT IT DOES

Every Sunday millions of Christians recite the creed. Some sleepwalk through it thinking of other things, some puzzle over the strange language, some find offense in what it seems to say. Perhaps few of them fully appreciate what a remarkable thing they are doing. Would they keep on doing it if they grasped how different it made them in today's world? Would they keep on saying these words if they really knew what they implied?

In a world that celebrates individuality, they are actually doing something together. In an age that avoids commitment, they pledge themselves to a set of convictions and thereby to each other. In a culture that rewards novelty and creativity, they use words written by others long ago. In a society where accepted wisdom changes by the minute, they claim that some truths are so critical that they must be repeated over and over again. In a throwaway, consumerist world, they accept, preserve, and con-

tinue tradition. Reciting the creed at worship is thus a countercultural act.

This quietly dramatic behavior deserves our attention. It is
worthwhile pondering what sort of thing the creed is and what
Christians are doing when they say it. The best way into the subject is through examining four terms that have been used for the
creed. Each points to a distinctive aspect. The four terms we will
examine are: profession of faith, rule of faith, definition of faith,
and symbol of faith. We will then examine what this profession,
rule, definition, and symbol do for the Christian community in its
worship and its life.

PROFESSION OF FAITH

The term "profession of faith" points to the way the creed
provides a statement of personal and communal commitment.
Faith is not science. Science seeks knowledge through description,
analysis, measurement, and prediction. Such knowing makes no
personal claim on the scientist. Knowing how a clam behaves does
not mean that you are personally committed to the clam. Science
seeks to be objective. What counts in science is not passion or commitment but verification. Scientists even dislike using the first-
person pronoun in writing. They prefer "it can be seen" to "I see."

Faith is just the opposite. It is always personal and subjective.
Faith cannot be verified by facts observable to all, because it deals
with realities that cannot be measured the way clams are measured, and because the realities it engages demand personal commitment. Faith that could be verified in the way that the basic
laws of physics can be verified would not be faith but a kind of
science.

Faith does not know a different world from the one measured and calculated by science, but it knows the same world differently. Paul says, "We look not at what can be seen but at what cannot be seen, for what can be seen is temporary, but what cannot be seen is eternal" (2 Cor 4:18). Such "seeing" demands a specific and embodied "seer." Faith's language is consequently not the scientific language of description, analysis, measurement, and prediction, but the language of "confession," "profession," and "bearing witness."

The New Testament is rich in such language. When Jesus declares that those who "confess" him he will also "confess" (Matt 10:32), the Greek term *homologein* suggests both recognition and personal commitment. Believers likewise "confess" that Jesus is Lord (Rom 10:9–10) and that Jesus Christ is God's Son come in the flesh (1 John 2:23; 4:2–3; 4:15; 2 John 7). Christian belief is a "profession" or "confession" (2 Cor 9:13; Heb 3:1; 4:14). Such confession is also called "bearing witness" (see, e.g., John 18:37; 19:35; Acts 2:40; 8:25; 1 Thess 4:6; 1 Cor 15:15; Rev 22:18).

If confession requires a personal commitment, how can we justify joining in a creed learned from the lips of others? Doesn't reciting the creed cancel authentic witness? Not really. Human freedom is always limited, not least by the many social roles we are expected to play. I am free, not when I am uninfluenced by any social role or obligations, but when I choose the confession I make.

Yes, the creed can be a sign of alienation, when its words mean nothing to me, or when I say them only to meet a social expectation. The creed is an authentic profession of faith when I find that the truth of my own experience in some measure corresponds to the words that I borrow from others to express that truth. It can be an authentic expression of freedom even when my experience at the moment does not seem to correspond with the words I speak. It is possible, after all, to place our bodies in witness to ourselves, as signs to ourselves, long before our thoughts and conscious desires have caught up.

Confession is obviously risky business. Because I can occupy only this place in the world and must speak from this particular perspective, I can never be sure that my perspective is true in any larger sense. I declare what is true "for me." But is it true for others as well? Other witnesses, speaking from other perspectives, will disagree with me. If people swear in court to opposite views of a car accident, they will surely also fight over matters of ultimate truth. I declare that God is real. But I am just as limited in my perspective as you are when you declare that God is an illusion.

And worse: to bear witness to the reality of God is to risk appearing foolish in the eyes of the sophisticated. Faith has, to be sure, its own ways of testing the truth of the creed. Is it consistent and cogent? Does it match the Scriptures? Most of all, what sort of life does it aid and support? It must be admitted, though, that such tests appear shabby and insubstantial beside the tests used by science. Medicines are tested by clinical trials and mathematical calculations are proven by the return of astronauts from space. Compared to the multiple and impressive ways in which scientific procedures find verification in our everyday lives—in every touch of the remote control and every casual scan of e-mail—the Christian's appeal to the story of Scripture or the lives of the saints to prove her creed seems pathetic and even a little desperate. To the extent that I also inhabit a world constructed on the basis of nonbelief, I risk appearing foolish in my own eyes as well.

The risk is greater than simply looking like a fool. I risk *being* a fool. When I bear witness, I risk my body as well as my mind. I might even die, as did Justin and his companions (see chap. 1).

But even when I recite the creed with others each Sunday, I expend my life in ways that cannot be recovered. If everything I say is false, I am wasting hours I could spend doing other things.

Can the presence of others reciting the creed and living this life beside me reduce my sense of risk? Yes, because their commitment can strengthen me in my own. Even flat-earth proponents gain strength from meetings. No, because the fact that many people agree with me does not diminish the possibility that we are all wrong and that I am a fool for joining them. I may still be a member of a flat-earth society.

Christian profession is therefore appropriately modest. Luther's famous statement, "Here I stand, God help me, I can do no other," is exactly right. We bear witness because this is the truth as we see it, or as we want to live it. We profess faith because from this place that our bodies occupy, the claims of the creed make more sense than not. But even when Christians make this profession together, the creed never turns into scientific truth. The Christian should candidly acknowledge that she speaks of things she does not fully understand, that she cannot demonstrate their truth even to her own satisfaction, and that many other people simply can't affirm what she does.

She should also remember that the profession of faith should not be taken as the entirety of faith. Belief and faith are closely related but n identical. Greek uses the same term for both (*pistis, pisteuein*), hile both Latin (*fides, credere*) and English use two separate terms. In its fullest sense, the New Testament term *pistis* ("faith" onnotes the entire human response to God, including belie rust, obedience, endurance, and loyalty. It is a response of the whole person. Belief refers only to the cognitive dimension of faith. Classical Christian theology has therefore distinguished between *fides quae* (the belief *that* God is one) and *fides qua* (the faith *by which* one responds to God).

Of what significance is this? One can hold a belief that something is true without letting the belief matter to one's life. The entire Christian creed can be treated as a set of beliefs that amount to no more than interesting opinions. This is the sort of "faith" that the letter of James scorns: "You believe that God is one. You do well. So do the demons, and they tremble!" (James 2:19).

Yet belief is not a trivial aspect of faith. Belief is both the condition for having faith and the initiation of faith. The letter to the Hebrews declares, "Without faith it is impossible to please God, for whoever would approach him must believe that he exists and that he rewards those who seek him" (Heb 11:6). Before one can "approach" God, one must "believe that he exists and . . . rewards." Approaching God stands here for the full response of trust and obedience to God's will. Without belief that God exists and rewards, however, one could never respond to him in trust and obedience. This is belief as the condition of faith.

But it is also the beginning of faith. Belief in the existence of God is more than agreeing to propositions like $2 + 2 = 4$ and "all systems tend toward greater entropy." Belief in the existence of God is already an act by which one "entrusts" oneself to a world that is not entirely defined by what can be seen and counted, heard, and accounted for. Belief is therefore not only the condition of faith but is also its beginning.

Finally, we must remember that we do not make this profession of faith alone. The Nicene-Constantinopolitan Creed recited by Christians every Sunday during the Eucharistic celebration begins "we believe." The formulation has several implications.

First, "we believe" says that in the creed we profess the convictions that bind us together as a community. We stand together and recite them in public. The creed in this form is a political statement: we declare that we are the people defined by these words.

Second, even as we say "we believe," we must acknowledge the different ways each of us actually believes. Each of us understands the statements of the creed in slightly different ways. Each of us holds it with different levels of intensity. Each of us lives by it with different degrees of integrity. On any given Sunday, I must admit that I am not sure how secure my conviction is that there is but one God, or (given my own tendency toward idolatry) how much my life reveals such a conviction.

Third, we also acknowledge that no one of us individually believes as much or as well as all of us do communally. The church always believes more and better than any one of its members. Does this mean that we act hypocritically when we say together "we believe"? Not at all: it is rather that we want to believe as the church believes, that we choose to stand together under these truths, in the hope that our individual "I believe" someday approaches the strength of the church's "we believe."

RULE OF FAITH

If the profession of faith points to the way the creed provides a statement of personal and communal identity, the second-century expression "Rule of Faith" (*Regula Fidei*) points to the way the creed provides a measure or norm for Christian identity, particularly how Christians should read their sacred writings and how they should live. The Latin word *regula* translates the Greek term *kanon*, meaning "a measure," or ruler. The same term is used for the authoritative collection of Christian writings, to say that these alone are the books that the church allows to be read in the liturgical assembly and uses in deciding the nature of Christian identity. It is not accidental that the same term was used for the scriptures and for the creed.

The creed provides a measure or rule for the proper reading of Scripture. Such a rule is necessary for a coherent communal understanding of Scripture. All Christians today are so shaped by the Rule of Faith (even when they are totally unaware that there is such a thing) that they do not recognize how wildly diverse readings of the Bible can actually be. Anyone who thinks that Scripture speaks clearly and unequivocally simply has not read it carefully enough. It is full of obscurity and conflicting views. Scripture therefore can reasonably be interpreted in many different ways. Many interpretations reveal the richness of Scripture. Others distort Scripture's witness. It may be a cliché to say that Satan can quote Scripture to his own ends, but it is a cliché supported by the Gospel accounts of Jesus' temptation (Matt 4:1–11; Luke 4:1–13).

How, then, can we tell one sort of interpretation from another? How can we distinguish between rich ambiguity and destructive deviance? In the second century, Irenaeus faced a challenge to Christian identity based precisely on a reading of Scripture that was both plausible and deeply subversive. Marcion of Sinope was a radical dualist who considered spirit good and matter evil. He argued that the creator God of the Old Testament was responsible for the disaster that is the material world with all its change and corruption. Jesus represented a good and previously unknown God who called humans to abandon their physical addiction and cultivate their spirit through fasting and celibacy.

Marcion claimed to get all these things from a sober and literal reading of Scripture. Does not Paul speak of the warfare between the flesh and the spirit (Gal 5:16–18)? Does he not say clearly that "it is good not to touch a woman" (1 Cor 7:1)? Does he not speak explicitly about the creator God when he says, concerning those who disbelieve the gospel, that "the god of this world has blinded the thoughts of the unbelievers" (2 Cor 4:4)?

To whom could he be referring, if not the creator God worshiped by those Jews who reject the good news concerning Jesus?

Marcion supported his entire dualistic and world-renouncing movement on the basis of these and many other scriptural texts. Marcionism claimed to be the real New Testament version of Christianity. The orthodox party, allowing marriage and demanding only moderate fasting, was a form of Judaism that had corrupted the pure gospel.

Irenaeus worked mightily—and brilliantly, it should be added—to refute each of Marcion's specific readings of Scripture. In the process, he established for all later readers the basic framework for interpreting Paul's difficult language. He demonstrated, through careful attention to the literary context of Paul's statements, that his words "flesh" and "spirit" do not signify a split between body and soul, but point to distinct ways of being human, living either in obedience to disordered passion (the flesh) or in obedience to God (the spirit).

But Irenaeus also recognized that such exegetical correction, however brilliant, was not sufficient to refute Marcion. The real force of Marcion's attack came from his overall interpretation of Scripture, the "code" that he said revealed what it really meant. Irenaeus saw that the orthodox needed in turn to make explicit their own "code for reading." This code is precisely the Rule of Faith. If it declares of God's Son that "he became flesh," it is impossible to hold that the flesh is evil, for God could not partake in that which is by its essence evil. When it declares that there is one God who is the maker of all things visible and invisible, it excludes the possibility of separate gods for separate realms.

The Rule of Faith guides the proper understanding of Scripture. It says that the two testaments do not stand only in a relationship of discontinuity but also one of continuity. It tells us that all created things are good, and that the one God is at work in all things. It does not exhaust the meaning of Scripture. It does not dictate how each passage of Scripture should be read. But it provides a code for reading that guides the faithful reader to the proper understanding of Scripture as a whole.

The Rule of Faith also provides a norm for Christian life. Humans tend to act in accordance with their convictions about the world. Of course, the relation between beliefs and actions is not absolute. We can, and often do, act contrary to our ideas. But this relation is nevertheless fundamental and important. If I think the world is a struggle for survival, I will distrust and battle everyone I meet. If I think that owning more means being more, and also think that there is only a limited number of possessions available, I will compete with you for these limited goods. On the other hand, if I believe that resources are infinitely available and that, in any case, no amount of having can increase being, I will share with you.

If people think that God creates the world, their life ought to reflect that conviction by thanksgiving, reverence, and sharing. But if they believe that the world is simply the result of accidental processes, they need not be grateful at all, but can take from others whatever they want and can get. Likewise, if they believe that God creates everything visible and invisible, they should refuse to regard or treat any part of the world as despicable or disposable. If Christians believe that the church is catholic, they should welcome diversity within the church. If they believe "in the resurrection of the body and life everlasting," then they should not act as if sustaining mortal life at all costs is a supreme good.

DEFINITION OF FAITH

The tradition also uses a third term, *definitio*, or "definition," for the creed. This word points to the way the creed provides the boundaries of Christian belief and therefore of the Christian community. To "define" means to draw a line around something, setting the limits between it and everything else. A definition excludes even as it includes. The definition of a square includes all rectangles of four even sides, whether large or small, but at the same time excludes all trapezoids and rhomboids and pentagons. The creed similarly defines the boundaries of Christian belief. In the process it also sets the boundaries of the Christian community. When I affirm its propositions I publicly identify myself with the community that is defined by them. When I deny these statements, I exclude myself from that community.

The defining character of the Christian creed was implicit from the beginning. Declaring that "Jesus is Messiah" denies that anyone else is Messiah (Matt 16:16). Proclaiming that "Jesus is Lord" denies lordship to all others (1 Cor 8:5–6). For 1 John, "confessing" and "denying" the truth about Jesus indicates who really belongs to the community of the beloved disciple (1 John 2:22–23; 4:2–4). We saw in the last chapter how the creed's development involved making affirmations more explicit and "definite." Earlier creeds are closer to piety because they have not yet been intellectually challenged. Later creeds increasingly become definitions in response to intellectual challenge. Against Marcion's cosmological dualism, for example, it became necessary to add that God is the creator of all things both visible and invisible. The line had to be drawn more clearly to definitively exclude Marcionite views.

The Arian controversy of the fourth century prompted the use of even more precise language to protect the integrity of Christian confession—and, above all, the logic of Christian piety. The Arians said that the Word of God is only a creature, and Jesus is not really the incarnate God. If this is true, all prayer and obedience directed to him is profoundly in error. Philosophical language entered the creed's description of the Son because that was the idiom used by Arianism to deny his equality with the Father. Scripture's language about Jesus as the "only begotten" (*monogenēs*) was too ambiguous. It was necessary to "define" the truth of piety more closely—to draw the line more closely—by stating that he was "one in being" (*homoousios*) with the Father and "begotten not made" (*gennētos ou genetos*).

The defining function of the creed remains important today. The Christian people affirm specific things as the truths by which they seek to live. They implicitly reject other things that other people might consider to be true. By believing definite things the Christian people become definite as well. It is a people that choose to declare and live by certain convictions and not others. Being Christian is not simply a matter of having certain attitudes or dispositions. It is a matter of living according to a specific view of the world and maintaining allegiance to the practices of the community that seeks to live according to that vision of reality. Christians cannot therefore agree with everyone about everything. To be a creedal Christian means inevitably to be a controversialist.

The term "definition" also suggests two limits to what the creed can do. First, even while establishing boundaries for and around the Christian people, the creed does not exhaust the meaning of Christian life and practice. Defining an equilateral triangle as one with three equal sides says pretty much everything, but it does not determine all the ways in which that figure might be put to use. The "definition" of a sport like baseball—which is found primarily in its rules—distinguishes the game from other team sports played with balls, but does not exhaust the possibilities of excitement, valor, excellence, and failure inherent in the sport as actually played. Within the rules, baseball can be played in distinctive ways and at many levels of competence. The creed defines the playing field for the game of Christianity, but by no means exhausts the possibilities for playing the game.

Second, still less can the creed "define" God or God's work in the world. God is not an object we can define. God has the maker's knowledge of the world, but humans do not have a maker's knowledge of God. Everything that humans can say about God comes through the process of God's self-disclosure in and through the world, a process that always remains elusive and uncontrollable—even, or perhaps especially, to thought. Christians believe that what they say in the creed is truth. They must also know that they cannot account for this truth, but must rather be accountable to it.

SYMBOL OF FAITH

The fourth term that has been used for the creed is the noun "symbol," which comes from the Greek verb *symballein*, used for the joining together of two objects (a ring, tablets, seals) as a sign of recognition and reception of others, and therefore as signifying a treaty. This term points to the way the creed provides a sign of reception and membership, and a way of affirming the community's shared story.

In the early church, the creed was referred to as a *symbolum* because it was handed over to those being initiated into the community as a sign of their reception. Together with the Lord's Prayer and other practices of the community that were kept from catechumens until they had been instructed properly, the creed thus "symbolized" the faith both of the church and of those being initiated, as they joined themselves together in the ritual of baptism.

The creed is a symbol of faith in the first instance, then,

because it provides a mutual sign of recognition between the believer and the faith community. The newcomer asserts what the community already holds true, and by that assertion identifies himself or herself as one who belongs to the faith community.

The creed is also a symbol in the sense that the spoken words point to and participate in the response of belief and commitment that they enunciate. When we say "Jesus is Lord," we are not making a general statement about reality, as if we were saying "Elizabeth is Queen of England." We affirm a personal commitment to Jesus' lordship with regard to ourselves. Jesus is *our* lord, whom we serve in our hearts and lives. The creed symbolizes this commitment.

Over time, the term "symbol" expanded to the sacraments of the church, classically defined as signs that affect what they signify. The gestures and words of the sacramental signs point beyond themselves. They open us to a deeper reality in which they participate. The Eucharist, for example, is a meal. The sharing of bread and wine symbolizes life together. But it also points to a participation in the body and blood of the Lord, who gave himself symbolically at his last meal with his disciples, before giving himself actually in his death on the cross. Ritual gestures like the sign of the cross are also symbolic. Tracing the cross on oneself is not an arbitrary sign of membership (like a secret handshake), but an invocation of the reality of the life of discipleship in the path of the crucified Messiah Jesus.

Is the creed also symbolic in this sense: that it participates in the realities of which it speaks? Here we need to pause a bit and think about the severe limitations of human language, particularly when we speak about God.

Let us begin with the candid recognition that all properly religious language claims more than it can demonstrate, define, or even understand. Although Paul says that Christians have been given "the mind of Christ" (1 Cor 2:26), he means only that Christians have been shown how to think about their lives in the pattern of Jesus the Messiah, not that they have been given the power to know the full mystery of God. Note how carefully Paul corrects himself in Galatians 4:9. He starts by saying, "Now that you have come to know God," but then adds, "or better, that you have come to be known by God." Again, in 1 Corinthians 8:2, Paul says, "If anyone thinks he knows something, he has not yet known as he should know. But if anyone loves God, this person is known by him."

For this reason, religious language is better regarded as mythic rather than as historical or as scientific. "Myth" does not mean "made up" or "untrue." Myth is language seeking to express a truth about the world and humans that lies beyond what we can test and prove. It seeks to express the basic truths of human existence: where do we come from, why are we here, and where are we going?

When Paul says, "God was in Christ reconciling the world to himself" (2 Cor 5:19), he speaks mythically. His terms "Christ" and "world" point to empirical realities. But their meaning is so dependent on a specific human story that they cannot be analyzed historically or scientifically. The terms "God" and "in Christ" and "reconciling . . . to himself" are beyond even the possibility of being demonstrated. God is not an object we can locate and measure. Reconciliation with God is not capable of being tested. Without such mythic language, Christians could not say anything about the world's origin or destiny in God.

Myth finds its natural expression in narrative, and the creed itself tells a simple story. It begins with God's work of creation and moves (in chronological order) through the Spirit's inspiration of the prophets, the Son's birth, suffering, and death for the sake of humans, his resurrection, ascension, and return as judge, and the inclusion of Christians into this story through their baptism, and their expectation of eternal life. Because God is the main character in this story, it is, in the most proper sense, mythic. Christians are, therefore, people who claim to live within a story whose protagonist is God—a character whose very existence cannot be demonstrated by the means of knowing most respected by the world.

But the real problem of the creed's language is not that it is mythic. The real problem is that its subject matter cannot be adequately expressed by any language, even that of myth. How can Christians responsibly mouth these words when in the strictest sense they do not know what they are saying? The real problem, then, is one of intellectual integrity.

It is just on this point that the Christian theological tradition is especially helpful. Theologians have tried to respect the distance between their language and their subject matter (the invisible God) by making a critical distinction between positive and negative ways of speaking about God, and insisting that we must use both to speak truly.

The tradition says first that we can speak of God in positive terms as though God were a character in the world. This is exactly what myth does. Theologians call this sort of speech "affirmative" or "kataphatic." But this language can distort reality when it is applied univocally to God as it is applied to people. Humans in touch with their own existence, for example, can properly speak of God as their "maker." But God is surely not to be understood as making heaven and earth in the way a watchmaker constructs a timepiece, or a carpenter builds a house. To speak only "affirmatively" about God runs the risk of creating God in our own likeness, to engage in a sort of verbal idolatry.

The theological tradition therefore demands that we also speak of God in a second way, called "negative" or "apophatic."

In this way, the positive affirmation we can legitimately make is nevertheless denied. The denial derives from the conviction that God's absolute otherness demands silence rather than description. In the apophatic way, we respond to the positive affirmation that "God is maker of heaven and earth" with the denial that "God is not the maker of heaven and earth in any manner known to us." The denial serves to protect us from reducing God to the level of our human ideas.

The positive and negative moments are joined dialectically in the third way of speaking about God, which the tradition calls "analogical." In this way, statements about God can be considered as true, but true in a way different from the way they are true in the case of creatures. In analogy, two things are both alike and unlike, but are more unlike than alike. Thus, we can say that God is "maker," but in a manner that is as much unlike as like the way humans are "makers." Analogical speech preserves the truth of the positive affirmation ("God is maker") and of the negative ("God is not maker"). Analogy helps solve a real problem with the creed's language because it enables us to see how we can say the words even though in the strictest sense we don't know what we are saying. Even as we affirm the statements of the creed as true, we know that they point to a reality beyond our understanding. We profess our faith not in the words but in the reality to which they point.

Another way of looking at the creed's language is as a set of "critical theological concepts." These are propositions we cannot explain or define, but whose denial leads to the distortion or loss of other truths. They are propositions that serve as conditions and controls for other truths.

I cannot prove that God is "maker of all things." And I certainly cannot explain *how* God makes all things. But if I deny this claim, I distort or even lose other truths about the nature of the world and our relation to it. I see the world as an instrument or plaything rather than a gift to be received in gratitude and awe. If it is not made by God, the world is mine to construct according to my desires and projects. Yet this attitude is named in the Bible as idolatry. It leads to a distortion of human relations and the use of the world. We accept the claim that God is "maker of heaven and earth," in other words, not because we can prove it, but because we see the consequences of its denial for human existence and the good of the world.

Other propositions in the creed can likewise serve as critical theological concepts, though none is so fundamental as the proposition that God is creator of all things. In fact, one of the most helpful ways of understanding the creed is to ask what effects logically follow from accepting or denying its claims. For example, what view of the human body and of the material world is implied by the proposition that we await the resurrection of the dead? What are the implications of a denial of the resurrection for a Christian sense of an ending, or goal to human life? How, in other words, do statements about God and God's work in the world shape the way people who believe them (and those who reject them) live?

This gives us some sense of how the creed functions as a "symbol of faith," even though our ability to speak of God and God's work is limited. The creed can be understood as a symbol of faith because through analogy it speaks truly about God—truly but inadequately—and, as a set of critical theological concepts, its statements provide the logic for the Christian way of life.

WHAT THE CREED DOES

We have seen how the creed can be held as a set of propositions. But it is more than a set of propositions to be analyzed. It is,
above all, a script that is performed every week by millions of
Christians throughout the world, as a part of worship. What the
creed *is* goes with what it *does* as an element in worship. The
creed performs five distinct but interrelated functions for
the Christian community in worship and in its life beyond that
context: it narrates the Christian myth, interprets Scripture, constructs a world, guides Christian practices, and prepares the Christian people for worship.

THE CREED NARRATES THE CHRISTIAN MYTH

The creed does not propose a philosophy of life but tells a
story with characters and a plot. It is a story about God and the
world, about God's investment in humans and their future. The
fact that Christian belief is embedded in the story says more than
any philosophy could about the Christian commitment to the
world—visible and invisible—as created by God.

It starts with God's creation and ends in the future life. But
the heart of the story is the birth, suffering, death, resurrection,
and ascension of Jesus, the Son of God, who shared our humanity
and transformed it by that sharing. When Christians recite the
creed on Sunday morning, they tell themselves and each other a
story that they already know but that bears such constant repetition, for it is a story unlike any other, a story that we must speak
to each other because so much of what we experience in the world
seems to deny the reality or the power of that story.

The story told by the creed is a myth in the sense discussed
earlier. It tells how God has entered the human story, or, perhaps

better, how God has enabled humans to enter God's own community of life. Because Christians tell this story over and over, they
know at a very deep level the answers to the three questions asked
by every religion and philosophy of life: Where do you come
from? We come from God, are created by God. Who are you? We
are God's children through Jesus his Son. Where are you going?
We hope to share in God's eternal life.

THE CREED INTERPRETS SCRIPTURE

The creed does not dictate how Scripture is to be read in all its
richness and diversity, but it provides an epitome or summary
that guides and directs the proper reading of Scripture. Apart
from the few places where it uses terms from ancient philosophy,
it draws all its language from Scripture. The story told by the
creed is itself drawn from the great story line of Scripture. It
omits great portions of Scripture, to be sure. It focuses on the
birth of Jesus and his death and resurrection, which means that
the focus is really on soteriology, the way in which humans have
been saved through God's work in Christ.

That this is less than a full or adequate representation of the
scriptural witness is clear. Nevertheless, the creed provides a
guide for the correct understanding of the heart of Scripture and
its overall intent. Any reading of Scripture that has it teaching of
multiple gods or the equality of evil with good, or that Jesus was
not fully human, or a sectarian view of the church, is, by the measure of the creed, a false reading. The creed unobtrusively but
effectively supplies the Christian people with the code for understanding its sacred text.

THE CREED CONSTRUCTS A WORLD

Those reciting the creed thereby construct a world based on
the Christian myth and Scripture. The world is not simply given

to us, so that its nature and meaning are self-evident. It is constantly under construction by us as we give meaning to it. To be sure, those building the world this way deny that they are the builders. They see themselves rather as describing the world that has been "given" to all by nature or God.

Only when we are exposed to other people's dramatically different understandings of reality do we begin to perceive that "the world" is a more malleable place than we had thought. Others understand the world in quite different terms. Thus, to claim—and to live by the claim—that our world is one that is being created by the one God who makes everything that exists is to make a claim that competes with other claims.

Not every construction of the world can be true. God either creates all that is, or God doesn't. But humans are not in a position to adjudicate between competing world constructions. Contemporary Christians—who have been brought to this awareness more sharply than in any previous age—recognize that their world is not everybody's world. The world as constructed by Hinduism or Confucianism is simply not the same world that is constructed by the Bible and the Christian creed. Christians must acknowledge, furthermore, that they cannot demonstrate the superiority of their world to that of others. They must, therefore, live in the tension inherent in what has been called the "post-modern condition": they affirm the truth of the world as expressed in the creed even as they know that other creeds construct other worlds that are just as believable—just as "livable"—as the Christians'.

Not least plausible among such competing worlds—and most pertinent to those Christians reciting their creed on a Sunday morning—is that constructed by the competing creed of capitalistic commerce. It defines the world not in terms of gift but in terms of possession, not in terms of cooperation but in terms of competition, not in terms of life-for-others but in terms of winner-take-all. The world constructed by commerce is all the more plausible because it actually runs things outside the church—even on Sunday. It is a world that even the Christians reciting the creed carry within their minds and often their hearts for the six days and twenty-three hours each week that they are not in church.

When believers stand together in the liturgy after the readings from Scripture and recite the words of the Christian creed, they affirm that the world as imagined by Scripture and constructed by the creed is the world in which they choose to live. They construct this world together by imagining together the world that the creed imagines. When they say the creed together, Christians explicitly articulate their vision of the world and at the same time implicitly reject other visions of reality. They choose to live their lives in adherence to these claims about reality, and none other.

THE CREED GUIDES CHRISTIAN PRACTICES

Because the creed constructs the world as one created by God the Father, saved by Jesus Christ his Son, and given life by the Holy Spirit, it also supports and guides the practices of the Christian community. It does not prescribe a full set of Christian practices. It does not tell Christians how to pray or to act in the world. But it does establish the right belief (orthodoxy) that lets us recognize right practice (orthopraxy). By providing an epitome of Scripture, the creed provides a bridge between the complex witnesses of Scripture and the moral lives of believers.

An obvious example is the way in which the confession of one all-powerful God as the maker of all things, visible and invisible, shapes our practices. At the level of piety, the perception of existence as a gift given moment by moment by an unseen power generates in us a sense of awe and wonder, of receptivity and thanksgiving.

At the level of politics, this same perception encourages a use of the world that is noninvasive, nonmanipulative, nondestructive. If God is equally and always the source of the smallest and the grandest creatures, of the infinite expanses of space as well as the minutest nuclear particles, then humans cannot arrogate to themselves what must always remain God's sovereignty over God's creation. They cannot narcissistically assume that God's prodigious energies are expended only for them and for their benefit, or that the special care that God has shown them in the gift of his Son exhausts God's capacity to care for all creation in God's own time and manner. They cannot, therefore, destroy God's earth for their own pleasure and profit and power in utter disregard of other creatures, as though creation was their possession to do with as they pleased rather than the precious gift of God that is given equally to all that exists and that is never removed from God's power or care. Precisely such convictions lie behind the Christian concern for the sanctity of life, the honoring of the body, the ecology of the universe, the sharing of possessions.

In similar fashion, our profession of "one, holy, catholic, and apostolic church" argues against any attitude or practice that would favor one of these qualities against the others. A practice in the church that led to disunity rather than unity, that tended to exclude rather than include, that had no roots in Scripture or tradition, and that failed to distinguish the church from the way of the world must be regarded as unacceptable. How much more coherent Christian identity and practice would be if it were consistently held to such a test!

THE CREED PREPARES THE WORSHIPING PEOPLE

The most obvious function of the creed is what it does liturgically for those who recite it every Sunday. The creed moves the people from the liturgy of the word to the liturgy of the Eucharist. Just as the recital of the creed at baptism marks the transition from being a catechumen to being one of the faithful, so—with less drama—does the recital at Mass accomplish the same transition.

This liturgical function of the creed came about by happy accident. Remember that the creed probably took its origin in baptism, in which saying the creed marked the point of transition by which someone entered the believing community. Later, we saw that the creed developed as a way to distinguish between right and wrong belief within the Christian community, leading to the elaborate Nicene-Constantinopolitan Creed that is the subject of this discussion.

This longer form of the creed apparently found its way into the Eucharistic liturgy first in the East, sometime in the sixth century. In the West, the Third Council of Toledo (589) stated that the creed should be included in the Mass, but located it immediately after the breaking of the bread. The point was for the people to refresh their faith before receiving communion. It was the Holy Roman emperor Charlemagne in 798 who directed that the creed be sung after the Gospel, and this eventually became the practice throughout the Western church, accepted formally by the Roman Church under Pope Benedict VIII in 1014.

Placed in the liturgy where it is now, the creed mimes the transition first accomplished by baptism, when catechumens entered fully into the life of the faithful. The first part of the liturgy is appropriately designated the liturgy of the word or of the catechumens. It is based on the ancient worship of the synagogue, and consists of readings from Scripture, preaching, and prayers. It was the part of worship that those not yet baptized— and therefore not yet either fully committed to the faith or received into it—could attend. After their baptism, as members of the faithful, they could also join in the liturgy of the Eucharist, from which they had formerly been barred.

The creed now effects that same transition for the worshiping congregation each week. The creed draws the readings of Scripture into a focus on the central mystery of the incarnation and redemption and the hope of a blessed resurrection. Thus it draws the gathered faithful to a clear focus and a shared commitment before they enter the sacred mystery of the Lord's Supper. It imprints on them more firmly the Christian myth, reminding them that they celebrate the work of God in Christ "for them and for their salvation."

By doing this, it reinforces the Christian symbolic world in which the sharing of life leads to greater and richer life. It both leads believers to the celebration of the Eucharistic mystery and directs them to live in ways fitting the mystery of the Eucharist. In short, the creed helps create each week an actively committed people, prepared to enter together into the mystery that shapes and nourishes its common life.

Chapter Three

WE BELIEVE IN ONE GOD

The language of the creed is exceptionally compressed, even cryptic. Each statement must be examined by itself and in combination with every other if we are to grasp something of the creed's meaning. In this and the following chapters, I attempt such an examination. Doing the job adequately would require a full-fledged doctrinal theology, a task beyond my abilities and the limits of this book. My aim is more modest. I want to provide Christians a better sense of what the words they declare each week in the liturgy mean, how they are grounded in Scripture, how they express the experience of the church, and how they affect the way one lives as a creedal Christian.

The creed's most radical and important profession comes right at the beginning: "We believe in one God." It is the root out of which all the rest grows. Without it, nothing more can be said.

We mean the God of whom we learn in Scripture, the Living God of Israel and the Father of our Lord Jesus Christ. As we begin to try to understand what the creed affirms about God, we should be aware that neither the biblical nor the creedal language about God is fully adequate to the mystery of which they speak. They speak truly but not fully. All language about God reaches into a mystery it cannot grasp or comprehend. Yet we need all the language we can get, since we recognize that, in the end, all language falls short.

In the previous chapter, I suggested some of the rich ambiguity of saying "we believe." I noted that saying "we" instead of "I" enables individuals to subscribe to the faith of a church that believes more and better than any one of them does; how belief is the indispensable beginning of all faith; how any profession of faith, whether individual or communal, entrusts the mind and heart to a truth that cannot be proven but can be lived.

We can now take all of that as read, and move to the content of this first statement, which most sharply distinguishes the inhabitants of the earth by the way it answers the question of whether we are alone or not. Let us begin by reflecting on what it means to say "God exists," and then consider the opening words of the creed phrase by phrase.

In saying these words, we declare that God exists (and thereby distinguish ourselves from agnostics and atheists). We say that God is one (and thereby situate ourselves in the biblical story). We declare that God is Father (and thereby articulate our relation to the Son). We say that God is almighty (and thereby respond to the mystery of evil and human suffering). We assert that God is maker of heaven and earth (and thereby declare what we believe God to be doing here and now).

GOD EXISTS

In saying that God exists, we passionately embrace a reality that embraces us. Our confession that God exists is not like an opinion about the existence of unicorns, for nothing depends on whether the claim that "unicorns exist" is true or false. It is not like an opinion about the future price of a stock, for although something may hinge on that judgment (my money), the stock market is just another part of the world, however unpredictable. The statement "God exists," in contrast, commits us to a fundamental posture toward everything else that exists. Everything else depends on whether "God exists" is true or false.

Different religious traditions have quite different understandings of the concept of God. They disagree on whether God is singular or plural, involved with humans or not, entirely good or both good and evil. But all religious people share something that unbelievers do not, and that is the conviction that when they say "God," they speak of something real, something that truly exists.

As a critical theological concept, the statement "God exists" suggests that the world we see and touch points to a power or powers beyond our own and outside our control, beyond our sight and touch, which must be taken into account even if we are to give an adequate account of the world that we can touch and see. To affirm the existence of God, then, means to affirm that the physical world, which can be measured and calculated, is not all that is.

The "more" of reality that is suggested by the word "God" cannot, in turn, be grasped or measured. To us, it looks much like "emptiness." The believer, however, insists that this simply shows the inadequacy of human measurement. And the believer turns the tables, by noting that the world we can measure cannot explain or account for itself. If it is not possible to prove the existence of God on the basis of what exists in the world, it is even more impossible to account for the existence of the world on the basis of itself.

The believer affirms that there is mystery at the heart of the world, a mystery that does not yield to direct examination, that refuses to be measured or manipulated, yet suggests its presence in every single thing that we can feel and taste and see and hear and smell in the world. The believer dwells in a world that is magical as well as mythic. The world is "full" even though it looks empty. The conviction that the world is not all there is does not diminish the worth of the world. Just the opposite: it teaches us to see the world as the most marvelous gift, a gift that, once given, can be studied, contemplated, and celebrated because it is freely given and not simply "there."

Believers—and they include the vast majority of humans who have ever inhabited the earth, since disbelief in God is a remarkably modern and relatively rare phenomenon—do not embrace this vision of reality as the end result of a process of reasoning about the world. It is for them the assumption or axiom that enables them to reason rightly about the world. For them, God is not a possible conclusion of reason but the necessary starting point for life.

Living on this basis, they inevitably consider agnosticism and atheism less as alternative intellectual possibilities than as fundamentally flawed ways of living in the world. They have the hardest time understanding the agnostic, the person who is neutral on the question of God's existence because it is "unknowable." Agnosticism is a contemptuous uninterest in the truth of the world. Because the question of God's existence affects the perception of absolutely everything else that exists and the way we deal with all that exists, agnosticism seems to the believer to be a form of atheism by default that pretends to be a refined and gentlemanly restraint on a difficult and unsolvable question.

Believers have considerable natural sympathy for the atheism that is based on philosophical and moral grounds. Such atheists see believers as people who refuse to grow up, precisely to the extent that they find depth and mystery at the heart of the world. The world, they insist, does not have such depth: "What you see is what you get." What is sometimes called humanistic atheism objects to the sort of "magical" thinking that I earlier ascribed to faith. They insist that what believers call "fullness" is simply "emptiness." They protest against belief as wish fulfillment or as denial of the world's evil.

A first type of humanistic atheism worries that believers deceive themselves. Belief in God is wish fulfillment that hides from people their real condition. Human existence is not beautiful and sweet, but nasty, brutish, and short. It is redeemed not by saviors from the sky but by the human resolve to make the best of a fundamentally bad deal through a morally conscious decision to live freely and fully precisely as human persons, unafraid and unapologetic. A second type rejects belief in God because of the pervasive presence of evil in the world. They point to the horrible deaths suffered by innocent children, the agonies of lingering and incurable diseases, the destruction of populations by random catastrophes or ruthless extermination. They take their stand on moral outrage, and think with Montaigne that "God's only excuse is that he does not exist."

Believers rightly honor the depth and passion of such humanistic atheism. Its astringent criticism of careless credulity and moral obtuseness, in fact, is closer to genuine belief than to its rejection. It serves the cause of authentic faith by reminding believers both that the human spirit can be noble and truthful apart from a professed belief in any God, and that formal profession of faith in God may in fact take the form of self-delusion and moral callousness.

The atheism that truly stands opposite authentic faith is the one described by Psalm 14. "The fool says in his heart, 'There is no God,' " and on the basis of that denial, lives a life of corruption and perversity (Ps 14:1–7; see also Ps 53:1–6). This "practical atheism" is based on a decision of the heart rather than a conclusion of the mind, and is expressed by serving oneself and oppressing others. Practical atheists have their "gods"—all humans must center their lives somewhere—but they are gods that are crafted according to their own desires. Practical atheism finds its expression in idolatry.

Scripture provides two extended treatments of this kind of atheism/idolatry. The Book of Wisdom stresses the foolishness of those who are "in ignorance of God and who from the things seen did not succeed in knowing him who is, and from studying the works did not discern the artisan" (13:1). It is slightly more sympathetic to those who are seduced by the beauty of things: "they search busily among his works, but are distracted by what they see, because the things seen are fair" (13:7).

Paul's letter to the Romans is harsher. Idolatry results from the choice to repress the truth about God that humans are able to know from the shape of creation (Rom 1:18–19): "though they knew God, they did not honor him as God or give him thanks, but they became futile in their thinking, and their senseless minds were darkened" (Rom 1:20–21). For Paul, lie precedes error: "claiming to be wise, they became fools, and exchanged the glory of the immortal God for images resembling a mortal human being or birds or four-footed animals or reptiles" (Rom 1:22).

The Book of Wisdom and Paul agree that idolators are "without excuse" (Wis 13:8; Rom 1:20), and that their atheism leads to violence and destruction (Wis 14:12–31; Rom 1:24–32). The scriptural analysis shows us that willfully to deny God's existence distorts our perception of the world and therefore distorts the way we live. The practical atheist does not see that the world is open to a great power and presence, but treats it as a closed system of cause and effect, with the only significant power being the human ability to manipulate the world. If the world is all there is and we are answerable only to ourselves, why should we care for anyone else, or use our power for anything but gaining our own goals?

The Book of Wisdom and Romans remind us that the awesome power of idolatry is found above all in its ability to shape the structures of society so that they suppress the possibility of perceiving the world in any way other than idolatrously. It is idolatry when much of the world is constructed on the basis of economic and political systems that foster radical individualism, that make competition the supreme value in life, that reward greed, that enslave families to endless work without meaningful rest or spiritual growth, that camouflage such slavery by an endless round of entertainment diverting attention from the deadening boredom of a life dedicated exclusively to acquisition of meaningless things, and that, through its control of the media, progressively convinces all the enslaved that this pattern is "natural" and "good" and "free."

Children born and raised within such a totalitarian system of meaning (even if it is called capitalism) can only with great difficulty learn to see the world in terms other than those given by these structures of society with their massive powers of persuasion. Before now, it was always possible to directly confront powers that did not derive from the sitters upon thrones—to see the stars in the vast emptiness of a cold desert night, to experience a terrifying storm at sea, to participate in the mysteries of birth and sickness and death within the home. What makes the present situation truly distinctive and threatening is that the idolatrous structures can so exercise their control, reinforced by the powers of the electronic media, that people are increasingly incapable of experiencing the "natural" world in ways that would expose as empty idolatry's claim to absolute control.

The pretense of idolatry to give life or identity or worth apart from God is always a lie. The pretense that the world is all there is does not lead to greater independence and freedom, but to ever greater degrees of dependence and slavery. And has the earth ever seen humans so dependent and needy and addicted as those now inhabiting contemporary Westernized countries?

GOD IS ONE

Now we can consider more closely the content of the proposition "God exists" as stated in the opening words of the creed. The structure of the creed reflects the Christian struggle to place a new experience of God through Jesus and the Holy Spirit in the church within a longer story, which is nowhere stated but everywhere presupposed. The creed grew out of the ancient confession of Israel, "Hear O Israel, the Lord your God is One" (Deut 6:4), but of that longer story, the creed retains only the first statement concerning God the Father, and the statement that the Holy Spirit "spoke through the prophets."

It is of the first importance, then, to be clear that the story of God's work in and through Israel is the implicit premise for God's new work in Christ. The creed acknowledges this with its brief but meaningful allusion to the entire scriptural world in its confession of "one God," meaning the God of Israel. The creed begins with a literary cross-reference—it says, in effect, "to know what this means, go read the Old Testament." It is impossible to understand what the creed goes on to say about Jesus and the Holy Spirit apart from the Old Testament. (And, as we shall see, for Christians, it is also impossible fully to understand the Old Testament apart from Jesus.)

At the start, Israel's profession of the Lord as one God may well have been an expression of what is sometimes called "henotheism," the claim that one people's god is superior to all others. Israel emerged as a people within a world that was everywhere polytheistic. Everyone agreed that the divine power was distributed among a group of superior beings who in administering the world sometimes competed and sometimes cooperated, but responded to the worship paid them by humans. Polytheism resembles most a vast and complex system of patronage. A people's warrior god, for example, might reward their worship by giving them victory over a rival nation. And since they conquered the other nation, their warrior god was superior to their rival's warrior god.

Polytheism is complex and inefficient—since the gods are not so very superior to humans and are beset by humanlike vices as well as virtues. But it is also capacious (there is always room for more gods) and forgiving—one god may do me injury, but another gives me help. Although the individual gods are fallible and fractious, the system as a whole is benevolent. As in all patronage, the main thing to know is how to work the system. Some Scripture passages suggest that Yahweh (the proper name of Israel's God; see Exod 3:14–15) was first conceived in terms similar to these, as the chief tribal god of the Hebrew people. Thus, we find language suggesting that Yahweh stands as the first among many gods (see, e.g., Ps 29:1; 82:1–6; 86:8–10; 89:5–8; 91:11). The triumph accomplished by Yahweh in creating a people out of nothing in the exodus of Israel from Egypt and in enabling this people to conquer the inhabitants of the land of

Canaan, in turn, could be viewed as the triumph of Israel's God over other tribal deities (see, e.g., Ps 44:1–8; 47:2–4; 59:5; 66:3–7; 68:1–10; 76:4–9; 78:11–16; 83:9–18): "The Lord is a great god," sings Psalm 95:3, "and a great king above all gods."

But the idea of Yahweh being "number one" among gods eventually led to the understanding that Yahweh alone was God, the one God of all the earth and of all peoples, the one source of all that is and the one goal toward which all is ordered. This change derived from reflection on the meaning of Israel's experience. Yahweh's powerful deeds in history had involved control over the powers of the earth itself (Ps 77:13–20; 105:26–42), and his creating a people out of nothing pointed to one whose power extended to the creation of the world (Ps 106:6–12; 104:3–8). Meditation on Yahweh's power to create "heaven and earth" (Ps 115:15) and all they contain (Ps 33:6–9; 65:6–13), including the innermost recesses of the human person (Ps 8:4–8; 139:13–18), led increasingly to the awareness that Yahweh was not only the "top god," but the "only God."

This understanding is made most explicit in the latter part of the Book of Isaiah. Here, the God of Israel is the creator of all things and is able to direct the affairs of all nations, selecting servants even from nations other than Israel to serve his ends. All the beings that the nations call gods are simply idols, the works of human hands. They have no real existence except that ascribed to them by worshipers. They cannot save but can only enslave their worshipers (see Isa 40:12–31; 42:5–9; 45:12–21; see also Ps 96:4–5; 135:5–18). "I am the first and I am the last; besides me there is no god" (Isa 44:6).

This robust and radical monotheism remains the heart of the religious faith of Judaism. The same understanding of God as one continues in the New Testament, but with a particular emphasis on the sovereignty of this one God over all peoples and not simply Israel. Peter says in Acts 10:34–35, "I truly understand that God shows no partiality, but in every nation anyone who fears him and does what is right is acceptable to him." And Paul in Romans builds his argument about righteousness through faith on the dual premise that God is the one God of all the earth and is also fair (or righteous): "We hold that a person is made righteous by faith apart from works of the law. Or is God the God of Jews only? Is he not the God of Gentiles also? Yes, of Gentiles also, since God is one! And he will make the circumcised righteous on the basis of faith and the uncircumcised through the same faith" (Rom 3:28–30).

This radical monotheism also severely challenges the inquiring mind and the pious heart. It challenges them because it seems to offer a poor answer to the issues sometimes called "the problem of free will" and "the problem of evil." The first one says that, if one God is the source of all that exists, how can creatures be held accountable for their actions? How can they truly be free? The second one says that, if God is the source of all things, is not God also responsible for evil as well as for good? For some, such a God is so paradoxical as to be unthinkable.

That was exactly the view of the second-century Christian teacher Marcion. He solved the problems of freedom and of evil by distributing power between two Gods and two realms of being. Material being is evil and spiritual being is good. The creator God of the Jews, described in the Old Testament, is responsible for everything evil. The God of Jesus, described in the New Testament (or at least that part he approved), has nothing to do with material reality, but is entirely spiritual. Humans are trapped within evil structures insofar as they participate in the material world, and can save themselves by turning away from the material world and toward the spiritual world.

Marcion therefore advocated a strict asceticism. Virginity is superior to marriage, for example, because refusing to bear children defeats the work of the evil God of the Jews. Fasting and abstinence from the affairs of the world speeds the process of spiritualization and therefore of salvation. Marcion dissolved paradox by distinguishing realms of power, in effect by reverting to a form of polytheism.

The orthodox party, represented by teachers like Irenaeus of Lyons and Tertullian, emphatically rejected Marcion's "solution." They defended the goodness of creation by insisting that Jesus participated in it through his incarnation. They insisted further that the same God who created the world is the one whom Jesus calls "Father." Evil, they said, is a distorted expression of human freedom. Salvation is not a matter of spirits escaping materiality but rather of healing the human spirit and transforming creation.

In the context of Marcion's challenge, in turn, the creed's statement that "we believe in ONE God" stands as an orthodox counterchallenge: the one God confessed by Christians is now emphatically understood as the God of creation and the God of the Old Testament, as well as the God of salvation. The New Testament story of redemption through grace continues the Old Testament story of creation and of covenant. The same God creates the world and re-creates it through the work of Jesus his Son. By insisting that oneness also means continuity, the orthodox teachers also maintained the paradox that Marcion tried to resolve. They stated, in effect, that with God it is not a matter of solving problems, but a matter of being caught up in mystery.

In the context of the creed, Christianity's monotheism challenges the other monotheistic religions, Judaism and Islam. While the radical monotheism of Christianity agrees with both of them in asserting that there is but one ultimate power that is the source and goal of all that exists, it differs from them in its profession of a God who is one, but who has been revealed as bearing the names of Father, Son, and Spirit.

It is something of a misnomer to speak of the "three monotheistic traditions of the West," as though the understanding of God in each tradition was the same. For Judaism and Islam, God's oneness is equivalent to God's singleness. But Christianity proclaims a triune God, a God whose oneness contains plurality. For both Judaism and Islam, the Christian ascription of divinity to the Son and Spirit is a kind of polytheism. In response to the Christian claim that Jesus was Lord, Jewish texts condemned as *minim* (heretics) those who spoke of "two powers in heaven." And the Qur'an denies divine status to Jesus precisely because "it does not befit Allah to have partners."

The trinitarian character of the Christian God will progressively be unfolded by the creed, as it speaks in turn of the Son and the Holy Spirit. The topic of the trinity itself will be taken up when we discuss the Holy Spirit. For now, it suffices to say that while Christians confess the oneness of God with Jews and Muslims, they mean by that oneness something quite distinctive.

GOD IS FATHER

The mystery of the trinity begins to be unfolded by the designation "father" for the one, all-powerful God, who is maker of heaven and earth and the father of Jesus Christ. Ancient people would have regarded the designation obvious for the chief god. The "natural" head of the household was the father. By extension, the "natural" ruler of the nation was the king. By further extension, the "natural" way to think of the god from whom all other gods and beings originated was as father. Such an idea required that all those of lesser status recognize the father's authority, but it equally demanded that the father govern well, protect, defend, and support those who were weaker, especially his children.

In Israel, the designation "father" was used relatively seldom for Yahweh, perhaps in part out of a concern not to identify the one God too closely with the sort of father-god who begets the entire divine family. When Yahweh is called father, it is as father of the people of Israel. Yahweh's "fatherhood" is revealed above all in his creating a people and nurturing it. The prophet Hosea has Yahweh say,

> When Israel was a child, I loved him, and out of Egypt
> I called my son . . . it was I who taught Ephraim to walk, I
> took them up in my arms; but they did not know that
> I healed them. I led them with cords of human kindness,
> with bands of love, I was to them like those who lift infants to their cheeks. I bent down to them and fed them.

In Psalm 68:5, God is called the "father of orphans and protector of widows." In this case, God's defense of the weak and helpless in a patriarchal and agricultural society is pictured as a form of adoption. The Lord can rescue in a way that human fathers cannot.

In the prophetic literature, there are only a few passages explicitly calling Yahweh "father." In contrast to the Psalms, these prophetic statements focus on the honor and obedience that should be paid to God (see Mal 1:6; Jer 3:19; Mal 2:10; Isa 63:16). Isaiah connects the title of father to God's creation of humans: "Yet O Lord, you are our father, we are the clay and you are the potter. We are all the work of your hand" (Isa 64:8).

In the Old Testament, Yahweh is "father," then, above all

through relationship (see Ps 103:13). In the New Testament, "father" becomes the dominant way of modifying the designation "God" (see 1 Cor 8:6). God's fatherhood involves not simply God's paternal relationship with humans, but above all, and in the first place, with his son, Jesus Christ. Christians understand God's fatherhood to be revealed most explicitly and clearly in the person of Jesus. We know God as father because Jesus calls him father, reveals himself as God's son, and through the gift of the Holy Spirit enables us to share in that filial relationship through adoption.

We can take a very quick look at several New Testament writings to get a sense of the richness and complexity of the New Testament's language about God as father. Matthew's Gospel puts every statement involving God as father in the mouth of Jesus. It is his own designation for God. He tells his disciples that God is "your father in heaven" (5:16, 45, 48; 6:1, 14, 32; 7:11, 21) or simply "your father" (6:4, 6, 8, 15, 18, 26; 10:20, 29), and he tells them to pray to "our father who art in heaven" (6:9).

But Jesus also speaks of God as his own father with a special sense of directness and intimacy. The clear implication is that God is his father in a way not entirely shared by others. He speaks of "my father in heaven" (see 10:32, 33; 12:50; 16:17) and "my father" (20:23; 25:34, 41). Midway through his ministry of healing and teaching, Jesus praises God as his father and declares his own special relationship to him as "the son":

I thank you, Father, Lord of heaven and earth, because you have hidden these things from the wise and intelligent and have revealed them to infants; yes, Father, for such was your gracious will. All things have been handed over to me by my Father; and no one knows the Son except the Father, and no one knows the Father except the

Son and anyone to whom the Son chooses to reveal him.
(11:25–27)

In John's Gospel, Jesus also speaks plainly about God as his
father, referring to "my father" (2:16; 5:17, 43) or simply "the
father" in relation to "the son" (3:35; 4:23; 5:19). His opponents
state, quite rightly, that "he was calling God his father, thereby
making himself equal to God," and in response (5:18–47), Jesus
both acknowledges the ways in which "the Son" shares the power
and authority of "the Father" and the ways in which the Son is
subordinate and obedient: "I can do nothing of my own. As I hear,
I judge, and my judgment is just, because I seek to do not my own
will, but the will of him who sent me" (5:30). He also says, "What
my Father has given me is greater than all else, and no one can
snatch it out of the Father's hand. The Father and I are one"
(10:29–30). It is not surprising that his opponents respond by
seeking to stone him for blasphemy, noting that "you, though
only a human being, are making yourself God" (10:33).

Jesus' farewell to his disciples reveals even more explicitly
the mysterious relationship between Jesus as Son and God as his
Father, as well as the human path to God through Jesus: "I am the
way, and the truth, and the life. No one comes to the Father except through me. If you know me you will know my Father also.
From now on you do know him and have seen him . . . I am in the
Father and the Father is in me" (14:6, 10). The full understanding of this relationship will only come to humans, Jesus says,
through the gift of the Holy Spirit (14:26; 15:26).

Paul's letters show the same relations between God as the
father of all and as the father of Jesus Christ. His characteristic
greeting concludes with the wish that his readers have "grace and
peace from God our Father and the Lord Jesus Christ" (see, e.g.,
Rom 1:1; 1 Cor 1:1; 2 Cor 1:2). God is simply "the Father of our

Lord Jesus Christ" (Rom 15:6; 2 Cor 1:3; 11:1). It is "the Father" who raised Jesus from the dead (Rom 6:4), and it is to "the Father" that Jesus will at last hand over the kingdom (1 Cor 15:24).

Paul says in Romans 8:29 that God wishes those he has chosen to be conformed to the image of his Son, so that he might be the firstborn of many brothers. They will be conformed to Jesus through the gift of the Spirit that comes from the resurrected Jesus (Rom 8:9–14). The Father does not give Christians a spirit of fear leading them back into slavery, but a spirit of adoption that enables them to cry out, as Jesus himself did, "Abba, Father!" (Rom 8:15; see Gal 4:6–7).

This very brief review of scriptural evidence indicates that the title "Father" is firmly rooted in the prayer life and prophecy of Israel, in the prayer life and perceptions of Jesus, and in the experience and prayer of the first Christians. In saying "God, the Father," the creed states as briefly as possible the precise character of God as revealed by Jesus Christ. This is the way Jesus viewed and addressed God—of that there can scarcely be a doubt—and it is as Jesus' Father that Christians now approach God, because they have been given that "spirit of adoption" that enables them to greet God in the same way as Jesus himself.

Learning to call "our Father" the one whom Jesus called "my Father," Christians approach God not as an impersonal force but as one having in the highest degree those qualities of knowing and loving that we associate with persons. The name "Father" suggests power and authority, but as Jesus has taught us, ours is a Father who not only brings to life but also raises to new life. As Jesus has taught us, furthermore, our Father blesses all beings with goodness. His sunshine and rain fall on the just and unjust alike (Matt 5:45–48). He cares for all, even the most insignificant creatures (Matt 6:26). He reveals his will to the little ones and the ignorant (Matt 11:25–27), and shares his rule with the poor in spirit, the meek, the sorrowful, the pure of heart, those who hunger and thirst for justice, those who make peace, those who suffer rejection (Matt 5:3–11). This Father can see the hearts of his human creatures and can therefore judge them not by appearance but by reality (Matt 6:4–6, 16). He knows what we need even before we do (Matt 6:8) and wishes us to receive what is really good for us (Matt 7:11).

He forgives us our sins when we are willing to forgive each other (Matt 6:14). He rewards, not those who simply call him Lord, but those who do his will (7:21), and has prepared an eternal home for those who seek to be perfect as he is perfect (5:48), that is, those who treat "the little ones of the earth" with the same care and tenderness that the Father shows toward them (Matt 25:31–46). As we have learned it from Jesus, the designation of God as Father seems personal and positive.

But is it so for everyone? Many female (and some male) Christians have become increasingly disturbed by the use of gender-exclusive language for God. The creed is a stumbling block for such Christians when it calls God "Father" and not "Mother," and when it speaks of Jesus as "Son" and as "becoming man." The concerns raised by such Christians are both real and serious. They arise from the hard experience of women within Christianity: with structures that elevate males above females (patriarchy), attitudes that diminish or destroy the value of women as persons (sexism), and language that tends to reinforce such structures and attitudes.

Speaking of God in exclusively male terms therefore seems to many contemporary Christians the supreme example of using language in a way hurtful to women. First, it projects on God human male qualities that are then regarded as "divine," reinforcing the arrangements of society that favor men by according them status and authority greater than that accorded women.

As Mary Daly says succinctly, "If God is male, then the male is God." Second, and perhaps equally important, it strongly implies that human female qualities cannot be ascribed to God, just as leadership within human societies should be denied to women.

Within Christianity, gender-exclusive language about God has served to support ecclesiastical sexism and power structures that have been bad for women. Recent arguments from the Vatican that support the refusal to ordain women to the Roman Catholic priesthood because priests represent Christ, and Christ is male, only make the point by reducing it to the absurd. As Elizabeth Johnson has noted, sexism is truly revealed when even the theoretical possibility of God's incarnation as a woman is rejected. If theologians really think it "unseemly" that God should have become human as a woman, little more need be added about the degree to which women are regarded as full sharers in the image of God!

Proposed remedies take three basic forms. The first is removing gendered language for God altogether. The second is replacing male language with female language. The third is supplementing male names with female names. The first and third options are the most appealing to the majority of Christians concerned about these issues (many still have not become conscious of them), since the second appears to be just as exclusive, only in the opposite direction. While it has some appeal to women who have heard nothing but "man talk" in the church since infancy, it is not clear how speaking of a goddess rather than a god improves things for long, except for those who actually prefer to celebrate the divine as a pure projection of their own gender, or for those who fundamentally want to leave Christianity altogether.

The first proposal, to eliminate gendered language for God altogether, has an abstract appeal, but its great deficiency is precisely that the Christian God is not an impersonal force, like destiny or fate, but a person. All human persons have gender (even those who are deeply ambivalent about their specific gender, and those seeking to change their gender)—no person is an "it." If we are to speak of God as person, then, we must either speak in terms of human genders or make up some new language about persons that combines genders, but that attempt, like all made-up languages, is bound to fail.

The third proposal, to supplement male language about God with female language, is the best. It has the advantage of preserving the sense of God as person. It reminds us that when we call God "Father" we do not mean that God is male. It is supported by passages in Scripture that speak freely of God in terms of female imagery. It expresses the fact that God is as much female as God is male, since God cannot be either female or male in the way that humans are male or female, since God is Spirit rather than body. And finally, it does not displace the specific symbolism of the biblical witness, which speaks of God as "Father" and "Son" as well as "Spirit."

There remains the question, however, of when and where such supplementary language about God should be used. I strongly oppose the growing practice of producing "gender-inclusive" translations of Scripture as well as of liturgical prayer, and would resist as well any attempts to modify the traditional language of the creed. These instruments of revelation, prayer, and profession are too fragile to survive such revisions. Revisions often make things only worse. For example, such revisions pay little attention to the requirement that every generation serve the genuine needs of those who come after it. Enlightened people in the pew today may understand what they mean by beginning the Lord's Prayer with the words "Our Father-Mother," but Christians three generations from now may not, and may not be in a position to, pray and profess in the manner that all Christians before them had done. It is a form of generational narcissism to change texts to suit one's own needs.

The appropriate settings for using supplementary female language for God, I suggest, are in theological discussions, in groups meeting for informal worship, in the reading of Scripture by those who know the appropriate ways to render the original languages in nonexclusive ways, and in every form of individual prayer.

Three final comments on this difficult subject may be appropriate. The first is the simple reminder that just as male language has been used to reinforce patriarchal structures to the diminishment of women, so has the actual human reality of fatherhood often been a powerful and beneficent reality for men themselves, for women, and above all, for children. By no means do all men or women find praying to God as Father an obstacle to true piety or psychological growth, because in their experience, their father maturely embraced and embodied the role of father. Calling God "Father" works well for them.

The second observation is another reminder, that Christian language about God as Father is not simply a projection from the human experience of fatherhood, still less from the patriarchal structures of society. The Christian understanding of God as Father is based on the way humans experienced God as creator, protector, and redeemer in the story of Israel, in the way Jesus bore witness to God as his Father, and in the way in which, moved by the experience of the Holy Spirit in their lives, Christians also have come to know God as their Father.

We do not call God Father because of our male parent. Rather, as Paul says in Ephesians 3:14, we come to understand all fathering because of the way God is Father: "For this reason [the way God has acted in the world through Christ] I bow my knees before the Father (*pater*), from whom all fatherhood (*patria*) in heaven and on earth takes its name."

Finally, we must also remember that *all* positive language about God must undergo the negative or apophatic reading I spoke of in the last chapter. We must say that God is "Father," but we must also say that God is *not* Father as we understand fatherhood, lest we simply and uncritically project human maleness on God. So we must use other names for God (including female ones) to remind ourselves that no single name adequately captures the fullness of God, even the one used by Jesus himself.

To think otherwise would be to limit God's own capacity to reveal Godself in ways beyond our control. Even when we, with great joy, call upon God as our Father, we must remember that before the mystery of God, all language must eventually fall away, and worship must fall silent to be true.

GOD IS ALL-POWERFUL

The designation of God as "almighty" or all-powerful (Greek *pantokrator*, Latin *omnipotens*) is at least as ancient as the second-century Roman creed given in Hippolytus's *Apostolic Tradition*. Together with "one," it helps define both "God" and "Father," and is defined by them. "One" concentrates all power in God and makes the distinction between God and not-God absolute. "Father" connotes a personal intelligence and will. In other words, God *can* do all things and God *chooses* to do certain things.

Within ancient polytheistic systems, it was not uncommon for the father-god to be regarded as supremely powerful. That notion may well lie behind the biblical usage from which this term derives, for in the Septuagint (the Greek translation of the Old Testament), the Hebrew expression for "Lord of Hosts" (see 2 Sam 5:10; Mic 4:14; Hab 2:13) is sometimes rendered as *pantokrator* and at other times as *kyrios tōn dynameōn* ("Lord of Powers"; see Ps 58:5; 67:11; 79:4). We picture Yahweh at the head of his army or his heavenly court. He is able to do whatever he wills.

The term "all-powerful" does not occur often in the New Testament (see 2 Cor 6:18; Rev 1:8; 4:8; 11:17), but the idea is there throughout. When Jesus prays in the garden before his death, he says, "Abba, my Father, all things are possible to you; take this cup away from me. Yet not what I will but what you will" (Mark 14:36). Likewise Gabriel tells Mary that she can conceive even as a virgin because "there is no deed that will be impossible for God" (Luke 1:37). About rich people entering the kingdom, Jesus declares, "the things that are impossible for humans are possible for God" (Luke 18:27). Paul emphasizes the power of God that can be known from the shape of creation (Rom 1:20), that is at work to save both Jews and Greeks through the good news (Rom 1:16), that is mighty enough to give life to a dead womb and raise Jesus from the dead (Rom 4:20–25), that is made known through his works in history (Rom 9:22), and that is sufficiently strong to restore Israel (Rom 9:23; see also 2 Cor 4:7; Col 1:11; Eph 1:19; 3:7; 3:20).

That God can do everything is the premise of all prayer in the biblical tradition. The apostles when persecuted pray, "Master, you are One who made the heaven and the earth and the land and the sea and everything that is in them" (Acts 4:24). Humans appeal to God because God is personal ("Father"), but their appeal is worth making only if God is all-powerful. Paul states memorably, if problematically, "we know that God co-works all things [an awkward translation, but important] toward good for those who love him" (Rom 8:28–30). Here is the problem that has caused the most profound questioning. How God can work all things for good is not obvious to human observation.

That God is working out all things is even less obvious. Paul ends his own long struggle to make sense of the relations of Jew and Gentile before God with an acknowledgment of the absolute distance between human reckoning and divine power:

> O the depth of the richness and the wisdom and the knowledge belonging to God! How inscrutable are his judgments and how undiscoverable his ways. For who has known the mind of the Lord? Or who has been his fellow-counselor? Or who has ever given him something first so that he might repay him? For all things are from him and through him and for him. To him be glory forever. Amen. (Rom 11:33–36)

Not everyone accepts Paul's answer. As we saw a few pages ago, many humanistic atheists protest morally against a God who causes or allows evil and relieves humans of the burden of freedom. If an all-powerful God "co-works" all things—no matter what humans choose—what does it matter if they can choose? And if an all-powerful God works for the good, why is there so much evil in the world? If humans are truly free, then God is not all-powerful. But a God who is benevolent yet powerless hardly seems worth rejecting. In brief, if we are to retain belief in an all-powerful God, then we must conclude that God colludes in evil, and if we are to retain belief in an all-loving God, then we must conclude that God is less than all-powerful.

Movements like process theology and liberation theology have tried to address this problem by saying that God is not really all-powerful. (What follows is a highly simplified picture of two complex and sophisticated positions.) Process theology appeals to the "Living God" of Scripture, who is always intimately involved with the world, and whose proper name, Yahweh, can be translated as "I will be who I will be." It understands God as also "in process" with the world—always evolving and changing with the world rather than standing apart from the world. What God "is," is "becoming." This clearly removes the note of "all-powerful" from God. God suffers as much from the powers of evil as creatures do.

Liberation theology combines this view with the political theology that arose from Marxist-Christian conversations in East Germany in the 1960s. It also appeals to the "biblical God," who thirsts for justice among humans, but can accomplish justice only through the social and political activity of human beings themselves. As humans fight oppressive social systems such as capitalism, sexism, and racism, they are in truth "co-working" with God toward the good. Liberation theology's God is entirely good, but not entirely powerful. God requires the participation of humans in order to accomplish the triumph of good over evil.

While process theology has appealed primarily to philosophical minds, liberation theology has considerable appeal for many contemporary Christians, especially the oppressed and those who strongly identify with the oppressed. This is precisely because it imagines a God who is at once intensely involved with this material, changing world, and is entirely on the side of good in its battle against evil. For many Christians, liberation theology supports an active engagement with the social order and a passion for social justice to a degree that "classical theology" never did.

It must be said, however, that both process and liberation theologies solve the theodicy "problem" at too high a cost. They have tried to solve how God, in Paul's words, can "co-work all things toward good for those who love him" (Rom 8:28) without taking sufficiently into account Paul's own declaration, later in the same letter, that God's judgments and God's ways are inscrutable: "who has known the mind of the Lord? Or who has been his fellow-counselor?" (Rom 11:34). By reducing the mystery of God's power and knowledge to the level of a problem, by insisting also that the "problem" of free will and the "problem" of evil must be understood within the frame of ordinary human understanding, such theologies diminish both the majesty and mystery of God, and diminish both the tragedy and hope of human existence.

The process and liberation understanding of God is both philosophically and religiously deficient. It is philosophically unsatisfying because the notion of God's "coming into being with the world" seems the most basic contradiction of the principle *ex nihilo nihil fit* ("out of nothing, nothing can come"). God is as unnecessary and as dependent as the world to which God is related. It is difficult to see how the absolute can arise out of the relative, the necessary out of the contingent, the eternal out of the temporal. It is religiously unsatisfying because it removes the need to pray and worship. How can we pray that God's will be done, if God is no more powerful than we are? How can we worship a God in the process of becoming—and needing our help?

Conceiving a God who is (apparently) more intimately involved with us and altogether on the side of the good comes at too high a price if that God turns out to be only a slightly improved version of ourselves—or the selves we would want to become. We have saved God's good reputation at the price of destroying God.

Two other comments are appropriate. First, while sin works in and through oppressive social systems, the mystery of evil is not fully to be identified with such systems. Hatred and prejudice recur in generation after generation, even when social structures have themselves been improved. And this is not even to mention all the ways that humans suffer and cause suffering not because of social structures but because of their own disordered hearts.

Second, although working for social justice is a necessary expression of the good news, a this-worldly vision of God's kingdom cannot address those deep dimensions of suffering and evil that demand more than social change, that demand the transformation of the heart and even the saving of the soul. Paul's words to the Corinthians retain their point: "If we have hoped in Christ for this life only, then we are the most pitiable of all people" (1 Cor 15:19).

If process and liberation theologies do not adequately answer the problems of evil and freedom as they challenge the claim that God is all-powerful, they have nevertheless contributed mightily to a more responsible way of thinking about and confessing God because they have made us face such questions squarely. In particular, they have reemphasized the truth of Paul's statement in Romans 8:28 that if God is working all things toward the good for those who love him, God is doing it by "co-working" (*synergein*) with us.

I am not able to provide a better answer to the problems posed for God's omnipotence by human freedom and the existence of evil. The answer cannot come from someone with only a limited human perspective. We cannot leap over the infinite gap between God and ourselves. We do neither God nor ourselves any service when we try to eliminate the gap by bringing God down to our level. But neither can we elevate ourselves to God's level. Paul asked, "Who has known the mind of the Lord? Or who has been his fellow-counselor?" (Rom 11:34).

But when we confess God as one and as Father and as all-powerful—all at once—we use the consistent language of Scripture and accept the unanimous testimony of the church from the beginning. We put ourselves within the worship and prayer of the faith community. We do not begin by trying to figure God out, but by bowing before God's unutterable majesty and power, as the source and goal of all that exists or ever has existed. When we stop looking at the mystery as though it were a problem to solve, and accept the mystery as that which has caught us up, that which defines us, and that within which we celebrate and suffer our human existence, *then* can we begin to think how the reality of human freedom and the presence of evil might be not the contradiction of God's power, but part of its fullest expression.

By this I mean that God's power is more obvious not in the depletion of creatures' power, but in its increase, God's freedom finds its most perfect expression in God's granting freedom to creatures. God's goodness is shown to its most astounding perfection in God's power to draw good even from what creatures experience as evil.

We confess these things. We cannot demonstrate them. When we think and speak of God, we are, as Paul says, like people "who are now seeing through a mirror, in a riddle" (1 Cor 13:12). This is our condition. We stand on this side of the abyss between us and God. We confess his power even when "through a mirror" we see all around us ways in which that power does not seem to be effective. We confess his goodness, even when "in a riddle" we experience all the ways in which evil appears as triumphant.

Paul says, "I know now only in part" (1 Cor 13:12). We are like beginners at chess. We have learned a few moves in a simple three-dimensional version. We cannot conceive what it would be like to play a million games simultaneously, or what it would be like to play those million games simultaneously in a million dimensions completely unknown to us. We are not yet where Paul hopes we will be: "Then I shall know just as I am known" (1 Cor

13:12). Until then, God's power is not for us to understand, but to obey, for God is God, and we are not.

GOD IS MAKER OF HEAVEN AND EARTH, OF ALL THINGS VISIBLE AND INVISIBLE

The designation of God as creator, or as "the one who makes" (*ho poiētēs*), grounds all the other statements of the creed. It is because God, the one, all-powerful Father, is the source of all things that God can also be revealer, savior, sanctifier, and judge of all. Because the heaven and the earth are not God but come from God at every moment, they reveal by their very existence the one who makes them (Wis 13–1–9; Rom 1:19–20). Because God has "maker's knowledge" of all things—that is, knowledge from within—God can judge justly as the one who "sees the heart" (Acts 1:24) and is not swayed by appearances (1 Pet 1:17). Because God loves what he has made, God seeks to save his world (Ps 65:1–13; 79:9; 1 Tim 4:10). Because the world is the bodily expression of God's Spirit, by his Holy Spirit God is able to transform the world and sanctify it (Ps 51:1–17; Rom 15:16; 2 Thess 2:13).

The phrase "maker of heaven and earth" derives from the very first words of Scripture (Gen 1:1; see also Ps 115:15), and thus connects God as the one, all-powerful Father with the story told in Scripture. By no means, however, does Scripture conceive of God's creative power as having been exhausted in the distant past or as fully described in Genesis 1–2. Psalm 104 celebrates creation as a wonder that God performs every day. Continuously God summons and controls the forces of nature, establishes and maintains the boundaries of the universe, calls into being and nourishes the plants and creatures of the world. God does this not once but always:

> These all look to you to give them their food in due season; when you give it to them they gather it up; when you open your hand, they are filled with good things. When you hide your face, they are dismayed; when you take away their breath, they die and return to their dust. When you send forth your spirit, they are created, and you renew the face of the earth. May the glory of the Lord endure forever, may the Lord rejoice in his works, who looks on the earth and it trembles, who touches the mountains and they smoke ... bless the Lord, O my soul. Praise the Lord! (Ps 104:27–35)

This God creates anew every day, this is a God who is totally in touch with the changing world because it is by his power that it comes into being and changes!

Further, Scripture clearly understands the deep connection between God's power to create the world and God's capacity to shape human events in history. Thus Isaiah mingles the language of creation and of new creation in history. The God who works in history, who "makes the things to come" (Isa 45:11), is "the Lord who makes you" (Isa 54:5) and who makes things new (43:19; 48:6). Isaiah links God's creative energies in the beginning, his constant renewal of the earth, and his work within human events:

> Thus says God, the Lord, who created the heavens and stretched them out, who spread forth the earth and what comes from it, who gives breath to the people upon it, and spirit to those who walk in it: I am the Lord, I have called

you in righteousness, I have taken you by the hand and
kept you, I have given you as a covenant to the people, a
light to the nations . . . I am the Lord, that is my name.
(Isa 42:5–8)

In the New Testament, God's continuing capacity to create is
expressed above all in the resurrection of Jesus from the dead
(Rom 4:17–24). For Paul, the resurrection of Jesus is so radical
that it can only be termed a "new creation" (2 Cor 5:17; Gal 6:15).
Christ is the "last Adam" (1 Cor 15:45), who is the "new human"
(Col 3:10) by whose image all other humans are measured and
into whose image the Spirit is to shape believers (2 Cor 3:17–18).

Nor is even the resurrection of Jesus and the renewal of humans (Rom 12:1–2) the end of God's creative activity. The Book
of Revelation joins the old creation to the new: in Revelation 14:7
we read, "Worship him who made heaven and earth, the sea and
the springs of water," and in 21:1–5, we read of a new creation:

Then I saw a new heaven and a new earth; for the first
heaven and the first earth had passed away and the sea
was no more . . . and he who sat upon the throne said,
"Behold, I make all things new."

This understanding of creation not simply as an event in the
distant past but above all as a constant and present activity of God
is the dominant testimony of Scripture.

We need to think of the Genesis phrase "in the beginning"
not in terms of time but in terms of causes. If we think about
"beginning" chronologically, then we may imagine creation as
initiated and completed by God long ago. God would be like an
ancient watchmaker whose work can still be detected from the intricate design of the timepiece, but who is no longer needed once

the watch leaves his shop, while it ticks away happily on its own, until it runs down.

But this is not at all how Scripture sees God's creative power. Scripture sees God as the breath that breathes through the world, giving it life at every moment. God causes the world to be at every moment. God is the world's "beginning," not once long ago, but at every moment.

The Christian confession of God as creator is not a theory about how things came to be, but a perception of how everything is still and is always coming into being. God's self-disclosure in creation, therefore, is not like the traces of the watchmaker in his watch. God is revealed in the world first of all not through the "whatness" of things, but through the "isness" of things. That anything exists at all is the primordial mystery that points us to God.

In this sense, everything that exists is equally capable of revealing God simply by its existence. However much they may differ in size and significance otherwise, a cell exists just as truly as a constellation and reveals God just as profoundly. A mussel and a mountain are equally fragile, equally dependent upon God for their existence. Viewed this way, all that is coming into being at every moment is also a miracle. Everything that is, is wondrous. This is the Christian view of reality: creation truly is magical, for it reveals the mystery at the heart of everything that is.

This vision of creation—which is simply the vision supposed by the entire weight of Scripture—is entirely compatible with theories of evolution, including the evolution of species. Such a view of God's creation is perfectly compatible with the evolutionary sense of the world as constantly becoming, constantly in process. The theories of the natural and biological sciences address, and can only address, the interconnecting causes of beings that have been or are now already in existence. They cannot account for existence itself. But concerning the sequence of becoming, the theories of the natural and biological sciences concerning the expansion of the universe and the evolving of species—the hypothetical character of which all genuine scientists firmly maintain even when they are substantially verified—are full of important insight that Christians neglect or deny at the cost of intellectual integrity.

It should also be clear that the peculiar exercise called "creation science" or "creationism" is a failed enterprise lacking such intellectual integrity. Trying to read the account of origins in the Book of Genesis as a source for scientific knowledge is both bad science and a disastrous misunderstanding of Genesis as a literary and religious text. Whatever else Genesis might be, it is not a scientific tract, not even by ancient standards. Only those desperate to save the "inerrancy" of the biblical text, and lacking any sense of how stories can be true without being accurate, will engage in such a dubious misuse of intelligence.

Genesis speaks the truth about the origins of the world, but not according to the standards of the natural and biological sciences. It speaks truth through literary and religious myth. It tells us plainly that everything existing comes to exist from a God who is not part of the world but who brings it into being by his power of knowing and loving (that is, by his "word"). It tells us that everything that has so been brought into being is good, and that humans particularly represent the creator among all other creatures because they bear God's likeness and image.

In short, the creed's statement that God is the creator of heaven and earth is not based on the natural science of antiquity but on the enduring truth glimpsed in part both by philosophy and religion, and magnificently attested by the prayers of Israel and the good news concerning the resurrected Lord Jesus Christ: God creates heaven and earth new every day.

VISIBLE AND INVISIBLE

The creed adds to "heaven and earth" the words "all things visible and invisible" (*panta horata kai aorata*). These words also have a scriptural basis (see the Book of Wisdom and Romans), but they seem at first to be redundant. What do they add to "maker of heaven and earth"? The additional words are a fine example of the creed as definition (one of the functions of the creed discussed in chap. 2).

It was possible to understand the biblical expression "heaven and earth" in ways that did not include everything that existed. This was in fact the case with the second-century teacher Marcion, who has already been mentioned. In Marcion's view, a lower God, the God of the Old Testament, is responsible for the visible creation (heaven and earth). The true God of Jesus is unseen, totally spirit, completely separate from the evil realm of the visible, material world. Marcionite readers could therefore not confess as one God both the creator of heaven and earth and the spiritual father of Jesus Christ.

The phrase "all things visible and invisible" therefore makes the language of Genesis 1:1 even more precise by making clear that those words include absolutely everything that exists. Not only things unseen but also the entire range of material reality comes from the one God, and it is all good. No part of creation is to be rejected. As Paul says against those who would prohibit marriage and the eating of certain foods, on the assumption that such participation in material things is polluting, "Everything created by God is good, and nothing is to be rejected, if it is received with thanksgiving; for then it is consecrated by the word of God and prayer" (1 Tim 4:4–5).

This clarification remains pertinent even today for those

Christians who suffer from the lingering effects on Christianity of the idea that matter—especially the body—is somehow evil. As expressed in the creed, the church rejected the explicit teaching that matter is evil and only spirit is good. But the explicit rejection of the disease still left the virus of dualism within Christian consciousness, particularly with regard to the human body, and most especially with regard to sexuality.

Christianity sanctified marriage and the begetting of children, in opposition to an explicit dualism that declared virginity the only way to please God. Yet within Christian piety, the celibate life has always been considered holier than the married life (as the roster of canonized saints attests). There has also remained a deep suspicion of the experience of pleasure in married sexuality. Thanks to the lingering effects of dualism, pleasure and vice are as closely linked in popular Christian consciousness as pain and virtue.

In the contemporary world, however, the opposite tendency is more apparent. Sexuality has been distorted in many ways, and the pleasure principle has driven out almost any sense of duty and virtue. The challenge for Christians is to find some way of affirming the goodness of all created things, including sexuality, including pleasure, without being corrupted by the idolatrous pansexuality and addictive hedonism of the current age. A good guide is provided by the Paul of 1 Timothy, who reminds us that all things created by God are good, but are also to be received in thanksgiving, that is, as gifts from God, not as ends in themselves. Paul also assures us in this same letter that "God supplies us all things richly, for our pleasure" (1 Tim 6:17).

For those living in the technologically advanced nations of the contemporary first world, however, the words "things invisible" may be more challenging than the words "things visible." The creed possesses for us a controversial edge quite distinct from the one it had in its first formulation, for those who profess the creed today tend to see the world in terms quite different than those of the Christians who first proclaimed it.

Almost all ancients assumed the superiority of the spiritual to the physical. Scripture was scarcely unique in assuming that God was more real than the world, and that the world included a variety of spirits, good and bad, who involved themselves in the lives of humans and the running of the universe. Demons and unclean spirits, whether independent agents or directed by a higher power like Satan or the Devil (Matt 4:10; Luke 10:18; Rom 16:20; 1 Cor 5:5; Gal 4:3, 9), regularly test, oppress, or even possess humans (see Mark 1:34; 3:15; 7:26; Luke 11:4–20; 1 Cor 10:20–21; 1 Tim 4:1; James 2:19). And for Paul, an adequate account of Christ's victory must include his sovereignty over the "powers and thrones and dominations and principalities" that operate at the cosmic level (1 Cor 15:24; Eph 1:21; 3:10; Phil 2:10–11; Col 1:15–16; 2:15).

The world of antiquity saw material reality, with all its changeableness and unreliability, its constant flow of birth and corruption, as a problem requiring explanation. That humans themselves had a "soul" or "self" which had a future beyond that of the human body was widely considered inarguable. Strongly dualistic impulses in philosophy and religion, indeed, considered the human soul as trapped in materiality, to find its freedom only when the body had been shed once and for all by death, or progressively through the process of asceticism. These impulses, as I have noted, found their way also into Christianity through Marcionism and Gnosticism. Thus, the creed found it necessary to include the creation of "things visible" among the works of the one God.

Today, however, the material world is taken to be all that is certainly real. The success of technology in controlling the forces of nature makes this assumption appear self-evident. The advances made by biological sciences, especially in medicine, provide a perfect contrast to the ignorance and bumbling of antiquity. On the basis of scientific methods, we conquer disease and are advancing on death itself. What did the mind of antiquity yield of comparable worth?

We can trace the demise of "things invisible." First to go were the various spiritual realities outside of humans—this was superstition. Then the soul was lost, replaced by mind. But now mind is quickly disappearing, because science is interested mainly in brains. The spiritual, outside and inside humans, has been lost, the "immortal soul" has been reduced to a tangle of complicated electronic circuitry.

Even among believers, the language and perceptions of Scripture and of most humans before the eighteenth European century now seem remote and even incredible. It is not at all clear how some sense of the spirit is to be recovered, or some awareness of the mystery of being that lies within and beyond the realm of the merely material.

Christians need to begin by insisting, first of all to themselves, then to each other, and finally to the world, that faith itself is a way of knowing reality. They need to insist that faith establishes contact with reality in a way different from, but no less real than, the very limited (though, in their fashion, extremely impressive) ways of knowing by which the wheels of the world's empirical engine are kept spinning. Christians need as well to cultivate practices that reveal and reinforce perceptions of the world that include "things invisible" as much as "things visible."

In particular, Christians need to claim the countercultural force of prayer, and to consciously and joyously embrace the political resistance inherent in worship. Every time we pray to God through the risen Lord Jesus, say "yes" to God and mean it, we also thereby say "no" to a world defined on the basis of matter alone, a world run solely on the basis of measurement and manipulation. In the practice of prayer, we confirm the truth stated by the creed that God creates heaven and earth, all things visible and invisible.

Chapter Four

AND IN ONE
LORD JESUS CHRIST

The longest part of the creed is devoted to the Son of God, Jesus Christ. It falls into two natural sections, the first describing his relationship with God the Father, maker of heaven and earth, and the second narrating his involvement with humanity, from his incarnation to his second coming (I will divide this second part into two chapters). We must take care not to turn this distinction into a division, for it is the *one* Lord Jesus Christ who is proclaimed in the creed. Focusing now on his "divinity" and then on his "humanity" should not lead us to separate them, for the entire effort of the creed is to assert both things about Jesus simultaneously: he is at once fully human and fully divine.

Before turning to the actual words of the creed, we must take an extended look at the scriptural witness it expresses, and the theological debates that led to its developing the way it did.

The earliest versions of the Christian creed moved directly from the statement of belief in one God as almighty father to the good news found in Jesus as Son of God. Thus, Hippolytus's *Apostolic Tradition* reads, "Do you believe in God the Father almighty? Do you believe in Christ Jesus, Son of God, who was born of the Holy Spirit out of the Virgin Mary and was crucified [etc.]?" Even today, the statements about Jesus' earthly life remain the least changed or developed. They stay closely connected to the narrative of Scripture.

But in the Nicene-Constantinopolitan Creed we say today, this simple story is preceded by other statements about the identity of Jesus that are the most elaborate and "technical" in the creed. Here we see most clearly how the creed developed as an instrument of polemic and definition, for it was precisely about the identity of Jesus—specifically how he was related to God—that the greatest and most divisive disputes within Christianity arose in the third and fourth centuries (the period in which the Nicene Creed was developed and officially approved). The present language of the creed shows a need to define ever more closely those core truths that were thought to be challenged by heretics.

For most Christians today, this is the least comprehensible part of the creed. Many of those reciting these words every Sunday do not understand what the words mean. Those who question the value of the creed as such find their best ammunition in this section, because it seems to focus on abstract philosophical questions rather than on the concrete facts of salvation.

To appreciate this part of the creed, it is helpful to understand the reasons it developed the way it did. The creed's order of exposition—beginning with the relationship of the Son of God to the Father and then his human existence—is not the order of discovery. The earliest Christians first experienced his humanity and then began to appreciate his divinity. In light of his resurrection, they began to see more clearly who Jesus had been all along and began to see him as more than a special human being. They saw him as God's unique representative to and among humans, as God's personal representation in human form, as God's only Son.

The creed does not ascribe divinity to Jesus as the result of a long development, as though the first Christians considered Jesus simply a man and only much later did their successors attribute divinity to him. The earliest Christians seem to have seen both his deepest sharing in their humanity and his divine power. Such, at least, is the evidence of the earliest writings, composed by those caught up by the experience of the resurrection.

THE PROCESS OF DISCOVERY

During his ministry, however, no one among Jesus' followers—and certainly not his opponents—fully appreciated who he truly was. At the very best, he was confessed as the Messiah (Mark 8:29) and Son of God (Matt 16:16), but as we have seen, such titles could scarcely have been intended to say that Jesus had a unique ontological relationship with God. As with the other titles given to Jesus, such as prophet (Luke 24:19; 6:14) and king (John 1:49) and Son of Man (Mark 14:62) and even savior (John 4:42), they were understood within the symbolism of Torah and the cultural and political realities of first-century Palestinian Jewish life. They pointed to the special role Jesus played among God's people, but they did not, indeed could not in that context, mean his distinctive and unique participation in the divine life. It was only *after* the disciples' experience of the resurrection of Jesus as an ongoing, personal, and transcendent presence that they understood these titles to mean that Jesus had this unique relationship with God.

The reader might well ask how I can say this, when the Gospels all portray Jesus as God's only Son whose deeds reveal the divine presence on earth. Let us look first at what the Gospels actually say about the way people saw Jesus during his ministry, and then at what the Gospels themselves tell us about the way they were composed.

First, each of the Gospels makes clear that despite Jesus' claims and wondrous deeds, neither his opponents nor his followers saw him for what he was. The same miracles and exorcisms that could evoke faith from some observers could evoke scorn and rejection from others (see Mark 2:1–12; 3:1–6). His opponents were looking for something else. Jesus' public behavior scandalized those seeking a messiah who followed the strict commands of Torah (see Luke 5:27–6:5; 7:31–8:3; 15:1–2). The manner of his death—crucifixion—seemed to certify that he was at least a failed and possibly a false messiah (see Gal 3:13; Deut 21:23). A consistent pattern of resistance (Matt 9:1–17; 12:1–14; 13:53–58; 15:1–14; 21:23–46) precedes their final rejection of him as a false prophet and their role in seeking his death (Matt 26:57–68).

As for Jesus' followers, each Gospel tells of the disciples' incomprehension (Mark 4:41; 7:18; 8:14–21, 31–37; 9:10, 33–41; 10:35–45; see even John 13:1–14:31; 16:29–33), which reaches its climax in the betrayal by Judas (Mark 14:10–11), the denial by Peter (Mark 14:54–72), and the abandonment by the rest of the disciples (Mark 14:50–52). The disciples were doubtful and confused (Mark 16:8; Matt 28:17; Luke 24:4, 16–24; John 20:14–15), and even disbelieved (Mark 16:14; Luke 24:11, 41; John 20:25), even in the face of the empty tomb and Jesus' appearances. Since the Gospel writers had every reason to suppress the sorry performance of Jesus' followers, all students of the New Testament accept the fundamental accuracy of their shared depiction. Neither Jesus' opponents nor his followers fully grasped who he was during his ministry.

So how did the disciples begin to grasp who Jesus was? In the letters of Paul and in the sermon usually called the letter to the Hebrews (written some twenty to twenty-five years after the death of Jesus and probably some twenty to twenty-five years before the first Gospel), we find not a recital of the resurrection as a historical event (see only 1 Cor 15:3–8), but the constantly repeated expression of the resurrection as the ongoing, personal, and transcendent presence of Jesus among his followers through the power of the Holy Spirit. It was because they were "in the Spirit" that they could confess that "Jesus is Lord" (1 Cor 12:3), that is, sharing God's life and sovereignty over creation. It was because they had all "drunk the one Spirit" (1 Cor 12:12) that they were "in Christ" (1 Cor 1:2) and indeed formed the "body of Christ" (1 Cor 12:27), the physical expression of the resurrection life of Jesus, Messiah and Lord.

The experience of Jesus' continuing power and presence made perfectly clear who he now was, the "Son of God in power through the Spirit of Holiness by his resurrection from the dead" (Rom 1:4; see Heb 1:1–13). But it also forced the question of whom he therefore *had* been before his exaltation to God's right hand and his share in God's rule over the world.

In Paul's letters and in Hebrews, the exaltation of Jesus by resurrection is more than a vindication by God of a good human being unjustly executed. It is the return of Christ to a position that is properly his. Paul declares that the one who by resurrection is called Lord began "in the form of God" and emptied himself out, taking the form of a slave (Phil 2:6–7). Paul calls Jesus the "image of the invisible God" (Col 1:15) and the "likeness of God" (2 Cor 4:4). God "sent forth his Son" to redeem humans (Gal 4:4), who were "chosen in him before the foundation of the world" (Eph 1:4). In him were "all things created" (Eph 1:16; see also 1 Cor 8:6). Paul may even—if some disputed passages be read from one perspective—call Jesus *theos*, the special title of God (Rom 9:5; Tit 2:11).

The letter to the Hebrews, similarly, says that God "created the world through [him]" (1:2) and speaks of the Son as one who "reflects the very glory of God and bears the stamp of his very nature" (1:3). Hebrews 1:8 also ascribes the title *theos* to the Son. Such statements are sometimes said to describe Jesus' "pre-existence." But how can someone exist before existing? How can "Jesus Christ" exist before Jesus was born in Bethlehem? "Pre-existence" is an unfortunate term, but it is the understandable consequence of creatures who live in time trying to speak about God who dwells outside time. We cannot speak of that which is outside time except in terms of time itself. Such language seeks to express in ways we can understand that, somehow, God was in the one we call Jesus from beginning to end, and that, equally, the one we call Jesus was, from beginning to end, in God.

The Christian experience of the resurrection, in short, did not follow as a natural result of the ministry of Jesus as recounted in the Gospels. It is rather the reverse: the Gospels follow as a natural process of reflection on Jesus' human ministry as a result of the Christian experience of him as resurrected Lord.

Second, the Gospels themselves, especially Luke and John, candidly acknowledge that they were written after and in light of this experience. In Luke 24, the three resurrection accounts each calls for a new insight into Jesus in light of his resurrection. In the first, at the empty tomb, the women are told to "remember how he told you while he was still with you, that the son of man must be delivered into the hands of sinful men and be crucified and on the third day rise" (24:6). Then, when Jesus joins the two disciples in their journey to Emmaus, he rebukes them for not knowing that he had to suffer before entering his glory: "And beginning with Moses and all the prophets he interpreted to them in all the scriptures the things concerning himself" (24:27). The story shows them learning how to find Jesus in Scripture and how to understand Scripture as pointing to Jesus. Finally, when Jesus appears to the disciples at another meal, he says to them, "These are my words which I spoke to you, while I was still with you, that everything written about me in the law of Moses and the prophets and the psalms must be fulfilled." And Luke adds, "Then he opened their minds to understand the scriptures" (24:44–45).

Luke interweaves these three revelatory moments with accounts of the disciples' reporting to each other experiences of encounter with the risen Jesus. He wants his readers to understand that even his own Gospel resulted from the reflections of those "eyewitnesses who became ministers of the word" (Luke 1:2), who remembered what Jesus had said and done in his ministry and had interpreted his acts and words in light of their new recognition of who Jesus really was, and in light also of a deeper grasp of how Scripture spoke of him.

John also tells his readers that a deeper understanding of Jesus by his followers came only after his death and the gift of the Holy Spirit. Jesus himself says this: "These things I have spoken to you while I am still with you. But the Counselor, the Holy Spirit, whom the Father will send in my name, he will teach you all things, and bring to your remembrance all that I have said to you" (14:25–26; see also 16:12–14). This deeper understanding of Jesus is precisely what his narrative provides. After Jesus' cleansing of the temple, the narrator comments, "When therefore he was raised from the dead, his disciples remembered that he had said this; and they believed the Scripture and the word that Jesus had spoken" (John 2:22). Commenting on Jesus' declaration that all those who came to him and believed could drink, for out of his heart flowed living waters, the narrator says, "Now he said this about the Spirit, which those who believed in him were to receive; for as yet the Spirit had not been given, because Jesus was not yet glorified" (7:37–38; see also 12:16; 20:9).

The evangelists interpret Jesus' sayings and deeds from the perspective of a deeper understanding of him given by the experience of the resurrection and the rereading of Scripture in light of his death and resurrection. What remains remarkable, in view of this, is how vividly human Jesus remains in their respective portraits of him: a man totally at home in the Judaism of first-century Palestine, with the words and gestures that fit that time and place. The Gospels should stun us most, not because they see Jesus as somehow divine, but that they so steadily and convincingly portray him as also utterly human.

Yet, written from the perspective of Christian faith in Jesus as God's Son, the Gospels contain an abundance of language pointing to God's presence in and through him already in his earthly life. In Mark, the designation "Son of God" appears at the beginning and end (1:1; 15:39) as a bracket around the story of Jesus. The demons recognize Jesus as "God's Son" and "God's Holy One" come to destroy them (Mark 1:24, 34; 5:1–20), and even the disciples catch a momentary glimpse of his identity as God's Son at the transfiguration (Mark 9:2–8). Matthew adds to these Jesus explicitly declaring himself as the Son who knows the Father and who reveals the Father to others (Matt 11:25–30), and speaks of Jesus' birth of the virgin Mary as a conception by the Holy Spirit (Matt 1:20). He brackets the story by identifying Jesus as "Emmanuel, which means God with us" at the beginning (1:23) and by the risen Jesus' declaration, "I am with you always, to the close of the ages" (Matt 28:20) at the end.

Luke also portrays Jesus' conception as the result of direct divine intervention: "The Holy Spirit will come upon you, and the power of the Most High shall overshadow you; therefore the child to be born will be called holy, the Son of God" (Luke 1:35). The prologue to John's Gospel, finally, states the conviction of all the early writers most explicitly. It begins: "In the beginning was the Word and the Word was with God and the Word was God" (John 1:1), then adds, "the word became flesh and dwelt among us, full of grace and of truth; we have beheld his glory, glory as of the only Son from the Father" (John 1:14), and then concludes, "No one has ever seen God; the only Son [or, as some manuscripts have it, "the only God"] who is in the bosom of the Father, he has made him known" (John 1:18).

Such a robust apprehension of Jesus as God's Son in the fullest sense was the church's faith from its earliest writings and through its first centuries. The only real exceptions seem to have been some forms of Jewish Christianity that appeared to deny his divinity and some Gnostic teachers, who so emphasized the divine character of Jesus that they ran the risk of denying his humanity. The innovation was not the "imposition" of a high Christology by the orthodox bishops of the fourth century, but rather the denial of that high Christology in the early fourth century by the Alexandrian priest Arius and his followers. Arius claimed that the Word was a creature, and therefore Jesus was divine only because God exalted him to divinity. Jesus was not already divine in his humanity.

The part of the creed we now examine did not exist before the Arian challenge. The orthodox saw the Arian position as a reduction of the mystery of Jesus to what seemed "reasonable," as one-sidedly emphasizing some scriptures and suppressing others, and above all, as denying the full Christian experience of Jesus. This section of the creed therefore is fundamentally a piling up of epithets to characterize Jesus Christ's relationship to God, precisely in order to safeguard the belief that Jesus Christ is our savior.

The Nicene theologians who argued for what we have now as the Nicene Creed maintained that salvation meant our sharing in God's life, and that only God can give us such a share in God's own life. A mere human cannot elevate other humans to the level of God. Christ therefore was not a human being who achieved divine status in the manner of the Greek heroes. Christ was rather the way in which God became human and through that humanity made it possible for all humans to share in the divine life.

THE SCANDAL OF DIVINITY

This unapologetic confession of Jesus Christ as divine scandalizes many who call themselves Christian. For fewer and fewer Christians is the robust Christology of the Nicene Creed truly the Rule of Faith. Many, consciously or not, subscribe to a modernized form of the Arian heresy. They share with their Arian forebears an explicit commitment to Scripture, but like them read the New Testament selectively. They share with their Arian predecessors a commitment to religion within the bounds of reason, and like them use reason to reduce the mystery of Christ to his humanity alone.

The modern version of Arianism finds perfect expression in the so-called quest for the historical Jesus that began in seventeenth-century England and found renewed vigor and notoriety recently in the Jesus Seminar. The "questers" seek "the real Jesus" based on what they think history shows, rather than on the faith of the church that "Nicene Christians" believe tells us what history means.

For them, historical study deals with verifiable events in time and space. The historical equals the real. If something is not historical, neither is it real. The historian must exclude divine causes as a matter of principle, because the divine is not an object that historians can study. This is legitimate. What is illegitimate, however, is the shift from recognizing that history cannot deal with wonders to saying that miracles cannot be known by any means, or that miracles do not happen. That shift is precisely what happened in the search for the historical Jesus "apart from faith." That which faith asserted is essential to knowing Jesus properly and fully was first excluded as historically unknowable and then increasingly denied. The "Real Jesus," therefore, could only be a Jesus stripped of divinity. But a Jesus stripped of divinity is just another human.

Such "historical Jesus" Christians don't seem to recognize the problem with their position. They prefer a Jesus who looks as much as possible like them. Alternatively, he should appear as much as possible like a powerful Jewish prophet of the first century. But if Jesus is simply like us, or if he is merely a powerful prophet of the past, why should he have any particular importance—or any claim on us? Why should we follow him rather than Hillel, another great Jewish teacher of the past? Why should Jesus matter more than Socrates or Confucius or the Buddha, or any of the great sages of the world? If God is not in Christ, devoting one's life to Christ is truly arbitrary.

To be Christian in any significant sense of the term is to claim that God is fully present in the human Jesus in a manner and fullness not realized in any other creature. It is to claim the way of knowing called faith, with the willingness to imagine the world that is imagined by the Scripture, so that when we look at the human Jesus we see also God's only Son and say with Paul, "It is the God who said, 'Let light shine out of darkness,' who has shone in our hearts to give the light of the knowledge of the glory of God in the face of Christ" (2 Cor. 4:6).

We therefore turn to the wording of this part of the creed in the same spirit of Paul, who proclaimed, "God was in Christ reconciling the world to himself" (2 Cor. 5:19). We gladly embrace the mythic character of our profession, knowing that myth expresses truths that history cannot reach. We do so not simply because we want to remain faithful to the full testimony of the Scripture and (up to very recently) the unswerving witness of the tradition, but most of all because we want to remain true to our own experience of God in Jesus Christ.

We are Christian in the first place, after all, not because Jesus was a splendid teacher of morals in first-century Palestine or because he had a particularly attractive vision for the ordering of society. We are Christian because somehow in Christ—through the sacraments, through prayer, through our suffering, through the words of our neighbors, or through the encounter with strangers—we have, in Christ's name, been touched and even transformed by God.

ONE LORD JESUS CHRIST

The name Jesus is the fundamental linchpin of the Christian confession. It translates the Hebrew name Joshua, which in turn derives from Yaheshua ("Yahweh = the Lord saves"). The angel Gabriel assigns the name and gives the interpretation: "you shall call his name Jesus, for he will save his people from their sins" (Matt 1:21; see also Luke 1:31). The name Jesus connects everything that is said about him in his relationship to God and everything that he did with respect to our salvation. It introduces everything in the creed that distinguishes Christianity from

Judaism and Islam, and begins to unfold the distinctive Christian understanding of God as triune.

The name, which belongs to a specific Jewish man of a specific time and place—"Jesus of Nazareth" (Acts 2:22)—grounds in history everything said about God's Son. The same grounding is given by the designation "Christ." The word, meaning "anointed one," is used in the Septuagint translation of the Old Testament to translate *messiach* (see 1 Sam 2:10; 24:7; 26:16; 2 Sam 19:21; Ps 2:2; 17:50; 19:6; 27:8; 83:9; 88:38; 104:15; 131:10). Jesus is God's anointed of whom Scripture spoke. God has anointed him with his own Holy Spirit, in order that he might proclaim the good news of God to all the outcasts of the earth (Luke 4:18; Acts 4:27; 10:38). Although in the eyes of his fellow Jews, "who seek for signs" of a genuine messiah (1 Cor 1:22), Jesus is a failed and possibly false messiah, for those "anointed" with his Holy Spirit (2 Cor 1:21), Jesus is truly God's Messiah of whom Scripture spoke, the fulfillment of the promises God made to Abraham and the patriarchs (Gal 3:14–18).

The experience of the crucified and raised Jesus showed that he is the firstborn of a new creation (2 Cor 5:16), a new Adam (1 Cor 15:45; Rom 12:12–21) who is the basis of a new humanity for both Jews and Gentiles (Gal 3:28; Eph 2:15; Col 3:10–11). In Jesus the Christ, we learn that the restoration God sought all along is the transformation of the human heart (Jer 31:31–34), and the law that God seeks to find in human hearts is that of the law of Christ (Gal 6:2).

The equation made between Jesus and Christ in the New Testament writings is absolute. In many cases, the simple designation *Christos* is used with reference to Jesus, with no need for clarification (see Rom 8:9–17; 9:1–5; 10:4–17; 1 Cor 10:4–11:3; Heb 3:6, 14; 5:5; 6:1; 9:11–28; 11:26). For Christians, Jesus simply *is* "The Christ" (see Matt 16:16; Mark 8:29; Luke 9:20; John 11:27;

Acts 18:5, 28). And the life that Christians live through the gift of his Holy Spirit they can designate simply as a life "in Christ" (Rom 6:11; 8:1; 1 Cor 3:1; 4:15; 2 Cor 3:14; 5:17; Gal 2:4; 3:16; 5:6; Eph 2:10; 4:32; Phil 1:13; 2:1; 3:14; Col 1:28; 1 Thess 4:16; 1 Tim 1:14; 2 Tim 1:9; Philem 8; 1 Pet 3:16; 5:10, 14).

The designation of Jesus as Lord (*kyrios*)—the third term in this phrase of the creed—is pivotal, since the Septuagint translates *Yahweh*, the proper name of the God of Israel (Exod 3:2–15), by the Greek term *kyrios*, for Greek readers, the name for the God who is the creator of heaven and earth, of all that is seen and unseen (see LXX Gen 2:4, 8; 3:1; 6:3; Exod 5:1; 6:1; 7:5; 15:26; 20:2, 5; etc.). Indeed, the use of "Lord" to mean "God" continues throughout the New Testament (see, e.g., Matt 1:20; 3:3; 22:37; Mark 13:20; Luke 1:6; 2:9; 3:4; 4:18–19; 19:38; John 1:23; 12:13, 38; Acts 2:34; 3:22; 4:26; 7:49; Rom 4:8; 9:28–29; 1 Cor 14:21; Heb 12:5; James 5:4, 21; 1 Pet 1:25; 3:12; Rev 1:8; 19:6).

For the earliest Christians to say "Jesus is Lord" (see Rom 10:9; 1 Cor 12:3; Phil 2:11) because of his resurrection meant that he had entered into the life of God and therefore shared in the power and authority of the Lord God, creator of heaven and earth. He was not merely a Jewish messiah as a "son of David" but was in virtue of his resurrection both "Messiah and Lord," who had been exalted "to God's right hand" (Acts 2:33–36). He is, as Revelation says, "King of kings and Lord of lords" (Rev 19:16), that is, supreme over all other earthly and cosmic powers (see Phil 2:10–11).

Rather than seek to distinguish the ways in which the one God can be Lord and Jesus also can be Lord, the first Christians simply embraced the reality in which they had been caught up. Indeed, the writers of the New Testament are particularly fond of the title *Kyrios* for Jesus. The full title, "Lord Jesus Christ"—the creed's wording—is one of the most frequently used designations for Jesus (see, e.g., Rom 13:14; 16:20; 1 Cor 1:2, 7; 2 Cor 1:13; 13:13; Gal 1:3; 6:14; Eph 1:2; 5:20; Phil 1:2; Col 1:3; 1 Thess 1:1; 5:9; 2 Thess 1:12; 2:1; Philem 3, 25; James 1:1; 2:1; 1 Pet 1:3; 2 Pet 1:8; Jude 4).

When we say these words of the creed, then, we declare that Jesus is our Lord, meaning that we recognize him as Lord of all and that we acknowledge his authority over our own hearts. We owe him the same worship and obedience we owe God. Indeed, by calling him Lord we imply that the worship and obedience we pay to the risen Jesus is the worship and obedience we pay to God.

To pay this obedience and worship to him is to deny it to any creature. As Lord, Jesus exercises absolute authority over our lives. We serve no created thing in preference to him. Thus, when pagan prefects demanded a choice between Christ and Caesar, Christians understood that this was a choice between the power of God as revealed in the world through the crucified and raised Messiah Jesus and the powers of the world as embodied by the Roman *imperium*. If they chose Caesar, the power of Rome assured that they would continue their mortal lives and, for the moment, escape death. They knew also, however, that if they chose Christ as Lord, they might die in their mortal bodies as a result, but they would live forever with Christ in the presence of God.

In light of this traditional understanding, the present-day objections to the use of "Lord" (as also to "King" and "kingdom") are particularly unfortunate and, in my view, wrong-headed. Some object to "Lord" and "King" being used for Jesus Christ because not only are lords and kings male, but they represent the unfortunate hierarchical arrangements of patriarchal social structures. Others object because "lordship" and "kingdom" suggest social arrangements in which some are more powerful than others.

Some translations of the New Testament seek to avoid offense by using soft near equivalents, like "sovereign" (who could be either male or female) and "dominion" (which does not demand a king). These ploys, while accomplishing gender neutrality, do not eliminate the power problem—a sovereign still rules and a dominion is still run by someone. Worse, they remove from the New Testament the terms by which Christians have understood themselves and their experience, not vis-à-vis each other, but in relation to God.

And these terms themselves offer an alternative to male domination and unjust social structures. If Jesus is our Lord, then none of us is lord over another. If Jesus is our Lord, then we can all be slaves of Christ, and none need be slave to another human. Being slaves of the Lord of the universe means that we are free from any enslaving creature and free to inhabit all of God's own freedom.

Such terms have been used to support male power in human social structures, and it is important vigorously to resist the automatic equation of theological terms with social realities. To do this, we must work to reform social structures and ideas about power to achieve full equality in dignity among humans and authority structures that enhance rather than detract from such dignity.

But we can do this precisely by means of a serious and sustained critique of the human tendency toward idolatry; that is, of applying to our worldly arrangements what should only be applied to God. And we can do this while recognizing and celebrating the truth of our existence in Christ: that it is by confessing him as one Lord that we thus have the freedom to engage and change the structures that do not reveal but obscure his Lordship over us all.

THE ONLY-BEGOTTEN SON OF GOD

From this point, the language about Jesus is directed to clarifying the conviction that he was, in the fullest sense of the word, God. Rather than provide a single crisp definition—how could any be possible?—the crafters of the creed piled phrase upon phrase, most drawn from Scripture but some not, in an effort to assert a single simple (but infinitely difficult) truth: that Christ came from and returned to God in a way that no other human has or will or could, because when he came from God he remained what he had been and when he returned to God he returned to his own place. This was needed in the face of the Arian position that sought to reduce the Son to the level of a creature, albeit a spiritual and "in some sense divine" creature. Creeds originally could move directly from "one Lord Jesus Christ" to an account of his human deeds. But in the early fourth century, the orthodox party had to affirm in as many ways as it could the uniqueness of this Son of God in comparison with any other.

Thus, Jesus is now designated as "the only Son of God" or, more literally, "only-begotten Son of God." In response to those who argued that Jesus was God's Son simply by adoption, in the same way that "all those led by the Spirit of God are sons of God" (Rom 8:14), the shapers of the creed needed to do more than show the ways in which Jesus is called God's Son throughout the New Testament. And they could not exploit those passages that referred to Jesus as the "firstborn," since these seemed to provide fuel for the alternative position.

They needed above all to emphasize those elements in Scripture that spoke of the ways in which Jesus was uniquely God's Son. In the Gospels, they found a voice from heaven declaring at Jesus' baptism, "you are my beloved son" (Matt 3:17; Mark 1:11;

Luke 3:22), and the same voice speaking from heaven at Jesus' moment of self-revelation to his chosen disciples, calling him "beloved son" (Matt 17:5; Mark 9:7; Luke 9:35; see 2 Pet 1:17). In the parable of the wicked husbandmen, they could also hear an echo of that announcement in the owner's decision to send to the vineyard his "beloved son" (Mark 12:6; Luke 20:13).

In Paul they found the description of Jesus as God's "own son," whom he did not spare from death (Rom 8:32). And Paul twice speaks of God "sending" Jesus, clearly implying that he was somewhere else (to use inadequate language) before coming among humans (Rom 8:3; Gal 4:4) to redeem humans "so that we might receive adoption as sons" (Gal 4:4). In 1 John they found the same language about sending a son to be the "expiation of our sins" and "savior of the world" (1 John 4:10; 4:14). In these passages, Paul and John strongly suggest not only that Jesus is divine but that it is through his being sent into the world that humans gain a share in his spirit and sonship.

BEGOTTEN FROM THE FATHER BEFORE ALL TIME

Jesus is the "only-begotten Son" of God. This term enables believers to speak of Jesus' relationship with the Father as Son and as God's only Son. The term may have been derived from Psalm 2:7, which was used by the first Christians as a way of expressing Jesus' sonship through his resurrection: "The Lord said to me, 'You are my son. This day I have begotten you (*ego semeron gegennēka se*).' " Paul cites the same verse in his speech about the resurrection in Acts 13:33 and in Hebrews in its argument that the Son is superior to the angels (Heb 1:5; see also 5:5).

Two passages in John's Gospel undoubtedly contributed to the use of this language in the creed. There can be no mistaking the fact that John asserts that Jesus is the unique Son able to reveal God because he is only-begotten. But in John it is not only the use of the term that asserts the uniqueness of Jesus' relationship with God, but the divine attributes that are ascribed to him. The first passage is John 1:14, from the prologue to the Gospel: "The Word became flesh and dwelt among us, full of grace and truth; we have beheld his glory, glory as of the only-begotten of the father." John affirms the divine character of the Son in three ways. First, the phrase "grace and truth" echoes the name of Yahweh revealed to Moses on the mountain (Exod 34:6). Second, the repetition of the term "glory" likewise evokes the presence of God among the people (Exod 24:16–17). The point is reinforced by the pun created by the verb translated "dwelt": *skēnoun* (to make a tent) recalls the *skēnē*, or tent of dwelling for God's glory in the wilderness (see Exod 40:34).

Finally, this embodied Word is "only-begotten" by God the Father. At the end of the prologue, John says that this "only-begotten Son" is "in the bosom of the Father" and "he has made him known"—suggesting an origin "from within" God the creator and the unique capacity to make God known (compare Matt 11:25–27 and Luke 10:21–22). A textual variant for this verse does not read "only-begotten Son," but "only-begotten God." It is attested by early and excellent manuscripts, and some scholars think this "harder reading" is what John actually wrote.

John uses language of the Son that Scripture associates with Wisdom as God's companion and helper in creation (see Prov 8:22–31; Wisd 7:22–30; Sir 24:1–31), as well as with the creation story that has God creating all things by his mere word (Gen 1:9)—deliberately evoked by the opening phrase of the prologue, "in the beginning" (John 1:1; Gen 1:1). John declares of this Word that was in the beginning: "the Word was with God and the

Word was God" (John 1:1–2). It was this Word that "became flesh and dwelt among us," whose glory was as of the only-begotten out of the father (1:14).

The second passage occurs in Jesus' discourse to Nicodemus (John 3:16–18):

> For God so loved the world that he gave his only [in Greek, "only-begotten"] son, that whoever believes in him should not perish but have eternal life. For God sent the Son into the world not to condemn the world, but that the world might be saved through him. He who believes in him is not condemned; he who does not believe is condemned already, because he has not believed in the name of the only [Greek: "only-begotten"] son of God.

In this passage John's use of verbs "giving" and "sending" suggest the Son's existence prior to his human appearance. The Son is the source of eternal life, which only God can give. He was sent for the salvation of the world, a task that no human could accomplish. All this is connected in the beginning and end of the passage to Jesus as the "only-begotten son of God."

The creed now clarifies the meaning of the term by adding "begotten from the Father before all time." The English translation used in the liturgy catches only part of the Greek, which can be translated as "the one who was begotten out of the Father before all the ages." The addition makes two things clear:

First, the "begetting" here is not physical. The creed is not talking about the birth of Jesus as a human. Rather, it takes place within the life of God. As temporal creatures we can speak of the eternal only in temporal terms, so we must use the phrase "before all time" or "before all the ages"—with an implied emphasis on "all"—to assert that this happened within God's own life, not as a physical process or human birth. Second, this begetting is not a making by God but a sharing by the Father out of himself. This the phrase "out of the Father" makes clear.

This language is both revealing and inhibiting. On one side, when the Son is said to be "begotten out of the Father before all the ages," we can grasp the metaphor in its positive dimension: we understand that the Son is not something made by the Father as part of creation, but is rather an extension or expansion of the Father's own existence. We recognize that our human offspring are not things we "make." They are not our possessions. They are bone of our bone, flesh of our flesh. They are "out of us" and share our substance, and are often, as the saying has it, our "spitting image."

But the metaphor also inhibits us, because our understanding of the relation of a father to a son is so bound up with biological parenthood. Our children are born helpless and dependent. They are less than we are. They are subordinate. They need to grow in order to become independent. Then we will die and they will replace us, only to have children of their own. It is difficult for us to think about an eternally begotten son without treating the begetting as something that happened in time and in the manner of a human birth.

Here is where the connection that John's prologue (John 1:1–18) drew between "the only-begotten Son" and "the Word" (with all its links to the wisdom tradition) was so helpful to the Nicene theologians—and us. Speaking of the Son as the Word enabled the Nicene theologians to think about begetting in spiritual rather than in physical terms. They could consider how the human mind generates thought in the form of a word (or words) before the human mouth expresses that word in speech. Although it is possible to distinguish mind and word in terms of cause and effect, it is clear that in terms of mental activity, they are also inseparable, and mutually defining. Also, when the word is spoken ("becomes flesh") in human speech, it remains the word of the thinker, and simply takes a new form. Our speech communicates our thoughts rather than that our speech creates our thoughts. The metaphor of the Word makes it possible to reflect on the relations between the persons in the trinity, interms of spiritual process rather than in terms of biological descent.

GOD FROM GOD, LIGHT FROM LIGHT, TRUE GOD FROM TRUE GOD

With the addition of these three phrases, you might well ask, "How many ways do we have to say the same thing?" Just in case describing Jesus as Lord, as only-begotten Son, and "begotten from the Father before all time" did not make the point, the creed adds three more phrases that make the meaning unmistakable. We mean: we are talking about God! The effect of them together is to make clear beyond all equivocation that our "Lord Jesus Christ" is divine.

The first and third phrases ("God from God" and "True God from True God") are virtually the same, and for the sake of efficiency, I will discuss them as one. The original Nicene version had all three, so did the Latin, and so does the English used by many churches. The official Greek version has only "Light from Light" and "True God from True God." Whether with two or three phrases, the repetition of the same preposition ("out of") that was used for "begotten out of the Father" serves to make these phrases hammer home the same point.

The phrase "Light from Light" is thoroughly biblical in origin. Light is the first thing created by God's word of command

(Gen 1:3–5). The Lord's presence was a light for the people of Israel during the plagues (Exod 10:3). In the Psalms, light is consistently associated with God: "The Lord is my light," says Psalm 26:1, and "in your light we shall see light" says Psalm 35:9 (see also Ps 42:3; 55:13; 77:14). Particularly striking is the language of Psalm 88:15, which declares blessed those who walk "in the light of your face." In Wisdom 7:22, wisdom itself is called "a reflection of eternal light."

Isaiah invites the House of Jacob "to walk in the light of the Lord" (Isa 2:5), and declares that the people who walked in darkness have seen a great light; "those who dwelt in a land of deep darkness, on them has light shined" (Isa 9:2). Most emphatically, Isaiah proclaims to the people:

> Arise, shine; for your light has come, and the glory of the Lord has risen upon you. For behold, darkness shall cover the earth and thick darkness the peoples; but the Lord will arise upon you, and his glory will be seen upon you, and nations shall come to your light, and kings to the brightness of your rising. (Isa 60:1–3)

In the New Testament, light is also associated with the divine presence. Paul says that God "alone has immortality and dwells in unapproachable light" (1 Tim 6:16). Peter speaks of God calling the chosen "out of darkness into his marvelous light" (1 Pet 2:9). Most dramatically, James says, "Every good and endowment and every perfect gift is from above, coming down from the Father of lights with whom there is no variation or shadow due to change" (James 1:17). This passage would prove powerfully attractive to those who crafted the creed, for at the same time that it speaks of the unchangeableness of the "Father of lights" who is "above," it also says that this God is the source of perfect gifts that are "coming down." The passage asks to be read together with the prologue of John's Gospel.

Before turning to that passage, however, we should note that Paul also uses light imagery for speaking about Jesus. In 2 Corinthians 4:5–6, he says that "the God who said 'Let light shine out of darkness' " shone in the hearts of believers "to give the light of the knowledge of the glory of God in the face of Christ." Paul draws together God the creator—who called forth the light—and Jesus the Lord. God's own glory "shines" on the face of Christ. He is "light from light." Immediately before this passage, Paul developed an elaborate contrast between the fleeting glory that shone on the face of Moses (Exod 34:30, 35) and the enduring glory on Christ's face. He concludes that we all, "beholding the glory of the Lord, are being changed into his likeness from one degree of glory to another; for this comes from the Lord, who is Spirit" (2 Cor 3:17–18).

From God to Christ to the believers, "light" stands as a metaphor for divine life and presence—in a word, for God's glory. The metaphor means less to us living in a world that is lit around the clock by electric power, far removed from those for whom light was a gift and a sign of God's providence, rather than a human product they could take for granted. Still, light is for us as for them a particularly happy metaphor, because among all things material, it comes closest to the spiritual. Since we do not so much see light as we see *by* light, moreover, light is an apt metaphor for God, who is never "seen" in the world but always the implicit premise by which the world is seen correctly.

It is John's Gospel that most exploits the metaphor of light in order to express the (inexpressible) identity and work of Jesus. In the prologue, John says of the Word that was with God and was God, "in him was life, and the life was the light of men. The light shines in the darkness and the darkness has not overcome it"

(John 1:5). This was, he continues, the "true light that enlightens every man, coming into the world" (1:9). John wants to identify the Word with the Life and Light that belong to God alone and that God gives to humans. John seems to be saying three things: that Jesus is the "true light" (I will return to this), that he enlightens all people, and that he is "coming into the world." This thematic declaration establishes the meaning of the metaphor that John uses throughout his Gospel.

Thus, in Jesus' conversation with Nicodemus, John has him say, "And this is the judgment, that the light has come into the world, and men loved darkness rather than light, because their deeds were evil" (John 3:19). Jesus is the light that exposes the reality of the world—its darkness or evil—and forces humans to choose for or against God.

In 5:35, the evangelist contrasts John the Baptist and Jesus (as he did earlier in 1:3–8) by having Jesus himself say, "He was a burning and shining lamp and you were willing to rejoice for a while in his light." John the Baptist is a lamp giving temporary illumination; Jesus is the true Light. Later, John has Jesus proclaim of himself: "I am the light of the world; he who follows me will not walk in darkness, but will have the light of life" (8:12). The statement shows how, even if John had never used the expression "Son of God," he would have made it powerfully clear through metaphor that Jesus is divine (see also 9:35; 12:35–36, 46). How striking it is that when Judas leaves the circle of Jesus' friends to betray him, John notes, "and it was night" (John 13:30).

The theologians who crafted the creed saw John's metaphor of Jesus as the Light "coming into the world" from "above" (see John 3:3, 31) and James's description of God as the "Father of Lights" who was unchangeable yet gave gifts "from above" (James 1:17), and Paul's language in 2 Corinthians 4:4–6 concerning the light of the glory of God shining on the face of Christ as providing full scriptural support for asserting of the Son that he is "Light from Light." And they were right.

Speaking of the Son as "Light from Light" is bold enough, but the creed's boldest stroke is to say of him that he is "God from God" and "True God from True God." It is bold because those Greek-speaking orthodox teachers certainly understood the specific resonance of the title *theos* ("God"). The Old Testament and virtually all of the New Testament restricts that title to God the Father. It is bold to apply the title to the Son despite the New Testament's own reluctance to ascribe it to Jesus Christ. It is possible that the title is given to Jesus in six passages (Rom 9:5; Tit 3:4; Heb 1:8; John 1:1 and 18; 20:28), but five of them are questionable. In the Pauline passages (Rom 9:5 and Tit 3:4), it is not clear whether God or Christ is the subject. In John 1:1, it is uncertain how strictly John wished the predicate "God" to have the full force of "God." In Hebrews 1:8, it is not clear how intentionally the author wishes Jesus to have the title "God" that he implies is his through the citation of Psalm 44:6–7. John 1:18 may not read "only-begotten God," but "only-begotten Son." Despite the difficulties in each case, sincere readers—especially those whose copies contained a text pointing that way—could certainly understand the New Testament as ascribing the title *theos* to Jesus. The decisive text is John 20:28, which is unencumbered by textual variants of any significance, and which has Thomas greeting Jesus with the words "My Lord and my God."

The characterization "True (*alēthinos*) God from True God" also depends largely on Johannine language. The adjective distinguishes the authentic from the false or the apparent. John 5:20 refers to "the true God," speaking of the Father, as does Jesus in the Fourth Gospel in his final prayer, when he addresses the Father as "true God" (17:1). But the association of "true/genuine" (*alēthinos*) with God also extends to Jesus. The Book of

Revelation refers to the resurrected Jesus as "the holy, the true" (Rev 3:7; 6:10), and John's Gospel speaks of the Son in 1:9 as the "true light," in 6:32 as the "true bread," and in 15:1 as the "true vine." This complex semantic linkage encouraged the bold designation of the Son as "True God from True God."

These two (or three) additional phrases—God from God, Light from Light, True God from True God—thus not only make the creed's point unmistakable, they illuminate its meaning by drawing on the rich metaphors of Scripture.

BEGOTTEN NOT MADE, OF THE SAME SUBSTANCE AS THE FATHER

These words are the least intelligible to present-day Christians, and must be placed in historical context if they are to be understood at all, much less appreciated. Here is the first appearance of language that is not derived from the Bible, and some reject it (and the creed as a whole) for that reason alone. To grasp why such language was thought to be necessary, we must recover something of the crisis the Council of Nicea was called to address. I sketched the basic history in chapter 1, and will now discuss only the ideas at issue.

This language developed through the struggle by Christian intellectuals (theologians) to express the nature of the one through whom they considered themselves to have been touched and transformed by God. From the second century forward, there was a tension between two emphases. Those who tended to focus on the humanity of Jesus tended to think of the relationship of the Son to God in terms of distinction and subordination. The extreme version moved toward ditheism—namely that the Father and Son were two Gods. Those who tended to focus on the divinity of

Christ tended to think in terms of unity, or a monarchical modalism that obscured full humanity. The extreme here was patripassionism, in which God the Father suffers on the cross.

Teachers in different regions of the church emphasized one side or another, and made use of extrabiblical language to bring some precision to the rich but ambiguous presentation of Jesus Christ in the New Testament. Tragically, the points of emphasis sharpened into points of conflict, not least because teachers in different ecclesiastical centers (above all, Antioch for the first emphasis and Alexandria for the second) read Scripture with different philosophical lenses.

Something very much like the creed's idea was nevertheless expressed frequently long before Arius (256–336). Thus, in the middle of the second century, in Justin Martyr's *First Apology*, for example, we find him speaking of Jesus Christ as the "only unique son begotten by God, being a first-born word and power . . . becoming a human being" (23). Here we see not only the emphasis on the singular nature of the Son as begotten by God, but the critical distinction between that "generation" (*gennētos*) and "becoming" (*genetos*) human. The distinction rests on only a few letters of the Greek alphabet, but is important. Similarly, Athenagoras says that the Father and Son are "out of one being," and continues, "The Son is in the Father and the Father in the Son, in the unity and power of the Spirit, Mind and Word of the Father, the Son of God . . . first begotten (*gennēma*) by the Father, not as a creature (*genomenon*)" (*Legation* 10).

At the beginning of the third century, Tertullian responded to Praxeas with a subtle statement concerning the trinity that fully anticipated Nicea: "Father and Son and Spirit are three, however, not in status but in rank, not in substance but in form, not in power but in appearance; they are however of one substance and of one status and of one power, because God is one, from whom these ranks and forms and appearances are designated in name as Father and Son and Holy Spirit" (*Adversus Praxean* II, 4). For Tertullian, the truth of revelation demanded making appropriate distinctions while maintaining a fundamental sameness in God.

Arius's teaching aggressively countered this tradition by emphasizing distinction at the cost of unity. He claimed to base his assertions on Scripture. His favorite texts included Proverbs 8:22; Acts 2:36; Romans 8:29; Colossians 1:15; Hebrews 3:2; John 17:3; 14:28, and the passages in the Gospels that suggested Jesus' ignorance (see above all Mark 13:32). Many of these passages can indeed be read as describing Christ as subordinate to the Father. But other New Testament texts lead in another direction. These, Arius tended to ignore.

More than that, he resolved to dissolve the mystery that lay at the heart of the Christian experience (being touched by God in our humanity) through a form of logical problem-solving. Arius exemplifies the theologian impatient with paradox. So in his *Letter to Alexander*, Arius states explicitly that the Son is a creature and, just as telling, that there was a time when he was not. The bishops at the Council of Nicea therefore considered themselves to be correcting a distortion, not inventing a new doctrine. They had to use the philosophical language of being because that had become the language of analysis, and because Scripture did not provide any term precise enough to say what they thought needed saying. They used the term *homoousios* ("one in being") to assert the unity of being of Father and Son, rather than *homoiousios* ("similar in being"). They considered themselves thereby not to be perverting but preserving the full testimony of Scripture.

They knew that it is impossible to state adequately how Father and Son are related. What they saw as essential to faith is to deny that the Son is simply an improved version of ourselves. An excerpt from one of the orthodox champions, Athanasius of

Alexandria, explains how he understood the words of the creed: "The Son is not only like to the Father, but that, as his image, he is the same as the Father; that he is of the Father; and that the resemblance of the Son to the Father, and his immutability *are different from ours*: for in us they are something acquired, and arise from our fulfilling the divine commandments. Moreover they wished to indicate by this, that *his generation is different from that of human nature*: that the Son is not only like to the Father, but inseparable from the substance of the Father; that he and the Father are one and the same." (*De Decretis Synodi Nicaenae* 20). I have added italics to show how what the orthodox theologians were denying is as critical as what they positively affirmed.

These debates and these distinctions do not make much sense to us today. It is nevertheless important that we see what is at stake, both for the ancient theologians and for us. These words do not significantly add to any of the words that were drawn directly from Scripture. Saying that the Father and Son are "of one being" says nothing more than that Jesus Christ is "God from God, Light from Light, True God from True God."

But it remains important to deny that the Son is a creature, for at stake is the reality of salvation. Is it God who saves us in Jesus or not? The creed says yes, Arius said no, not exactly. The Nicene theologians sought to protect the reality of redemption by God by resisting the reductionistic rationalism of Arius. For many Christians today, a version of that reduction is deeply appealing. For them, the creed is as great a scandal as the divinity of Jesus itself.

THROUGH WHOM ALL
THINGS WERE MADE

Arius had exploited Old Testament passages that had portrayed wisdom as the first of God's creatures, acting as an assistant in the creation of the world (see Prov 8:22–31; Sir 24:1–9). The Nicene bishops now complete their statement about the "pre-existent" Christ by asserting that "through [him] all things were made." Arius had defined the Son as a "thing made" (*poiēma*). The creed had in its first line called God the Father "maker" and now declares the one who is "begotten not made" (*gennēthenta ou poiēthenta*) to be the one through whom God has made "all things." It follows that, if he is the one through whom all things are made, he is not one of the things made.

In light of the titles ascribed to the Son, the crafters of the creed would not view his role in creation as that of a lesser god (such as would be possible if Proverbs and Sirach formed the only scriptural basis), but fully as the work of God. They would read the Psalm's statement "by the word of the Lord were the heavens established," and understand it to mean the "Word [who] was God" in John 1:1.

The prologue to John, in fact, is one of the three New Testament witnesses to the Son's role in creation: "all things were made through him and without him was not anything that was made" (John 1:3). The creed adopted John's language and its insistence on the inclusiveness of the Son's creative role. The second witness is Paul, who clearly considers the Son as active in creation, referring in 1 Corinthians 8:4–6 to "one Lord Jesus Christ, through whom are all things and through whom we are." Paul not only asserts that "we" as Christians came into being through Jesus Christ, but that "all things" came into being through him.

The Son plays a role not only in the second but in the first creation.

Likewise in Colossians, Paul speaks of the "Son of his love" (1:14) in these terms: "He is the image of the unseen God, the first-born of all creation, because in him all things were created in the heavens and on the earth, things visible and things invisible, whether thrones or dominions or rulers or authorities: all things were created through him and for him" (Col 1:15–16). We can see here, by the way, the selectivity of Arius's reading of Scripture. This was one of his favorite texts, because of the line "first-born of all creation," but the entire passage argues against his position, for Paul emphasizes that all things were created through him, and that he was not merely God's agent, because all things were also created for him.

The third witness is the prologue to Hebrews, which says of the Son through whom God has spoken in the last of days that "through him also he created the ages." On this point the language of the creed could not be more faithful to the expressions of the New Testament concerning the Son of God.

In the section of the creed we have examined in this chapter, we have found stated that all things are from God the Father and all things are equally through God the Son. Later we will see that the Spirit is equally to be "worshiped and glorified." What we have learned about God in creation and salvation and sanctification, the creed proposes, tells us not only what God does but also who God is. The revelation of God through Jesus Christ and the Holy Spirit draws us into the mystery of God's own life. And since the goal of salvation and sanctification is to give humans a share in that life, the mystery of the trinity also reveals something of who we are and what we are called to reveal within creation.

We must wait for the articles dealing with the Spirit and the church to consider this more fully, but it is important to see the implications of the elaborate and sometimes technical language that has been dedicated to the divinity of Jesus Christ. What is at stake is not only who Jesus is, but who God has shown Godself to be, and therefore also what salvation truly is. We learn now that God is fully and deeply implicated in and involved with creation, so much so that the one who comes among us as a human person is making explicit a presence that is already and always implicit in the creation-at-every-moment that is "through him."

We learn also that the incarnation is not an afterthought, a rescue operation carried out by God's subaltern, but is implicit from the beginning in the Son's active agency in the creation that happens at every moment in our evolving world. We learn, finally, that when Genesis says that male and female are created in the image of God (Gen 1:26), we are allowed to think that this image is already implicitly ordered to the image of Christ into which, in the new creation, we are being transformed (2 Cor 3:17–18; Col 3:10–11), since all things created are already created "through him" who is the "image of the unseen God" (Col 1:15).

Chapter Five

WHO FOR US . . .
BECAME HUMAN

✠

"Who for us . . . and . . . our salvation . . . became human."
Here is the heart of the creed. Here is the expression of that experience that led pious Jews to break with tradition and proclaim
their belief that there are two powers in heaven. Here is the story
that for Christians defines the difference between the old and the
new age, between the first and the new creation. Here is the confession of Jesus as the incarnate Son of God that arose out of the
church's powerful experience of his resurrection.

The creed's first statements about Jesus, we have seen, were
included to defend the full richness of his designation as Son of
God, as the church reflected on its experience of Jesus and faced
challenges to it. But the next statements spring less from reflection upon experience than from the witness of the experience itself. Here is the heart of the earliest community's confession of
Jesus, found in the barest possible narrative about his birth, suf-

fering, death, resurrection, exaltation, and return as judge of the living and the dead.

This part of the creed above all makes clear that the profession of faith does not seek to replace Scripture but only to provide a norm for the faithful and adequate reading of Scripture. Everyone recognizes that this spare account has none of the richness of the Gospel stories. No one can find here the vibrant and living person who is so vividly portrayed by Matthew, Mark, Luke, and John.

But complaints that "the creed leaves a blank where Jesus should be" miss the point. The creed, as we have seen, is not the only instrument for expressing the faith of the community. It stands together with all the other elements of the church's tradition, including its worship and its Scripture, in a mutually interpretive relationship. No single element of the tradition can capture all the truth of the reality in which believers have been caught up. Each element works together with the others to convey the truth as fully as it can be conveyed in language. The Gospels can be interpreted in any number of ways, not all of them compatible with the church's sense of who Jesus is and who the God he reveals is. The creed provides a guide to the correct hearing of the Gospels—and the Gospels (indeed all of Scripture) provide a guide to the proper reading of the creed.

If the narrative summary is meant to provide a guide for the reading of the Gospels, the right selection of the elements included in the summary is critical. The creed says, in effect: these are the parts of the story that you must include and on no account omit if you are to render the story of Jesus correctly. What are these elements? The creed states first the manner of his conception and birth as a human being, then the manner of his death, then his resurrection and ascension, and finally his coming again as judge. To these, it adds the conviction that his rule will have no end. The entire sequence is introduced by the interpretive phrase "for us men and for our salvation," which is echoed by the words "for us," before "he was crucified under Pontius Pilate."

This part of the creed is only in part about the human story of Jesus that is past. It does not tell a story that is finished and over. His resurrection, exaltation, and never-ending rule is part of the present story of every believer, and his return to judge is part of the future story of all humanity. Further, by using the pronoun "who" in this section, the creed makes clear that the one whose story it tells is the same person as the "Lord Jesus Christ" spoken of in the previous section. The one who enters into humanity bears with him all the fullness of divinity (Col 2:9). In the previous chapter, we asked why phrases like "God from God" were being used for Jesus and tried to discover their basis in Scripture or logic. In this section, the basis for what is said is clear. Each of the statements about Jesus derives from the Gospels. Our task now is therefore slightly different. We need to ask why these elements and only these elements have been selected as essential to the correct confession of Jesus, and why all the elements of the story are thought to be necessary "for us men and for our salvation."

FOR US MEN

With these words "for us men and for our salvation," for the first time since the beginning of the creed, the speakers enter the narrative. Up to now, they have been speaking entirely about God's identity and work. Now they declare their interest in the story: what happened, is happening, and will happen in and through Jesus Christ, they assert, is all for them. The creed does not imply that only those who speak these words are the intended recipients of God's gift. It means that those who make this profession differ from others in the way they acknowledge the "for us-ness" of the gift, but the Greek version of the creed in particular makes clear that all humanity is potentially included. It uses the gender-inclusive *anthrōpos* (humanity) rather than *anēr* (male). If the translation "for us men" is retained for the sake of tradition, therefore, it must be interpreted in an inclusive manner to mean "humans."

The creed says, then, that the Son of God became human and suffered and died as other humans do, for the sake of humans themselves. Now, this is the sort of assertion that Christianity's critics delight in as demonstrating the terminal narcissism of believers. How, they say, can we imagine the all-powerful creator of the universe being so concerned with one part of the population of one tiny planet in all this vastness as to become one of those creatures? First they posit a God of such magnitude, then they pretend that a God of such magnitude could care about creatures so small. Better to face a meaningless existence facing the void of nonbeing than submit to such delusion.

The gap is just as scandalously wide as the critics say. The creed does in fact posit a God of literally unimaginable power and magnitude—creator of all things visible and invisible!—and does assert that this God, for the sake of humans, entered into their history. But three facts eliminate any reason for humans to take pride in this.

First, the creed modestly declines to declare what the almighty God has in mind for creatures other than humans, what gifts God has or is giving them, and what divine plans they may figure in or have figured in. The creed does not restrict God's benevolence or saving activity to humans. The creed merely celebrates the saving care that God has shown humans in Christ Jesus.

Second, by identifying humans as the reason for God's entering this world, the creed (with Scripture) also identifies humans as the problem with this world. The world—including humanity—that God declares as good in its creation (Gen. 1:9, 11, 18, 21, 25, 31) does not cease being good (1 Tim 4:4). But as Paul says, human disobedience to God led to a distortion of creation (Rom 1:18–32; see also 8:20). Creation awaits its liberation through the liberation of humans as children of God with Jesus (Rom 8:19, 28–29). If God became human for our sake, we are identified as the cause of the distortion of creation that God became human to repair.

Third, the creed does not suggest that humans uniquely deserve divine attention and care, but rather that in such care, God is revealed truly as love. The term used by the New Testament for God's love is *agapē*, which means what we today might call a "pure love": a disposition that seeks the good of the other, not because of any benefit to oneself, but simply for the sake of the other. Both Paul and John use the language of *agapē* for the self-donation of God through Jesus Christ. John has Jesus himself declare to Nicodemus, "For God so loved the world that he gave his only son, so that everyone who believes in him may not perish but may have eternal life" (John 3:16). Paul speaks of Jesus as the one who "loved me and gave himself for me" (Gal 2:20), and tells his Ephesian readers, "Be imitators of God as beloved children, and live in love, as Christ loved us and gave himself up for us, a fragrant offering and sacrifice to God" (Eph 5:1–2).

The phrase "for us men," then, does not suggest that humans are so overwhelmingly important that God had to become human, but declares that the mystery of God is love. John says in his first letter, "Whoever does not love does not know God, for God is love [*agapē*]. God's love was revealed among us in this way: God sent his only Son into the world so that we might live through him. In this is love, not that we loved God, but that he loved us and sent his Son to be the atoning sacrifice for our sins" (1 John 4:8–10). To put it simply, when we look at Jesus, we do not learn how we are, but how God is. The incarnation "for us men" reveals God to be a passionate and (by some measures) almost a careless lover, who is willing to hide or even lose himself in order to elevate the creatures made in his image to whom God is so oddly yet powerfully committed.

AND FOR OUR SALVATION

To the words "for us men" the creed adds the phrase "and for our salvation." It appears to be a small addition, but it was critical to all the debates about Jesus and the trinity in the ancient church. The reason that the early Christians argued about the full divinity of the Son and his sharing fully in humanity is because the answers radically affected our salvation. Although these debates often involved complicated arguments and technical terminology, the orthodox side tried to remain faithful even in the most abstract matters to the experience of the church and the testimony of Scripture.

If salvation were simply a matter of correcting some mistaken ideas that humans held, then Jesus need be no more than a good teacher sent by God in the manner of Moses. If salvation were simply a question of rectifying social structures that were oppressing the people, then Jesus need be no more than a faithful prophet sent by God in the manner of Amos or Isaiah. If salvation, in short, were simply a human matter, then Jesus needed to be only a human being.

But what if the New Testament speaks about salvation in terms quite other than didactic or political? What if the witness of the New Testament—and the life and practice of the church from the beginning—regarded salvation as something far more than the adjustment of thought or of social structures? Then the agent of salvation must fit the nature of salvation. If the salvation witnessed by the Scripture and experienced by the church could come only from God, then the agent of that salvation, Jesus Christ, must be considered fully divine (because we have received from him what only God could give) just as he is fully human (because we have seen and heard him as a human like us). And this is exactly what the earliest witnesses to the experience of Jesus tell us.

The best way to know what the early Christians meant by "salvation" is to observe what they said about their new experience. We must pay attention not simply to the words that speak of "salvation" in isolation, as though this were a matter of a dictionary definition, nor simply to the witness of diverse writings in isolation, as though this were a matter of literary analysis. Rather, we must listen to what all the earliest Christian writers say about the life they describe as their own, not as something they hope for, not as something they plan for, but as something that has happened to them and is continuing to happen to them.

The most astonishing aspect of the earliest Christian claims was that they seemed so disproportionate to their actual worldly circumstances. Christian communities were small, isolated, beleaguered, disliked. Christianity was a tiny sect of Judaism centered on an executed criminal, having no claim to power of any manifest sort, and seemingly an infinite distance from any historical significance.

Yet from the first, believers made cosmic claims. They were to witness to the ends of the earth (Acts 1:8) and make disciples of all nations (Matt 28:19). The world was theirs: Paul tells the Corinthians, "the world or life or death or the present or the future, all are yours, and you are Christ's, and Christ is God's"

(1 Cor 3:22). And they claimed this, only some twenty years after Jesus' shameful crucifixion! Paul insists that they are to judge the world and judge the angels (1 Cor 6:2–3). He says that members of the church help to reconcile the world to God (Rom 11:15; 2 Cor 5:19) and anticipate the world's liberation (Rom 8:20–22) as the place where God's plan for the world is being revealed (Eph 3:9–10).

These are truly remarkable claims. Given the actual social status of the first believers, one would be justified in regarding them as megalomaniacs. But since they were also well aware of their actual situation—they were persecuted, they were enslaved, they were poor, they included few important people, they continued to die, they continued to sin—on what basis did they make such cosmic claims? They made such claims because they had experienced something that justified making them.

What was that experience? The earliest writings expressed this experience in several ways. They had been liberated, they said, from those cosmic forces that, in the perceptions of antiquity, dominated humans and kept them in subjection. They were no longer captive to "the elements of the universe" (Gal 4:3, 9) and the "powers and principalities" (Rom 8:38; 1 Cor 2:6–10; Eph 2:1–10; Col 1:13; 1 Pet 3:22). They were freed as well from repressive systems of human law, which such cosmic powers had used to keep humans in bondage (Rom 6:15–23; 2 Cor 3:6–18; Gal 3:23–4:7; Col 2:8–23; Eph 2:14–15). They were freed from their fear of death, which accompanied their bondage to sin (1 Cor 15:54–57; Rom 8:14–15; Heb 2:14–15; 1 John 4:17–21).

A central symbol for this experience of freedom among the first Christians was salvation (*sōtēria*). It is of the first importance to remember that when Christians spoke of salvation in their earliest writings some twenty to thirty years after the death of Jesus, they did not speak of it as a theory or an ideal. Their language expresses an actual human experience, which they said was not something for the future but something real now. They were "being saved" (see Rom 1:16; 10:10; 1 Cor 1:18, 21; 15:2; Eph 2:5–8; Phil 1:28; Tit 3:5; James 1:21; 1 Pet 3:21; 2 Pet 3:15; Jude 3; Rev 12:10).

What are the external signs of this salvation? The New Testament uses two terms that were widely admired in Greco-Roman philosophy of the time: freedom (*eleutheria*, see Rom 6:18–22; 1 Cor 9:1, 19; 2 Cor 3:17; Gal 5:1, 13; James 1:25; 1 Pet 2:16) and free speech or boldness (*parrhēsia*, see Acts 2:29; 4:13, 29, 31; 2 Cor 3:12; Eph 3:12; 1 Thess 2:2; Philem 8; Heb 4:16). Freedom is connected to another set of terms, including release, deliverance, redemption, liberation, and salvation. To be free means to be transferred from a negative to a positive condition. But it also means gaining positive capacities formerly lacking. Thus, Paul says, "for freedom Christ has freed you" (Gal 5:1).

The term "free speech" or "boldness" thus means that believers have an ability to confront opposition without fear, to approach danger confidently, to express their identity in every circumstance with confidence and courage. The qualities of freedom and free speech are found in these texts not as ideals for which Christians strived, but as realities in their lived experience. They "have" freedom and free speech, and exercise these capacities in their lives now.

Christians of the first generation spoke also of certain states in which they now found themselves, including peace (Rom 5:1; 14:17; 1 Cor 7:15; 2 Cor 13:11; Eph 2:17; 4:3; Phil 4:7; Col 3:15; James 3:18) and joy (Acts 13:52; Rom 5:3; Gal 5:22; Phil 2:2; 1 Pet 4:13; 1 John 1:4). In these writings "peace" sometimes refers to harmony between people, but that harmony is connected to a condition of peace between humans and God. "Joy" refers to a kind of contentment and sense of fittingness that is not the same as happiness, but is rather compatible with distress and even with tribulation and suffering (1 Thess 3:6–9; Heb 12:1–3; James 1:2; 1 Pet 4:13).

Christians also claimed as their own certain dispositions, such as faith, hope, and love (1 Cor 13:13; 1 Thess 1:2–3; 1 Pet 1:3–9). These dispositions are not abstract, but show themselves in the way Christians live. Hope does not grieve at the death of community members (1 Thess 4:13), faith resists temptation and endures persecution (1 Pet 5:9; Heb 11:32–38), and love is neither arrogant nor rude (1 Cor 13:5).

In terms of the Christians' experience, then, salvation meant both liberation from a negative condition (defined primarily in terms of slavery and fear) and the gift of a positive one (defined primarily by a freedom that revealed itself in states, dispositions, attitudes, and behavior). At root, the Christians claimed the experience of *power*. The terms used for such power are diverse. It can be called authority (*exousia*; see 1 Cor 8:9; 2 Cor 10:8; 2 Thess 3:9), or energy (*energeia*; see 1 Cor 12:6; Gal 3:5; Eph 3:20–21; Heb 4:12), or power (*dynamis*; see Rom 1:16; 1 Cor 1:18; 2 Cor 6:7; Gal 3:5; 1 Thess 1:5; 2 Tim 1:7; Heb 2:4; 1 Pet 1:16). Outwardly, this power was expressed in "signs and wonders" (Acts 4:30; 5:12; Rom 15:19; 2 Cor 12:12) such as healings, prophecies, and speaking in tongues, but above all in the bold proclamation of the good news (2 Cor 4:7; 1 Thess 1:5; 2 Tim 1:8). Inwardly, it was expressed in the spiritual transformation of those who received it (Rom 12:2; 1 Cor 2:16; 2 Cor 3:18; Gal 3:5; Eph 4:23; Col 3:10; 1 Pet 1:22).

The first Christians claimed that this power did not come from themselves but from another, to whom it properly belonged (Rom 1:4; 16:25; 1 Cor 1:24; 5:4; 12:3; 2 Cor 1:4; 6:7; 12:9; 13:4; Eph 3:16, 20; Phil 3:10, 20–21; 2 Tim 1:7; Heb 5:7; James 4:12; 1 Pet 1:5; 2 Pet 1:16; Jude 24). God the creator is the source of the power that has touched and energized them (Rom 4:17; 1 Cor 1:28–30; 2 Cor 4:6). They speak of this power not as something wished for but as something present and effective. As Paul says, "The Kingdom of God does not consist in talk but in power" (1 Cor 4:20).

Because God had empowered them, Christians considered themselves to be part of something radically new in the world, whether they described it in terms of a new covenant (1 Cor 11:25; 2 Cor 3:7–18; Heb 9:15), a new life (Rom 6:4; Eph 4:24), or even a "new creation" (2 Cor 5:17–18). In antiquity, this claim to "newness" was distinctive, for in matters of religion, old was always better than new. But the Christians were not claiming novelty; they were claiming that the structures of their existence had been fundamentally transformed. They knew that God's work was not finished. They looked forward to God's final victory (1 Cor 15:20–57; 1 Thess 4:13–5:3; 2 Thess 2:8–12; Heb 9:28; James 5:7–11; 1 Pet 1:7–9; 2 Pet 3:10–13; Rev 21:1–22:5). But they insisted above all that their present experience was the inauguration (and fundamental accomplishment) of that cosmic victory.

The powerful sense of present experience can be detected simply from the New Testament's use of the simple word "now." In the single letter to the Romans, for example, Paul declares that *now* God's righteousness is being revealed (3:21, 26), *now* they have been made righteous (5:9), *now* they have been reconciled to God (5:11), *now* they are freed from sin (6:22), *now* they are discharged from the law (7:6), *now* there is no condemnation for God's people (8:1), and *now* the mystery of God is being revealed (16:26). In another place, Paul says, "Behold, *now* is the acceptable time, *now* is the day of salvation" (2 Cor 6:2; see also Gal 4:9; Eph 2:2; Col 1:22; Heb 9:26; 1 Pet 1:12; 1 John 3:2).

The prayers of blessing that Christians shared with their fellow Jews spoke less about God's mighty works in the past or the hope of their renewal in the future. Christians gave thanks constantly for God's present and continuing work among them now, and prayed that he would continue that work (see Rom 1:8–14; 1 Cor 1:4–9; 2 Cor 1:3–7; Eph 1:3–14; Phil 1:3–11; 1 Thess 1:3–5; 1 Pet 1:3–8). It is important to note here that this work was not only individual but also communal. The moral exhortation to "become what you are" is directed to communities, exhorting them to realize "salvation" by living as a people discerning and doing God's will in every circumstance (see Eph 4:1–5:20; Phil 2:1–13; Col 2:20–3:17; Heb 12:18–13:17; 1 Pet 1:21–2:3; 1 John 3:16–18).

Three phrases occur repeatedly when the New Testament speaks about power and the Christian experience of power: eternal life, forgiveness of sins, and Holy Spirit. The first seeks to express the quality of the life that they have been given, and does so by referring to it as "eternal life" (*zōē aiōnios*). The term is found in all the Gospels (Matt 19:16–17, 29; 25:46; Mark 10:17, 30; Luke 18:30; John 3:36; 4:36; 5:24; 6:54; 17:2), in Acts (13:46–48), in the letters of Paul (Rom 2:7; 5:21; 6:22–23; 2 Cor 5:4; Gal 6:8; 1 Tim 1:16; Tit 1:2; 3:7), and in the first letter of John (1:2; 2:25; 3:15; 5:11, 20). The expression is not used mainly of a future life, but of the present life. Those who have been given it share in some sense in God's own life, even as they continue their earthly existence.

The second phrase, "forgiveness of sins," expresses the removal by God of everything that prevents full reconciliation between God and humans. This term (or its equivalents) is also found throughout the New Testament literature (see Matt 1:21; 9:2, 5–6; 26:28; Mark 1:4; 2:5, 7–10; Luke 1:77; 5:20–24; 7:47–49; 24:47; John 1:29; 20:23; Rom 3:20; 5:20–21; 6:11, 18; 8:2; 1 Cor 15:3; Gal 1:4; Col 1:14; Heb 1:3; 1 Pet 2:24; 2 Pet 1:9; 1 John 1:7; 2:2; Rev 1:5). Just as no human can give a share in God's life ("eternal life"), so only God can forgive sins. This is precisely the point of the controversy reported in the three Synoptic Gospels when Jesus declares the paralytic man's sins forgiven: the legal observers protest that only God can forgive sins, and Jesus responds with the bold assertion that the Son of Man has authority to forgive sins (Matt 9:5–6; Mark 2:7–10; Luke 5:21–24).

Matthew and Luke each connect the salvation brought by Jesus specifically to the forgiveness of sins. Matthew says that the name Jesus is given to him, "for he will save his people from their sins" (Matt 1:21). Luke has Zechariah speak of John as the forerunner who will "give knowledge of salvation to his people by the forgiveness of their sins" (Luke 1:77). Luke similarly describes the mission of Jesus' followers as preaching "repentance unto the forgiveness of sins" (Luke 24:47), just as John has Jesus bestow the Holy Spirit on his followers so that, "if you forgive the sins of any, they are forgiven them" (John 20:23).

The third phrase is simply "Holy Spirit." We will have much more to say about the Holy Spirit later. For now, I simply observe the way in which the phrase occurs as an element in describing the early Christian's experience. They claimed, as I have shown, freedom, boldness, joy, peace, perseverance in suffering, and newness of life, and they had all these because they had experienced God's power. With remarkable consistency, the source of this power is said to be the Holy Spirit. Indeed, for all practical purposes, the term "Holy Spirit" in these writings corresponds to the word "power."

It is the Holy Spirit that works mighty deeds among belivers (Gal 3:5), empowering them in their proclamation of the good news (Acts 4:8; 1 Thess 1:5; 2 Tim 1:6) and in their very profession of faith in Jesus as Lord (1 Cor 12:3). It is the Holy Spirit that brings about the transformation of their consciousness (1 Cor 2:12; Tit 3:5). This Holy Spirit is not an impersonal force. It is not a symbol for what they have accomplished for themselves. It is the life-giving presence of the risen Lord: "Because you are sons, God has sent the Spirit of his Son into our hearts, crying, 'Abba! Father' " (Gal 4:6). As Paul says in 2 Cor 3:17–18, "Now the Lord is Spirit and where the Spirit of the Lord is, there is freedom. And we all, with unveiled faces, beholding the glory of the Lord are being changed from one degree of glory into another; for this comes from the Lord who is Spirit" (see also 1 Cor 2:12; Rom 8:11).

That Paul is speaking about a power of life far beyond that of humans is made clear in 1 Corinthians 15:45: "The first man became a living being; the last Adam became a life-giving Spirit." The connection between the Holy Spirit and the early Christian experience of God's power is, as these references show, a Pauline emphasis, but almost all the other New Testament writers draw the connection as well (see John 20:21–23; Luke 24:47–49; Acts 2:1–4; Heb 2:4; 4:12; 6:4; 1 Pet 1:12; 3:18; 1 John 3:24; 4:13; Jude 19; Rev 2:7; 4:2; 19:10).

The overwhelming testimony of the New Testament to the early Christian experience of salvation is that it changes humans themselves both individually and communally. It not only removes them from the power of those things that enslave them (sin, law, death), but it energizes them with a power that is God's own. The forgiveness of sins, the gift of the Holy Spirit, the sharing in eternal life, these constant emphases in the New Testament literature are summarized by the bold statement in 2 Peter 1:3–4:

His divine power has given us everything needed for life and godliness, through the knowledge of him who called us by his own glory and goodness. Thus, he has given us, through these things, his precious and very great promises, so that through them you may escape from the corruption that is in the world because of lust, and may become participants of the divine nature.

In the understanding of those earliest Christians who composed the writings of the New Testament, in short, salvation was not merely a rescue or even a restoration. It was an elevation. Paul declares that "the free gift is not like the trespass" (Rom 5:15), and argues "how much greater" is the effect of Jesus' work on all humans than the effect of Adam's disobedience on his descendants (Rom 5:12–21). He expresses the disparity crisply in Romans 6:23: "the wages of sin is death, but the free gift of God is life eternal in Christ Jesus our Lord." So understood, salvation can be accomplished only by God. To return to the creed's "and for our salvation," for the writers of the New Testament and for those who sought to represent its witness and their own experience of the faith adequately, therefore, the divinity of Jesus Christ is as axiomatic as his humanity, and for the same reason.

It is a sad fact that this robust understanding of salvation, which truly is "good news," has progressively weakened among those professing themselves to be Christian. The causes are complex, but among them, surely, are the Christians' failure convincingly to display the power and energy of the Holy Spirit within transformed persons and communities, and the tendency to focus obsessively on sin as the condition from which humans have been rescued, to the neglect of the "how much greater" condition salvation brings.

The first is the more important and devastating. The strong sense of salvation as a participation in God's life, remember, depends on the strong experience of liberation and power, not as something hoped for in the future, but happening already in present-day lives. The reality of the resurrection was convincing because people acted freely and powerfully through the Holy Spirit. If people are living and speaking and acting in a manner that goes beyond their normal capacities, then some other power must be at work in them. The "witness" of early Christian communities was not primarily through their preaching, but through the quality of their lives. The greatest miracle supporting the claims of Christians was the transformation of their lives and the creation of transforming communities.

Now, this experiential evidence has never completely disappeared from Christianity. If it had, then Christianity itself would long ago have disappeared. Saints of every stripe have revealed in every age the power of God at work for salvation. But that spark of life has all too often been routinized, formalized, even suppressed, within churches more concerned with surviving than with salvation.

When Christians lack the strong experience of a transformed life in the present, it is all too easy for them to think of salvation primarily in terms of a future positive condition—sharing God's life in the future—that is made possible because God has rescued them from the negative condition of sin. And once the focus is on human sinfulness, it was natural to think of salvation primarily, if not exclusively, as only a remedy for sin. And if the focus is on the human situation rather than on the free gift of God, it is all too easy to lose sight of the "free gift" and to inquire into the magnitude of the sin that required a divine agent to remedy it. Christian theology loses its sense of proportion when theories of atonement diminish the love of God in precise proportion to their exaggeration of human importance.

I do not want to suggest that the human predicament is not real or that sin is not important. I will in fact return later to the "forgiveness of sins," and in that place discuss the contemporary loss of the sense of sin. That loss of sin-consciousness has left many present-day Christians without much sense of salvation. Without a traditional sense of sin, and without an appreciation of grace as an elevation of the human condition, they struggle to make sense of salvation. They likewise struggle to make sense of the role of Jesus. Some are willing to accept as adequate the dramatically reduced Christology offered by the "historical Jesus," portrayed either as a countercultural teacher or as a prophetic critic.

Such a minimal Christology offers a Jesus who is at best a guide, whose teaching inspires, or an example, whose protest against injustice evokes imitation. Salvation therefore means following moral teaching or participating in social reform. When Christian salvation is reduced to these options, there is little surprise that several secular salvations and alternative spiritualities appear at least as attractive, even among those considering themselves Christians.

HE CAME DOWN FROM HEAVEN

The mythic character of the Christian narrative is most obvious in the two spatial expressions that bracket the human story of Jesus in the creed. Here we have "he came down from heaven," and later we see "he ascended to heaven." The pattern of descent and ascent is common in stories about the gods. In world mythology, high places tend to get associated with the divine realm just as the lowest places represent the farthest distance from the divine. To speak of the deity's approach to humans would require speaking in terms of "descending."

When we call this language mythic, we acknowledge that spatial and temporal terms are inadequate for speech about God. If Christians ever did live in a "three-deck universe," they do so no longer. Christians understand that speaking of Jesus' "ascension" cannot mean his physical ascent into space, and that awaiting his "return on the clouds of heaven" cannot mean a physical arrival via vapor. We acknowledge once more the inadequacy of human language. How can we speak of the eternal God as being far or near, as approaching or leaving? Understood literally, such speech can actually be blasphemous. But is it much better to say, "God's implicit presence to creation in Christ becomes explicit"? This is more abstract but it is still inadequate. And there is the more important consideration: by becoming human, the divine Word does in fact enter the empirical realm, and can in fact be spoken of in the language of time and space.

Perhaps the writers of the New Testament did think of heaven "up there" and of God in the sky beyond human sight. We cannot be sure. What is certain is that we do not, cannot, think in such terms. To think of God in such terms would be illegitimately to reduce God to a material and limited existence. We take the language of "descending" and "ascending," then, as symbolic. The creed stretches speech into new shapes to express what it is not made to express. But what does it seek to express?

In this place, the writers of the creed clearly depended on the language of the Fourth Gospel. John has Jesus use such language of himself in his bread-of-life discourse, speaking of "the bread coming down out of heaven and giving life to the world" (John 6:33, 50, 58), and then applying the image to himself: "I have come down from heaven to do the will of the one who sent me" (6:38; see also 6:42). In this language, "heaven" designates the place of "the one who sent me," namely God. As the one who has "come down," Jesus is no longer in that place, but among humans, in order "to do the will of the one who sent me."

The language of heaven and earth therefore expresses not a change in place but a change in condition from the divine realm to the human. In John's Gospel, Jesus is the one who breaks the boundary between creator and creation by entering as the Word "through whom all things were made" into the flesh, and then returning to God (1:3, 14; 13:1). John insists that the Son alone accomplishes this movement from and back to God: "No one has ascended into heaven except the one who descended from heaven, the Son of Man" (John 3:13).

John is not the only one who struggles to express the reality of continuity-within-discontinuity in the incarnate Jesus. Paul speaks of a change or exchange in status. He says that the one who did not know sin became sin so that in him we might become God's righteousness (2 Cor 5:21). He says that Christ, though rich, became poor for our sake, so that through his poverty we might become rich (2 Cor 8:9). Most dramatically, he speaks of this transition in the "Christ Hymn" of Philippians 2:6–11 in terms of an emptying out (*kenosis*), involving a metamorphosis, or change of form and appearance:

> Though he was in the form of God [he] did not regard equality with God as something to be grasped, but emptied himself, taking the form of a slave, becoming in human likeness (Phil 2:6–7).

The author of Hebrews likewise speaks of Christ "coming into the world," while saying, "See, I have come to do your will, O God" (Heb 10:5–7), and says of the Son "through whom he also created the worlds" (Heb 1:2) that "for a little while he was made lower than the angels" (Heb 2:9).

The phrase "he came down from heaven," therefore, cannot help being mythic, for it seeks to communicate in human speech what human speech cannot express. It wants to say two things at the same time: first, that the Jesus Christ whom we encounter in the flesh is "from *heaven*," that is, of divine origin; and second, that the Jesus Christ whom we encounter in the flesh is "*come down out* of heaven," that is, he is truly among us in our world.

HE WAS INCARNATE BY THE HOLY SPIRIT AND THE VIRGIN MARY, AND BECAME HUMAN

A more literal rendering of the Greek is: "and being made flesh out of the Holy Spirit and Mary the Virgin, and becoming human." Three immediate observations can be made. First, the phrase is carefully constructed so that "being made flesh" and "became human" stand in tension with each other and balance each other. Second, the agency of enfleshment is equally the spirit designated as holy and Mary designated as virgin. Third, the effect of the whole statement is to affirm both the divine agency at work in Jesus' incarnation and his genuine participation in the human condition.

We should note that the translation used in the liturgies of many churches (the Catholic and Episcopal churches, for example) and in the Catechism of the Catholic Church is freer than it should be. In the original, there is no mention of the power of the Holy Spirit or of Jesus' being born. Such translations soften and explain a harder original.

Faulty translation aside, the language causes two difficulties for modern readers, in its apparent gender exclusivity and its assertion that Christ was born of a virgin. The first we addressed earlier, and I will only point out again that the Greek original, based on the noun *anthrōpos* ("human being") rather than *anēr* ("male"), is gender-inclusive. All of the alternatives lose something of the meaning of the original. In short, if we cannot agree among ourselves to say "man" and mean "human being rather than male," then we should use some version of "human," for that is what the creed intends to say.

The second difficulty is the notion of the virgin birth. The language of the creed clearly derives from the annunciation accounts of Matthew and Luke. In Matthew, Mary is said to be pregnant before she and Joseph had intercourse, leading Joseph to seek to divorce her quietly (Matt 1:18–19). But he is told by the angel of the Lord not to fear taking Mary as wife, "for that which is begotten in her is out of the Holy Spirit" (Matt 1:20).

Matthew interprets this by citing Isaiah 7:14 in the Septuagint version: "Behold the virgin will be pregnant and give birth to a son, and they shall call him Emmanuel." In Luke, Mary is identified at once as "the virgin" (Luke 1:28) to whom the angel announces that she will "become pregnant and bear a son and shall call his name Jesus" (1:30). When Mary objects that she has no experience of sex ("I do not know a male," 1:34), the angel responds, "the Holy Spirit will come upon you and the power of the Most High will overshadow you. Therefore also the holy one born shall be called a son of God" (1:35).

There is no doubt that ancient Christian writers understood the New Testament to teach that the conception of Jesus was a miraculous intervention by the Holy Spirit, bypassing normal sexual intercourse between a male and female. The shapers of the creed undoubtedly understood the language of Scripture in a literal and biological way. And the development of Mariology within Roman Catholicism, which insisted on the "perpetual" virginity of Mary, extended that literalness considerably.

The decision to read the virgin birth literally rather than symbolically became, in turn, the touchstone of "biblical" versus "progressive" Christianity in the early twentieth-century fight between fundamentalists and Modernists—a fight that continues unabated in the early twenty-first century. For "biblical Christians," the virgin birth is listed as one of the fundamental doctrines at the same level as the divinity of Christ as a test of a wholehearted obedience to the "inspired word of God" (another of the fundamentals), no matter how hard to understand or accept for the modern mind. For "progressive Christians," an equally vehement rejection of a literal virgin birth has become the test of a "reasonable" Christianity, as opposed to a pre-Darwinian obscurantist fanaticism passing itself off as Christianity.

Each side has its own absurdities. Those claiming an absolute fidelity to Scripture prove to be typically selective, ignoring (or explaining away) those passages of the New Testament that speak plainly about Jesus having brothers and sisters (see Mark 6:3), including an important leader of the early church, James, "the brother of the Lord" (see 1 Cor 9:5; 15:7; Gal 1:19). Those claiming a "progressive" version of Christianity are just as selective, rejecting God's capacity to create a human person apart from sex, but still (as some do) accepting God's capacity to create the world out of nothing, or God's capacity to raise a human person from the dead.

What makes each side especially absurd is that the progressive's objection to the virgin birth is not really a defense of reasonableness but a misdirected rejection of the supernatural altogether, while the conservative's defense of the virgin birth does not really celebrate God's capacity to work wonders in creation but instead limits that capacity. How absurd to think that the God who is able to create all things through the Word cannot enter humanity through the Word and through the processes of sexuality that God has created as good! What Matthew has Jesus say to the Sadducees on the matter of the resurrection life can be said equally to both sides of this sad disputation: "You are wrong because you know neither the scriptures nor the power of God" (Matt 22:29).

The plain fact is that it is neither possible nor important to know the biology of Jesus' conception and birth. The God who creates all things can create a human apart from sex, but it does not follow either that he does, or did in the case of Jesus. Likewise, the conception of the Messiah through the sexual intercourse of Mary and Joseph could be just as "holy" and just as much "out of the Holy Spirit" as a conception that did not involve human sexual intercourse.

When finally we shift from a preoccupation with biology, we can begin to notice what is important in the creed's statement. And what is most important is that the incarnation of God's Son came about through both divine and human agency.

This is the first of two times that the Holy Spirit is named in the creed (I will devote much more attention to the second mention in chap. 7) and serves here to link the Spirit particularly with Jesus. These words tell us that the Spirit of God that blew on the waters in creation (Gen 1:2) and stirred the prophets to ecstasy (1 Sam 10:6, 10) and speech (Ezek 37:1), the Spirit those same prophets foresaw as a sign of the messianic age (Isa 11:1–3; 61:1–2; Ezek 37:1–14; Joel 2:28–32), is active in the life of the Son who "came down from heaven." This Spirit is active in the birth of the Messiah Jesus (Matt 12:20; Luke 1:35), comes upon Jesus in his baptism when the voice proclaims him as God's beloved Son (Luke 3:21), guides him in his ministry (Luke 4:1, 16; 10:21; see Acts 10:38), and is poured out on his followers upon his resurrection (Acts 2:1–5), finding among those who are baptized and drink the one Spirit (Acts 2:38; 1 Cor 12:13) a living body and temple as a dwelling place (1 Cor 6:12–20).

In this instance, as in virtually all the times the New Testament uses this name, "Holy Spirit" stands for the effective presence and power of God among humans. To speak of "God among us" (Matt 1:23) for the incarnation, then, is equivalent to saying "out of the Holy Spirit."

The significance of Mary's presence in this pivotal statement is perhaps the more intriguing. She is, after all, one of only three humans mentioned in the creed. Besides Jesus, only Mary and

Pontius Pilate represent the human race, and, as with so much in the creed, they do so in mythic and balanced fashion. Pilate stands for the world that rejects the claims of God and kills God's messenger who bodily bears that claim. Mary stands for the world that accepts the claim of God and gives birth to the embodiment of God's presence in Jesus the Messiah.

Mary locates Jesus within the common experience of all humanity. He too was, as Paul says, "born of a woman" (Gal 4:4). Jesus has a human mother, bears human genes, carries the imprint of human evolution. But Mary also signals that Jesus is born of a particular people living, as Paul says, "under the law" (Gal 4:4). Mary lived as a Jew in Nazareth (Luke 1:26), a small hill town of Galilee, and during the reign of Caesar Augustus gave birth to Jesus among conditions of poverty in the Davidic city of Bethlehem (Luke 2:1–7). Just so specific and homely is the humanity of the incarnate God, who takes on the human condition within the body of a young Jewish woman.

Just as Jesus (Joshua) bears the name of the liberator of the people who brought them into the land of promise (Josh 1:1–10), Mary bears the name of Moses' sister Miriam, who was, like her brother, a prophet (Exod 15:20–21). Luke's Gospel in particular develops the character of Mary as a woman of faith. In response to the angel's announcement, she identifies herself as a servant of the Lord and says, "Let it happen to me according to your word" (Luke 1:38). And like her prophetic forebears Miriam and Hannah (see Exod 15:20–21; 1 Sam 2:1–10), she interprets the work of God in history in light of her own experience and the words of Scripture (Luke 1:46–55).

Luke sees Mary as a model for those who "believe in all that the Lord has spoken" (1:45) and "hear the word of God and keep it" (8:21). Her words, indeed, find echo in her son's prayer at Gethsemane, "Let not my will but yours be done" (Luke 22:42).

Is it too much to think that the human Jesus learned such faithful obedience from her? Is it any surprise that Luke includes Mary among those male and female followers of Jesus who received the prophetic gift of the Holy Spirit on the day of Pentecost (Acts 1:12–14)?

All this is interesting, but why did "incarnate by . . . the Virgin Mary" find a place in the creed? Because it says something important about the nature of salvation. If salvation were a matter of rearranging the systems of the human world, the savior's conception and birth would not matter, and attention would focus on his public actions and accomplishments as an adult. But such salvation would only help people living within those social arrangements, and never accomplish more than a temporary improvement. But if, as Christians believe, the salvation brought by Jesus Christ fundamentally altered the structures of human existence itself, the moments of conception and birth are deservedly singled out by the creed, for the full sharing of the human condition by God's Son is fundamental (Heb 2:14–18). In this moment we see the astonishing love of God, expressed by the willingness not only to create or sustain but to become one among those creatures who alone choose not to recognize or accept the very source of their being.

How more vulnerable could God be than to become, in Jesus, both the gift and the reception of the gift, both the "yes" of God to humans and the "yes" of humans to God (2 Cor 1:20)? In this moment we also see the full implication of God's creating humans "in the image and likeness of God" in the first place (Gen 1:26). God creates humans in his image as a preparation for that human, Jesus, who would perfectly reflect the glory of God as God's image (Col 1:15), and so also perfectly reflect the glory of God to other humans so that they might be transformed accord-

ing to that image into the fullest realization of their humanity
(2 Cor 3:17–18; Col 3:10).

FOR US

In the creed's pattern of descent and ascent, the section beginning with his crucifixion for our sake and ending with his burial marks the lowest point. The one who "for us came down from
heaven" now experiences the most shameful form of violent
death and is buried in the earth. In the Apostles' Creed, the descent is even steeper, as it adds that Jesus "descended into hell," a
confession that is rich in significance but which I will not take up
here, in order to stay focused on the Nicene-Constantinopolitan
version.

It should be noted that the English translation provided by
the Catechism of the Catholic Church and that used in the liturgy
of many churches again expands the original slightly, by adding
the word "died" or "death," after the phrase "crucified for us under Pontius Pilate." The Greek has simply, "he suffered and was
buried."

The creed jumps from the beginning of the Messiah's human
life to its ending. Here is the "gap where Jesus should be" of
which many seeking the "historical Jesus" complain. Why doesn't
the creed, they ask, elaborate the human deeds of Jesus, his miracles, his sayings, his reaching out to the outcast of society, his as-
sociating with sinners, his opposition to the established powers of
society? The answer to this fairly silly objection, I have suggested,
is twofold. First, the creed is only one instrument of Christian
self-definition. It does not replace the rich portrayals of Jesus in
the Gospels, but points to the elements in those portrayals that are

essential to our salvation and would be sufficient for our salvation if we did not know anything else. The creed does not try to draw believers away from the Jesus of the Gospels but rather to direct them toward that Jesus.

Second, the creed reminds us that God transforms our humanity not because a Jew in antiquity spoke in parables or welcomed strangers or forgave sinners, much less criticized the social structures of the day, but because that Jew was himself the Son of God. It is who Jesus is that makes him the savior of humanity, not what he did or said. For this reason, moving from Jesus' birth to his death "for us" says all the creed needs to say.

"For us" recalls the "for us men and for our salvation" with which this section on the incarnation begins. This time, it refers to the decision of the human Jesus to die the death he did. That Jesus died means that he shared our humanity fully and faithfully to the end, but he did not have to be crucified. He could have avoided confronting the powers of the world that resist the claim of God, or he could have acted as their agent, and either way, die in comfort. The phrase "for us" points to the fact that the Son of God accepted execution as an act of solidarity with his fellow humans. In the life of the human Jesus, then, we discover, explicitly displayed, the same "existence turned toward others" of God that we found implicit in creation itself.

The phrase is thoroughly scriptural. In Paul, we find expressions like these: "Christ died for the ungodly" (Rom 5:6), "Christ died for us" (Rom 5:8), "Christ died for our sins" (1 Cor 15:3), "for our sake he became sin" (2 Cor 5:21), "Christ loved us and gave himself for us" (Eph 5:2), "Christ became a curse for us" (Gal 3:13), and others (Rom 14:15; 15:3; 1 Cor 1:13; 8:11; 2 Cor 8:9; Gal 1:4; 1 Tim 2:6; Tit 2:14).

In Paul, the meaning of Jesus' existence as a whole is expressed by his dying "for our sake." Jesus is the human whose character was entirely defined by his saying "yes" to God (2 Cor 1:19–20) even to death (Rom 3:21–26; 5:12–21; Phil 2:5–11). That obedience to God took the form of a life of self-giving to others, which, through the power of the Holy Spirit, is the pattern disciples themselves are to follow. As Paul says in Galatians, "I live now no longer I, but Christ living in me. The life I now live in the flesh, I live by the faith of the Son of God, the one who loved me and gave himself for me" (2:20), and "Bear one another's burdens, and so fulfill the pattern of the Messiah" (literally, the "law of Christ," 6:2).

Other New Testament writers equally understand the human Jesus as the one for others. Hebrews says that Christ died "in order to sanctify the people by his blood" (Heb 13:12). Peter declares that Christ "bore our sins in the body to the tree" (1 Pet 2:24), that "Christ suffered, the righteous for the unrighteous" (3:18), and that "Christ suffered for you" (2:21). This understanding pervades the Gospels, and finds explicit expression in the statements made by Jesus himself. In Mark 10:45 Jesus declares, "The Son of Man came not to be served but to serve, and to give his life as a ransom for many." In Luke's account of Jesus' last meal with his disciples, he tells them, "This is my body, which is given for you," and "This cup that is poured out for you is the new covenant in my blood" (Luke 22:19–20). And in John, Jesus says of himself:

I am the good shepherd. The good shepherd lays down his life for the sheep . . . I lay down my life for the sheep . . . for this reason, the father loves me, because I lay down my life in order to take it up again. No one takes it from me, but I lay it down of my own accord. I have the power to

lay it down, and I have the power to take it up again.
(John 1:11–18)

Ancient biographies gave careful attention to the death of their protagonists, because the manner of death was thought to prove the quality of their life. The wit and wisdom of Socrates found validation in the cool style with which he faced state execution. The courage of Zeno was demonstrated by his contempt for his executioners.

The manner of Jesus' death was critical for the same reason. If God had cursed his death as a criminal, his entire life would have been shown to have been a sham and a fraud. But if he (like Socrates and Zeno) died as a righteous person, however paradoxically, then, however paradoxically, his execution as a criminal proved the righteousness of his life.

For this reason, the Gospels' passion stories, while not in the least avoiding the scandal of Jesus' death—they show Jesus fearful, betrayed, denied, abandoned—interpret it from the prophets (especially Isa 52–53) and the Psalms (especially 21 and 68). They show Jesus dying not by accident but by choice (Mark 14:41; 15:2–3). In Mark's Gospel, for example, Jesus knew in advance what he faced and nevertheless remained faithful to God's claim on him (Mark 8:31; 9:31; 10:33). He understood that he was fulfilling God's plan in Scripture (Mark 14:27, 49). He died in radical obedience to his father (14:36). He was not guilty but innocent (Mark 15:6–15). By his dying words, he expressed not despair but confidence in God's vindication (Mark 15:33). Like other New Testament writers, the Gospel authors insist that Jesus died "for us," and because of this, the manner of his death turns out to be not a demonstration of his failure as a messiah, but the demonstration of his character as God's Son (Mark 15:39).

HE WAS CRUCIFIED

That Jesus did not die from natural causes but rather was executed as a criminal by means of crucifixion by command of the Roman prefect, is a statement on which both believers and nonbelievers can agree. The writings of the New Testament uniformly testify to it, both in story (Matt 27:15–37; Mark 15:1–39; Luke 23:28–49; John 19:19–30; Acts 3:13–16; 4:27) and in letters (1 Cor 1:18–2:8; 2 Cor 13:4; Gal 3:1; Phil 2:8; Col 1:20; 1 Tim 6:13; Heb 12:2; 1 Pet 2:24). It is also significantly confirmed by ancient outsider sources, including Tacitus, Josephus, and Lucian of Samosata. This statement about Jesus is the one statement in the creed historians as historians make with confidence, though as historians they can make diverse judgments as to what it means. The meaning of this fact is, to be sure, where believers and unbelievers diverge. Believers add the words "for us," and confidently confess the death of this ancient man as the willing self-donation of the Son of God. For believers, the bare historical facts do not say enough about Jesus. In order to state the truth about the death of Jesus—"God was in Christ reconciling the world to himself" (2 Cor 5:19)—Christians gladly embrace the language of myth. But myth is not the same as fantasy. The mythic statements made about Jesus are grounded in a historical figure. Historical facts do not save. But God saves within a history that we can (however inadequately) identify and describe.

The statement in the creed is typically spare, communicating only the essential reality with no narrative development. We find none of the richly elaborated Gospel passion accounts. We are made to focus, therefore, not on the betrayal, denial, and abandonment of Jesus' appointed disciples, nor on the quiet fidelity of his female followers, nor on the participation of the Jewish leadership in the plot that led to his public execution. Instead, we are made to focus on the means of execution, its political sponsor, Jesus' own intention, and his suffering.

Crucifixion was a particularly cruel form of execution, even by the standards of antiquity. Especially when nails rather than ropes were used, it combined an intensely painful form of torture with slow asphyxiation. Crucifixion was not used for the noble, but only for enemies or slaves. Thus, Romans punished the slave rebellion of Spartacus and the rebellion of the Jews with mass crucifixions. Crucifixion therefore shamed the one crucified. The Jews themselves could apply to someone crucified a passage from Deuteronomy, "Cursed be everyone who hangs upon a tree" (21:23). In this view, only a sinner could suffer such a death, and therefore a crucified person, being under a curse, could not be the source of life and blessing for others. If Jesus was a crucified messiah, he was certainly a failed messiah—and in all likelihood a false messiah.

These associations are embedded in the New Testament. Paul speaks of Jesus' obedience unto death as that of a slave (Phil 2:7–8). He says that on the cross, Christ "became a curse for us" (Gal 3:13), and that "for our sake the one who did not know sin became sin" (2 Cor 5:21)—note the phrases "for us" and "for our sake"—and he proposes the cross to the Corinthians as the measure of how God's power worked through weakness and God's wisdom worked through foolishness (1 Cor 1:25). The letter to the Hebrews says that Jesus "despised the shame of the cross" (Heb 12:2) and that believers who again sin in effect "[crucify] again the Son of God and [hold] him up to contempt" (Heb 6:6).

Part of the joy of being Christian is celebrating the profoundly paradoxical character of God's salvation through Jesus Christ. The incarnation is scandal enough: that the Lord of all universes should enter a single time and space in the form of an infant baby born to impoverished parents. Already in the birth of Mary's child is revealed the paradox of wealth in poverty, wisdom in foolishness, strength in weakness. That the incarnate God should not only experience death, but the most shameful form of violent death as an executed criminal!

Here is extreme paradox. And here is the reason why the earliest Christian language is so filled with tension and energy, as it strives to express how blessing can come through one cursed (Gal 3:6–14), freedom through a slave (Gal 5:1), righteousness through one made sin (2 Cor 5:21), wealth through one made poor (2 Cor 8:9), wisdom through such obvious foolishness (1 Cor 1:25), strength through weakness (2 Cor 13:4), and life for all through one man's death (Rom 5:12–21). This brings us joy, because if we experience blessing, freedom, righteousness, enrichment, wisdom, power, and life through means so contrary to anything humans could ever conceive, we know we are in the hands of our God.

UNDER PONTIUS PILATE

The same joyful realization, however, also carries with it the reminder that worldly authorities actively oppose this power at work through the crucified Messiah Jesus. The words "under Pontius Pilate" remind us that imperial authorities hate challenges to their absolute power to order the world as they wish. Jesus died a violent but also a legal death.

The reminder has two sharp edges. The first is the memory that when Christians have most followed the pattern of Jesus' life, they have also come most clearly and painfully into conflict with political rulers and have often followed Jesus not only in manner of life but also in manner of death. The second edge is the memory that when Christians have relied on the power of the state to advance their own goals, or, even worse, imitated in the life of the church the values and practices of the state, they have lost their distinctive identity and have become oppressors of others.

Mary and Pontius Pilate represent these two edges, which are the two poles of human status and response to God. Mary is young, female, poor, Jewish, and—pregnant out of wedlock—socially and religiously suspect. Yet through her faith, God brings life to the world—at the cost of a sword piercing her own soul (Luke 2:35). Pontius Pilate is mature, male, wealthy, Roman, and safely wed (see Matt 27:19). Yet through his moral obtuseness, a holy and righteous one was taken to the cross and a murderer released, and through his legal concession, "the author of life was killed" (see Acts 3:13–14). Those reciting this profession of faith do well to pause and reflect on these two examples.

HE SUFFERED

The New Testament also attests throughout that Jesus suffered in his life and death. The predictions of his death that the evangelists place in Jesus' mouth as he journeys to Jerusalem are rightly called passion predictions—"passion" in Greek meaning "suffering"—for the "great suffering" of the Son of Man is emphasized in them (see Mark 8:31; 10:34). The theme is especially prominent in Luke, who has the risen Jesus reminding his followers how "it was necessary for the Messiah to suffer these things and so enter into his glory" (Luke 24:25). Paul proves to the Thessalonians that "it was necessary for the Messiah to suffer and to rise from the dead" (Acts 17:3). Similarly, Peter says that "Christ suffered in the flesh" (1 Pet 4:1; see also 1:11).

It is Jesus' suffering above all that demonstrates God's full embrace of our human condition. The Son of God did not live his human life safely above the plane of human suffering as a dispassionate observer, but entered fully into the struggle of human life. The Son of God did not end his human life when he chose, but died in agony as a young man arrested violently in the prime of his life, subjected to official and popular mockery, scourged, spit on, crowned with thorns, and nailed naked to a cross in a death of hideous shamefulness and horrifying pain.

The letter to the Hebrews especially notes the "appropriateness" of such suffering for the Son of God:

> For the one who sanctifies and those who are sanctified are from one. For this reason he is not ashamed to call them brothers . . . since, therefore, the children share flesh and blood, he himself likewise shared the same things, so that through death he might destroy the one that has the power of death, that is, the devil, and free those who through fear of death were held in slavery. It is clear that he did not come to help angels but the children of Abraham. Therefore he had to become like his brothers in every respect . . . because he himself was tested by what he suffered, he is able to help those who are being tested. [Heb 2:10–18]

As this passage suggests, Jesus' suffering is important to us not only because it demonstrates his full sharing in our humanity and the extreme to which the divine love will go for us, but also because it reveals something essential about the human condition itself. Human suffering—so often identified as intrinsically evil—can be as much a sign of life and growth as a sign of decline and death. It is capable of being transfigured, and has been transfigured by the suffering of Jesus Christ.

This is a difficult and delicate point. Some today, who regard themselves as Christian theologians, reject any language about suffering as oppressive, especially for women and persons of color who have been mistreated by dominant social systems. Some even repudiate the cross itself, because the cross has been used to deprive women and other powerless peoples from a full participation in the blessings of human life, by claiming that it requires them to suffer oppression passively.

The language of the cross and discipleship understood in terms of suffering, they insist, represents a strain within Christianity—some even call it sadomasochistic—that feeds the savage tendencies of some people and the self-destructive tendencies of others. Such language, they say, ought to be removed from the Christian lexicon. When it is removed, presumably, oppression and suffering might be eliminated as well.

The protest is a variation on the complaint made about the tradition's patriarchal language, except that it cuts even more closely to the heart of how salvation was revealed through Jesus Christ and therefore to the heart of the Christian understanding of the good news. A response must begin with a candid acknowledgment of the partial—indeed substantial—legitimacy of the complaint. A strain of masochism in some Christian piety has celebrated suffering almost for its own sake. A strain of sadism has imposed the virtues of sacrifice (especially self-sacrifice) unequally on the oppressed. The language of suffering, like the language of service, can be and has been used to legitimate the unfair and even inhumane treatment of humans taken in bondage—women, the poor, and racial and other minorities.

But having acknowledged this, we must also insist that such practices and such use of language are distortions of the good news rather than the logical expression of the good news. The distortions are corrected, not by excising the language, but by correcting both language and practice in light of a better understanding of suffering, especially what suffering means when the creed says the Son of God suffered.

Just as it is wrong to glorify all suffering, for example, so is it equally disastrous to consider all suffering as something evil. Suffering is simply the pain caused by change, which can be good or bad. The absence of pain, indeed, can mean a lack of growth. If at the physical level, pain can be the sign of injury or disease, so is it as often the sign of birth and growth. If pain at the emotional level is a sign of distress, so also is it a sign of great love and longing. At the mental level, pain results from confusion and mental conflict; these accompany mental growth as much as mental decline.

Suffering is neither all evil nor all good. It is simply the consequence of being conscious creatures. It can diminish us or enlarge us. We can—if we are clever and lucky—avoid suffering and live anesthetized lives, but only at the cost of being shallow and giving up those pleasures and joys that come only through suffering. Suffering that is imposed on us can destroy us, but suffering we embrace can ennoble us.

It must be said with the greatest possible vigor that eliminating the language of suffering or constructing an ideal without suffering is even more distorting and destructive than the abuses of the language of suffering.

Such forms of discipleship are widely popular today. One form is the "Gospel of Success," so frequently proclaimed by televangelists, who propose that allegiance to Jesus as savior will lead to prosperity, health, and the overcoming of all mental anxiety. There is no Gospel character at all to this form of "evangelical" Christianity. Another form no less a distortion is an ideal of liberating peoples from all alienating and oppressive social structures, which reduces the reality of suffering to a matter of economic or social inequality. There is some Gospel character to this, for the good news is liberating and seeks the freedom of persons, but the "freedom for which Christ has freed us" (Gal 5:1) goes deeper than political and social arrangements—it goes to the transformation of human existence itself.

The writings of the New Testament do not allow anyone to impose suffering on others. Nor do they allow anyone to acquiesce in others inflicting pain on people, especially the vulnerable. But it expects Christians to accept the suffering that comes to them as a result of their profession and practice of faith. The New Testament regards such suffering to be a form of participation in the redemptive work of Jesus himself (Col 1:24) and a means of personal transformation into the full maturity of the Son of God (Rom 8:18–30; 2 Cor 4:13–5:5).

What will this kind of suffering look like? The first letter of Peter and the letter to the Hebrews especially develop the link between the suffering of Jesus and that of disciples. In 1 Peter 2:19–21, we read that those who endure suffering when they have done right have God's approval, because they are following Christ's example: "For to this you have been called, for Christ also suffered for you, leaving you an example, so that you should follow in his steps."

In Hebrews, as we have seen, Christ's suffering is a sign of his full participation in our human condition (2:10–18) and of his ability to represent us as priest before God, as "one who in every respect has been tested as we are, yet without sin" (Heb 4:15). Hebrews goes even deeper, however, by proposing that the entire character of the Messiah's life was expressed by the words it attributes to him upon his entering it, "Behold I have come to do your will, O God!" (Heb 10:7). The very process by which he became obedient Son, moreover, involved suffering: "although he was a son, he learned obedience from what he suffered, and having become perfect became the cause of salvation for all who obey him" (Heb 5:8–9).

This process, in turn, is the one into which we are invited by the God who calls us into a share in his Sonship. The suffering we experience is a means by which we, too, can "learn obedience" and become perfected in the manner of Jesus: "you are enduring for the sake of an education" (Heb 12:7). For these New Testament witnesses, suffering is not that from which Jesus frees us, but that which Jesus has transfigured into a means for us to share in salvation.

AND WAS BURIED

The final moment of Jesus' earthly existence noted by the creed is that he was buried. Once more, we find the tradition of Jesus' burial both in Paul and in the Gospels.

Writing to the Corinthians around the year 54, Paul provides a summary of the good news that he had himself received and had handed on to them, and "by which you are being saved if you hold firmly to the message" (1 Cor 15:1–2). It begins, "that Christ died for our sins in accordance with the scriptures, and that he was buried." Note that Paul reports this in an unadorned fashion. It is simply one of the "facts" about Jesus that he received from the first believers, therefore within some few years of Jesus' death. He does not suggest that, like the death for sins and like the resurrection on the third day, these are matters predicted by the scriptures.

The same matter-of-factness about the burial is found in the Gospel narratives, with several small variations (see Mark 15:42–47; Matt 27:55–66; Luke 23:50–55; John 19:38–42). More striking is the strong agreement on the basic characters and actions, and above all on the fact of the burial itself. That Jesus was buried and remained in the tomb for some length of time certainly serves to confirm the reality of his death. Compare Martha's comment concerning her brother Lazarus, "Lord, already there is a stench because he has been dead four days" (John 11:32), and the resurrection of a body so thoroughly dead must also be regarded as an act of God.

But another dimension of the burial is equally ancient and important. The burial symbolizes Jesus' descent into the realm that in ancient cosmology was most removed from "heaven" or the place of God's dwelling. He goes "under the earth," which in the Psalms is called *sheol*, and in the Greek translation, *hadēs*. In Peter's speech at Pentecost, he quotes Psalm 16 in connection with Jesus' death: "You will not abandon my soul to hades, or let your Holy One see corruption" (Acts 2:27).

This connection may help account for the conviction that Jesus, after his death, entered into the dungeons of the lower depths in order to free those most distant from the divine presence, a motif that was subsequently termed "the harrowing of hell" or, in the Apostles' Creed, "the descent into hell." In Ephesians 4:5, Paul asks cryptically, "when it says 'he ascended,' what does it mean but that he had also descended into the lower parts of the earth?" The conviction is stated more clearly by 1 Peter 3:18–20:

He was put to death in the flesh, but made alive in the spirit, in which also he went and made a proclamation to the spirits in prison, who in former times did not obey, when God waited patiently in the days of Noah.

Peter continues, "For this is the reason the gospel was proclaimed even to the dead, so that, even though they had been judged in the flesh as everyone is judged, they might live in the spirit as God does" (1 Pet 4:6).

The descent of Jesus into hell is, in this view, an expression of God's universal will for salvation and a part of his cosmic victory, so that every tongue, even those "under the earth," should proclaim that Jesus is Lord (Phil 2:10). In terms of the movement of the creed, the burial represents the nadir of downward descent, the ultimate expression of Jesus' sharing the human condition, even to the depositing of the flesh in the soil like a seed (John 12:24; see 1 Cor 15:35–41).

Chapter Six

HE ASCENDED . . . AND
WILL COME AGAIN

Having reached its lowest point in the burial (and descent into hell), the story of Jesus now begins to swing upward again, as the creed speaks of his resurrection, ascension, and enthronement at God's right hand. This part of the creed most clearly reveals the inadequacy of a Christianity based only on the "historical Jesus" and its distance from traditional Christian faith. For such a Christianity, Jesus' story ends with his death. We can decide who he is and what he means only from the facts of his ministry in ancient Palestine. But for creedal Christians, Jesus' story does not end with his death. It continues into the present and into the future, more powerfully than before.

AND ROSE ON THE THIRD DAY, ACCORDING TO THE SCRIPTURES

The statement follows Paul's declaration in 1 Corinthians 15:3, "he was raised on the third day according to the scriptures." The creed uses the active verb "he rose" instead of Paul's "he was raised." The variation is typical in the New Testament, which uses both the passive—suggesting the divine activity even when God is not explicitly named as subject (see, e.g., Matt 16:21; Rom 4:24)—and the active—sometimes God as subject (see Acts 2:24; 1 Cor 15:15; 2 Cor 1:9) and sometimes Jesus (Mark 8:31; 1 Thess 4:4).

The New Testament has a similar variation concerning "the third day." Some passages speak of the resurrection occurring "after three days" (Mark 8:31; 9:31; 10:34; Matt 27:63; Luke 24:21), but most have it "on the third day" (1 Cor 15:3; Luke 9:22; 18:33; 24:7; Acts 10:40; Matt 16:21; 20:19). The Gospels agree that Jesus was killed on the day before the Sabbath, that is, a Friday (see John 19:31; Luke 23:56; Mark 15:42; Matt 27:62), and that his empty tomb was discovered on "the first day of the week," that is, our Sunday (Mark 16:1–2; Matt 28:1; John 20:1; Luke 24:1), so "on the third day" is accurate enough. Less clear is how this "third day" is in fulfillment of the Scriptures.

Indeed, the resurrection itself is not clearly foretold by the Scriptures, much less that it should take place on "the third day." The resurrection hope was discovered in the Psalms and the prophets after the fact (see Luke 24:25–27). Isaiah 53:10–11, read by the first Christians as about Jesus, the suffering servant of the Lord, contains a hint: "he shall see his offspring and shall prolong his days . . . out of his anguish he shall see light." And Psalm 16:8–11—cited by Peter at Pentecost (Acts 2:25–28)—promised an escape from death for God's chosen one: "I keep the Lord always before me; because he is at my right hand I shall not be moved. Therefore my heart is glad and my soul rejoices, my body also rests secure, for you do not give me up to Sheol, or let your faithful one see the pit. You show me the path of life."

Two prophetic passages contain the phrase "the third day." Read in light of the experience of Jesus' rising, they have a deeper resonance. Jonah says that the prophet was kept in the belly of the whale for three days and three nights (Jon 1:17). The connection to Jesus' resurrection would seem obscure, if Jesus were not reported as using it as a parallel for himself: "Just as Jonah was three days and three nights in the belly of the sea-monster, so for three days and three nights the Son of Man will be in the heart of the earth" (Matt 12:40). The second passage is Hosea 6:1–2:

> Come, let us return to the Lord; for it is he who has torn, and it is he who will heal us. He has struck down, and he will bind us up. After two days he will revive us; on the third day, he will raise us up, that we may live before him.

The tradition concerning the third day owed something both to the actual timing of the experience and to the careful examination of such fragile scriptural precedents.

The creed here reduces a complex body of evidence to the two propositions that pertain to "us . . . and . . . our salvation": that Jesus rose from the dead and that he ascended to his Father's right hand. The truth of the resurrection is not simply that Jesus is no longer among the dead, but that he now shares the life and power of God. The resurrection, the ascension, and the enthronement express the truth about Jesus in the present. Because the creed provides only the outline of faith that guides the reading of Scripture and the discernment of life, it says nothing about the experience of the resurrection from the side of believers—which the New Testament speaks most about—but speaks only of the cause of that experience in the story of Jesus.

It therefore leaves out what follows the resurrection and enthronement of Jesus, namely the sending of the Holy Spirit into the hearts of believers for their transformation in his likeness. I am focusing here on what the creed says explicitly, but I hope that readers will appreciate from my earlier discussions how these few and spare statements point to the powerful and transforming experience of Jesus Christ as life-giving spirit (1 Cor 15:45) that alone makes sense of and gives life to the bare bones of this mythic account.

The existence of Christianity is inexplicable apart from the experience and conviction that the story of Jesus did not end with his death, but rather entered into a new and more powerful phase. As Paul argues in 1 Corinthians 15:13–19, responding to some who said that there is no resurrection of the dead:

> If there is no resurrection of the dead, then Christ has not been raised; and if Christ has not been raised, then our proclamation has been in vain [or "empty"], and your faith has been in vain ["empty"]. We are even found to be misrepresenting God, because we testified of God that he raised Christ—whom he did not raise if it is true that the dead are not raised. For if the dead are not raised, then Christ has not been raised. If Christ has not been raised, your faith is futile [or "foolish"] and you are still in your sins. Then those who have died in Christ have perished. If for this life only we have hoped in Christ, we are of all people most to be pitied.

Paul's language is extraordinarily strong. As much as any subsequent critic of Christianity, he recognizes that everything hinges on this article of the creed (see 15:1–3), and yet it is the article that most conflicts with any other human experience and is therefore the most difficult to assert. In a word, Paul acknowledges that if Jesus is not resurrected, the gospel is a lie, preachers (like himself) have been false witnesses, and Christians have been gullible and self-deluded fools who have wasted their lives. Nietzsche could not have put it more crisply.

Paul saw clearly that if Jesus was important only for what he did during his mortal existence, he was of no value to the Corinthians who gathered in his name. Jesus may have been a good teacher or a powerful prophet, but if he was not resurrected, he was at best a moral exemplar like other teachers or prophets. If he had not overcome mortality, he could not lead others to a share of life greater than the merely mortal. If Jesus is not raised, Christianity is simply another cult or ethical society, and not a particularly attractive one.

The same is just as true today. Those contemporary forms of Christianity that focus only on the humanity of Jesus believe in vain. They have, sadly, capitulated to the mind of the Enlightenment that I discussed in the Introduction. If religion can hold as true only what is "within the bounds of reason," and if "reason" is defined in terms of the empirically verifiable, then the resurrection is excluded by definition. But if the resurrection is excluded, why should Christians continue to revere Jesus, who is then only one of many figures from antiquity worthy of attention and honor? If Jesus is only the "historical Jesus," then Christianity is a delusion and a waste of time. But if Jesus is raised as Lord, everything changes radically.

The resurrection creates the need to write the New Testament in the first place. The belief in a crucified messiah whose resurrection was understood as a powerful sharing in God's life forced the early Christians to interpret the Scriptures and account for Jesus' ministry. He was manifestly a failed messiah by any Jewish measure. He did not restore the people to prosperity and safety, did not establish the rule of Torah. And he was probably also a false messiah, since he led the people astray and did not live according to the norms of Torah.

The pre-conversion Paul was thus utterly consistent as he persecuted the church in defense of Torah. If Jesus was not raised, then Torah correctly considered him "cursed" (Deut 21:23). His life and death stood in opposition to Torah as it was understood by its righteous interpreters. But when Paul encountered the resurrected Jesus, he needed to reconcile that experience of Jesus as the Holy One with the testimony of Scripture. So also with the other writers of the New Testament compositions: they needed to write because they needed to account for this paradoxical experience of God in a crucified messiah, but they needed to account for a crucified messiah only because they experienced him as alive with the power of God.

The New Testament speaks about the resurrection, then, in varied and complex ways. When, for example, Christians spoke about the power of the Holy Spirit among them, they were speaking by implication of the resurrection of Jesus (see, e.g., 1 Cor 12:1–3). And when they spoke of God "raising Jesus from the dead" with reference to their own lives (see, e.g., Rom 6:1–11), they were likewise alluding to that event. These ways of speaking about the resurrection dominate in the earliest writings (the epistles): it is spoken of less as an event of the past than as a cause of their present existence.

Revealingly, these early letters offer no stories about the resurrection as a past event. The most explicit attention given to the resurrection as an event in the past is found in 1 Corinthians

15:3–8, where Paul summarizes the good news by which his Corinthian readers are being saved. After stating that Jesus was "raised on the third day according to the Scriptures" (15:4), Paul lists Jesus' appearances to various witnesses after his resurrection:

> He appeared to Cephas, then to the Twelve. Then he appeared to more than five hundred brothers at one time, most of whom are still alive, though some have died. Then he appeared to James, then to all the apostles. Last of all, as to one untimely born, he appeared also to me . . . whether it was I or they, so we proclaim and so you have come to believe.

Two points in this dense summary deserve attention. First, Paul tells us that the resurrection of Jesus was among "the things of greatest importance" (15:3) not only to him, but to all the first believers. If it were untrue, not only he but they would be "false witnesses concerning God." Paul claims that Cephas and James and the Twelve, and "all the apostles," preach just as he does. And he says this to a church that knows Cephas and other "super-apostles" (1 Cor 1:10–11; 12:11), and could counter his claim were it untrue. They as well as those among the five hundred who were still alive were not witnesses of the distant past, but active members of the congregations, whose testimony could be sought and obtained.

Second, Paul's list of witnesses does not match precisely those who appear in the Gospel accounts. Notably absent from Paul's list, but present in the Gospel accounts, are the women who play, as I will shortly show, such a key role both in the empty tomb and appearance stories. Absent also are Cleopas and the other (possibly female) disciple who journeyed with Jesus to Emmaus. None of the Gospels contains an appearance to "the Twelve" as such, since Judas was excluded from that circle (see the mention of "the eleven" in Matt 28:16; Mark 16:14; Luke 24:9, 33). Present in Paul's list but absent from the Gospel accounts are James and the "five hundred brothers at one time," unless we (roughly) harmonize this with Luke's Pentecost story (Acts 2:1–5). We can be fairly sure that stories now found in the Gospels were circulating in some form already when Paul was writing, as suggested by his use of certain sayings of Jesus that appear also in the Gospels (see, e.g., 1 Cor 11:23–25).

We can explain the differences between Paul and the Gospels in two ways. One is that, for some political purpose, Paul and the Gospels were correcting each other. Perhaps Paul chose to ignore the stories involving women (this is the usual supposition) in favor of a more "official"—and male—list of witnesses. The other possibility is more reasonable. The traditions of the resurrection varied for a considerable period of time—we will find that the Gospels do not agree even with each other—and it was more important to the first believers to know that there were witnesses among them and that their own lives were transformed than that the historical account was accurate in every detail.

As for the Gospel accounts, it is vital to note that the experience of the resurrected one does not arise from these stories. Rather, these stories seek to express and interpret the experience. Although undoubtedly based on real experience and early tradition, they are not simply reports of the resurrection. The stories have been selected and shaped to instruct the readers of the Gospels. In their present form, the Gospel accounts reflect the ongoing experiences and convictions of the believing community over a period of some forty years.

The Gospels contain two basic types of resurrection stories. The first concerns the empty tomb. The second concerns Jesus' appearances to his followers. The basic form of the empty tomb story is the same in each Gospel (see Mark 16:1–8; Matt 28:1–8; Luke 24:1–11; John 20:1–10): followers of Jesus come to the tomb to anoint him after his burial and discover that he is not there; they are told by one or more messengers to deliver the message that he has been raised. The accounts vary considerably, however, in detail: of those going to the tomb, the number and identity of the messenger(s), the nature of the message, and the followers' response to the announcement. So sharp are these discrepancies that it is impossible to speak simply of a standard "empty tomb account." We have, rather, a set of interpretations of an empty tomb experience.

Besides these differences, the accounts also have certain apologetic details that respond to the charge that the resurrection was a hoax perpetrated by the apostles—a charge made explicit in Matthew 28:11–15 (see also 27:62–66). Thus, the stone is said to be too heavy to be rolled away by any human, and the empty tomb is a surprise to the visitors. Likewise, when the other disciples are informed, they remain incredulous.

The empty tomb by itself, however, does not and could not give rise to the resurrection experience or the conviction that Jesus is Lord. The main point of these accounts is that Jesus is not among the dead. As Luke puts it, the women are seeking "the Living One" among the dead, and he is not there (Luke 24:5). Rather, as Mark has it, he "goes before" them (Mark 16:7). Like the tomb itself, these stories lie open for new encounters with Jesus. He is not where he was (his old life is closed), but his new life cannot be defined precisely in terms of time and space (he goes before them). The linens left behind give silent testimony to the one freed from the binding of death (John 20:6–9).

The second type of resurrection story is the appearance account (see Mark 16:9–20; Matt 28:9–10, 16–20; Luke 24:13–49; John 20:11–21:23). These stories also vary in detail concerning who had the experience, where, and in what circumstances. They also respond to an implied charge, this time that the resurrection was somehow unreal. Thus, some stress the reality of Jesus' resurrection body in order to make the point that the one who now lives is continuous with the Jesus whom they knew before (see John 20:26–28), and others, that the experience of his presence was not to be thought of in terms of a ghost or phantom (see Luke 24:36–43).

But three other features give the appearance accounts their special character. The first is the sudden, surprising, and unpremeditated nature of the encounters with Jesus. He intrudes into the midst of his followers. They do not make him appear through prayer or ritual, and they are frightened when he does appear. Second, Jesus appears among his followers in an altered form, so that he is not necessarily recognized and may even be mistaken for a gardener or a fellow pilgrim. Third, he appears as a more powerful and commanding presence.

These stories are dominated by the powerful words spoken by Jesus to his followers. He interprets the Scripture concerning himself. Above all, he commands them to proclaim his presence to others. The disciples experience Jesus in the imperative mode. He is Lord.

These Gospel stories must be read in the context of the whole New Testament witness concerning the resurrection. If the Gospel accounts were the only ones considered, the resurrection of Jesus might (with some difficulty) be understood as a resuscitation. But to take only these Gospel stories as the basis for the Christian confession of the resurrection, much less as an adequate expression of that reality, is the most fundamental mistake in reading them. The rest of the New Testament's witness insists that Jesus did not return from the dead to continue his former life. That would be good news only for him and his friends and family. It would not be a new creation. It would not be good news for all humanity for all ages.

The resurrection is, the whole of the New Testament witness insists, Jesus' entry into the life and power of God. To express that truth, the New Testament uses the language not only of resurrection, but the symbol also of Jesus' ascension and enthronement at God's right hand. To those symbols we must now turn, but all the while remembering that we deal with the same reality, the same passage of the human Jesus from mortal death to the life of God.

HE ASCENDED TO HEAVEN, AND SITS ON THE RIGHT HAND OF THE FATHER

This statement completes the creed's witness concerning the resurrection of Jesus. As we have seen, that Jesus is no longer among the dead is only one part of the resurrection. The other is that he now lives with God's own life and power. His resurrection, then, is not resuscitation, a return to mortal life. It is Jesus' entry as a human person into the immortal existence of God. This is, indeed, a "new creation" (2 Cor 5:16).

The New Testament has a number of ways to express Jesus' new and more powerful form of existence. One of the most frequent is to speak of him as sharing royal power with the Father. The royal enthronement in Psalm 110:1 here plays an important role, even when it is not cited in full (as in Acts 2:25; Heb 1:13): "The Lord said to my Lord, 'Sit at my right hand, until I make your enemies a footstool for your feet.' "

Thus, simply the phrase "on the right hand" suggests such a sharing in power (see, e.g., Matt 27:29; Mark 10:37; Rev 2:1), as does the reference to Jesus "sitting at the right hand" (see Matt

26:46; Mark 14:62; 16:19; Luke 22:69; Acts 2:33; 5:31; 7:55–56; Rom 8:34; Eph 1:20; Col 3:1; Heb 1:3; 8:1; 19:12; 12:2; 1 Pet 3:22; Rev 5:1, 7), and the declaration that "all things are subject" to him (see, e.g., 1 Cor 15:27; Eph 1:22; Phil 3:21; Heb 2:8; 1 Pet 3:22). Similar to the language about Jesus' enthronement is that about his "exaltation" (see Acts 2:31; 5:31; John 3:14; 8:28; 12:32, 34), and of his "entering glory" (see Luke 24:26; Acts 7:55; 1 Cor 15:40–43; 2 Cor 4:6; Phil 3:21; 1 Tim 3:16; Heb 2:7, 9; 1 Pet 1:11; Rev 5:12–13), and of his being "glorified" (see John 12:16; 13:31–32; 17:5; Acts 3:13). All these terms point to Jesus' continuing authority and supreme status. They do not portray Jesus as absent but as powerfully present: he now rules creation together with God the Father. He is not less active and powerful than in his earthly ministry, but more active and powerful, as the visions of the exalted and all-powerful Christ in the Book of Revelation show (see Rev 1:17–20; 2:2–6, 13–17; 19–29; 3:1–22; 5:1–14).

Another way of expressing Jesus' new and more powerful life is to speak of him "ascending" or "being lifted up." This corresponds to the language that spoke of his "coming down" or "descending." John's Gospel frequently has Jesus speak of "going" and "going back" and "ascending" to the Father (see John 13:1; 14:3, 12, 28; 16:5, 10; 17:11, 13). He tells his disciples, "I came from the Father and have come into the world. Again I am leaving the world, and am going to the Father" (John 16:28). When he appears in hidden form to Mary in the garden after his resurrection, he tells her, "I am ascending (*anabainō*) to my Father and to your Father, to my God and your God" (John 20:17).

Paul rarely uses this imagery, but we find a trace in Ephesians. Applying Psalm 68:19 to Jesus, Paul says,

> Each one of us was given grace according to the measure
> of Christ's gift. Therefore it is said, "When he ascended

on high he made captivity itself a captive; he gave gifts to his people." When it says, "he ascended" what does it mean but that he had also descended into the lower parts of the earth? He who descended is the same one who ascended far above all the heavens so that he might fill all things. (Eph 4:7–10)

Jesus' ascent is the premise for the sharing of the gifts (of the Spirit) with others (Eph 4:11–16). The ascension of Christ is not a distancing from us but the condition for a new form of intimacy with us. Likewise in 1 Timothy 3:16, Paul states:

He was revealed in flesh, vindicated in Spirit, seen by angels, proclaimed among Gentiles, believed in throughout the world, taken up in glory.

1 Peter 3:22 also uses this kind of language as well as the symbolism of enthronement: "baptism . . . now saves you . . . through the resurrection of Jesus Christ, who has gone into heaven, and is at the right hand of God, with angels, authorities, and powers made subject to him."

So although the *story* of Jesus' ascension appears in only two New Testament writings, Mark and Luke-Acts, the *conviction* that Jesus is now in heaven and "exalted," and "glorified," and "enthroned" is found everywhere in the New Testament.

The two stories are themselves problematic. The first is extremely short and is found only in the "longer ending" of Mark's Gospel absent from the oldest and best manuscripts of the Gospel. The best scholarly opinion is that these words were not part of the composition written by Mark, but were early on appended to Mark to make up for what appears to be a truncated ending: "So then the Lord Jesus, after he had spoken to them, was taken up into heaven and sat down at the right hand of God" (Mark 16:19). Luke provides a version both in his Gospel (Luke 24:51) and in the beginning of his second volume, the Acts of the Apostles (Acts 1:9–11), but they do not entirely agree. The Gospel has: "Then he led them out as far as Bethany, and lifting up his hands, he blessed them. While he was blessing them, he withdrew from them and was carried up into heaven." In Acts we read:

When he had said this, as they were watching, he was lifted up and a cloud took him out of their sight. As he was going and they were gazing up into heaven, suddenly two men in white robes stood by them. They said, "Men of Galilee, why do you stand looking up toward heaven? This Jesus, who has been taken up from you into heaven will come in the same way as you saw him go into heaven."

The fact that Luke himself has provided two distinct versions of the same event—both remarkably restrained—liberates us from the tedious work of trying to literalize either of them and argue that the ascension is a historical event. As in the case of the resurrection narratives, let us recognize that the experience and conviction of Jesus' exaltation are not to be identified with the story, and also that these narratives are written to suggest through their choice of symbols the deeper significance of the event.

Luke's placement of the Acts account immediately after Jesus' promise that his followers would receive the Holy Spirit and become his witnesses (Acts 1:8), as well as its symbolism, tells us what significance the ascension has in his writing. There is, for example, an obvious literary link between these two men in white garments and the two men who speak to the women at the tomb (Luke 24:4–5). The form of the men's question to the disciples echoes the challenge the two men put to the women coming to the tomb: "Why are you seeking the Living One among the dead?" followed by the correction, "he is not here but has been raised" (Luke 24:5–6). Here we have, "why do you stand looking up toward heaven," followed by the correction, "he will come in the same way" (Acts 1:11).

It is clear what the problem was with the women seeking the Living One in the tomb. But what is wrong with the disciples gazing into heaven? The clue is offered by the literary prototype of Elijah. Before Elijah was taken up, his follower Elisha requested from him a double portion of the prophetic spirit. Elijah said he would receive this gift only if he *saw him departing* (2 Kings 2:10). Elisha did see him ascend in the fiery chariot and whirlwind and did receive a double portion of the spirit. Luke's emphasis on the disciples' seeing him as he ascends (Acts 1:9) picks up this idea: we know that they will receive the promised Spirit. But to do so, they must obey the command to return to the city and await that empowerment.

The message of the two men then serves the same double function as that given to the women. By seeking Jesus in the tomb, the women are able to certify that he is not there but raised, but they are told to "remember" how this was a fulfillment of Jesus' own prophecy (Luke 24:6–8). The empty tomb account looks backward to the story of Jesus. The disciples are able to confirm that Jesus has ascended, but they are not to stand there gazing, for (as Luke's subsequent account will show) Jesus' presence will be with them even more powerfully in the outpouring of the Spirit they are about to experience (Acts 2:1–5). The ascension looks forward to the empowerment and ministry of Jesus' prophetic followers.

One final point worth noting is the insight Luke provides through the way he arranges the sequence of stories in this part of his narrative. Luke is a storyteller. It is by following his narrative sequence "in order" (see Luke 1:3; Acts 11:4) that we are able to grasp the theological truth he seeks to express. Luke provides the fullest array of post-death stories of any of the Gospels. He has an empty tomb account (24:1–12), several appearance stories (24:13–49), two reports of the ascension (Luke 24:51; Acts 1:9–11), and, finally, the story of the bestowal of the Holy Spirit on Jesus' followers at Pentecost (Acts 2:1–5), which Peter's speech interprets as the sign that Jesus has been raised (2:14–36). When we read these stories in sequence, we see that Luke has provided us with insight into the mystery of the resurrection as a dialectic of Jesus' absence and presence.

The empty tomb says that Jesus is absent from the realm of mortality. He is not among the dead, but neither is he simply somewhere else. He is now "the Living One." The appearance accounts say that the raised Jesus is now present to his followers, but not in the manner of his mortal life. He can appear and disappear suddenly, manifest himself in the guise of a stranger, and speak as commanding Lord. The ascension says that Jesus must transcend earthly life altogether, be "absent" from humans in his former manner in order to be fully "present" at God's right hand. But this "separation" and distance serve, finally, as the premise for his more intimate and powerful presence to "all flesh" through the gift of the Holy Spirit.

The creed's statements about the resurrection and exaltation of Jesus express the truth about Jesus now. They are the premise for the church's worship and practice. If these statements are false, everything that the church does "in the name of Jesus" is an empty shell, for "Jesus" can refer only to a dead man of the distant past, and not a powerful Lord of the present whose presence defines our present. When the church gathers "in the name of Jesus," it gathers in the name of nothing if Jesus is not Lord.

When the church prays and heals and prophecies "in the name of Jesus," it engages in self-deception and delusion if Jesus does not now act in the world with the very power of the creator.

But if the creed speaks the truth, then the question we put to Jesus is not nearly so important as the question Jesus puts to us. If the creed speaks the truth, that Jesus now lives at the right hand of the Father, then "learning Jesus" is not a matter of scholarly enterprise and casual reading about a teacher of the past, but a matter of obedience to the one who presses upon us at every moment, encounters us in the sacraments and saints and strangers, and calls us to account.

HE WILL COME AGAIN
WITH GLORY TO JUDGE
THE LIVING AND THE DEAD

That God is judge of the world follows logically from the fact that God is creator. As the one who brings all that is into existence at every moment, God has power over all that is (God is "all-mighty") and has "maker's knowledge" of all things. God is uniquely able to judge the world rightly because God alone knows the world from the inside and exercises dominion over it. That God judges the world also shows that creation is not a casual affair for God but rather a passionate commitment. God wills that what God creates as good should end by being good.

The conviction that God judges the world, and judges justly, is constantly affirmed in the Old Testament (Gen 18:25; Deut 32:36; Exod 5:21; LXX Ps 5:10; 7:8, 11; 9:39; 49:6; 53:1; 57:11; 67:5; 74:5; 134:14; Sir 32:12; Isa 30:18; 33:22; 63:7; Jer 11:20; Ezek 7:8; 11:10; 18:30). Two notions are embedded in the understanding of God as judge. The first is that God sees clearly and decides fairly between humans on the basis not of appearances or bribes but on the basis of their deeds. The second is that the Lord who sees into the hearts of humans also acts to redress the wrongs that humans do to each other. Thus, when the Lord is asked to "judge the orphan and the poor" (LXX Ps 9:39), the plea is that God provide for them what their oppressive neighbors have taken away by force or guile. For the Old Testament, consequently, God's "justice" is not simply a matter of dispassionate bookkeeping in which human actions are tallied, but a passionate involvement on the side of good against evil. Thus, an appeal to God's justice is often a cry for the rectification of a world gone awry through human wickedness (see, e.g., Gen 18:19; Deut 33:21; LXX Ps 5:8; 10:8; 21:31; 30:1; 44:4; 70:2; Hos 10:12; Amos 5:7; Isa 5:7; 9:7; 33:5; 48:1; 9:24; 22:3).

The New Testament maintains both dimensions of the Old Testament's understanding of God as judge. God judges the world and the hidden things of humans (Rom 2:11, 16; 3:6; 14:4, 10; 11:32; Heb 10:30; 12:23; James 4:12). At the same time, the revelation of the good news through Jesus is a revelation of "the righteousness of God" in the sense of God's righteous intervention in human time and space to rectify God's world, to show, as Paul says in Romans 3:26, that God "is righteous and makes righteous."

Distinctive to the New Testament, naturally, is the conviction that Jesus is not only the agent of God's salvation but also shares God's role as judge. No more emphatic testimony could be given to the earliest Christians' convictions concerning the divinity of Jesus, or his powerful present life with God, than this, that Jesus is judge. Thus, when Paul declares in Romans 2:16 that God will judge the secrets of humans "on a day," he adds that this will be done "through Christ Jesus" (Rom 2:16). And as he affirmed that all will stand before the judgment seat of God (Rom 14:10), so does he say, "for all of us must appear before the judgment seat of Christ, so that each may receive recompense for what has been done in the body, whether good or evil" (2 Cor 5:10).

These affirmations of Jesus' sharing in God's prerogative of judging human hearts were written within thirty years of Jesus' execution as a criminal. The conviction that Jesus will "come again as judge" is rooted in the experience of him as powerfully alive with God's own life through his resurrection. To "come again," Jesus must be alive in a manner that transcends mortality; to "come as judge," he can only be alive with the very power of God.

In many New Testament texts, the "coming" and "judging" will happen in the future. In Acts 17:31, for example, Paul proclaims that God has "fixed a day on which he will have the world judged in righteousness by a man whom he has appointed, and of this he has given assurance to all by raising him from the dead" (see also Acts 10:42; 2 Tim 4:1, 8; 1 Pet 4:5). But in the Gospel of John, what other witnesses speak of as in the future is sometimes portrayed as a feature of Jesus' human ministry. Sometimes this is called a "realized eschatology." John's language about Jesus and judgment is a prime example.

John's language is difficult to sort out because he typically plays on the several possible meanings of a word. The Greek verb *krinein*, for example, can mean "to judge" and also "to condemn." John has Jesus say to Nicodemus, "Indeed, God did not send the Son into the world to condemn/judge (*krinein*) the world, but in order that the world might be saved through him. Those who believe in him are not condemned/judged (*krinein*), but those who do not believe are condemned/judged (*krinein*) already, because they have not believed in the name of the only Son of God" (John 3:17–18).

Jesus' words following this statement make clear that Jesus' coming into the world as "the light" is already a call to decision and thus a judgment on the decision made. It is when light comes into the darkness that not only light but also darkness can properly be named. The one who chooses darkness once the light has been revealed thereby refuses the light, and therefore comes into judgment or condemnation (3:18–20).

But although John sees the first coming of Jesus as itself a judgment or crisis for the world, the evangelist retains as well the more traditional sense of a future judgment. Thus, in 12:47–48, Jesus declares at the end of his public ministry, "I do not judge/condemn anyone who hears my words and does not keep them, for I came not to judge/condemn the world but to save the world. The one who rejects me and does not receive my word has a judge; on the last day the word that I have spoken will serve as judge."

Equally ambiguous with regard to present/future judgment is Jesus' discourse found in John 5, which stresses the equivalence in authority between Father and Son:

Very truly I tell you, the Son can do nothing on his own, but only what he sees the Father doing; for whatever the Father does, the Son does likewise. The Father loves the Son and shows him all that he himself is doing, and he will show him greater works than these, so that you will be astonished. Indeed, just as the Father raises the dead and gives them life, so also the Son gives life to whomever he wishes. The Father judges no one but has given all judgment to the Son, so that all may honor the Son, just as they honor the Father. Anyone who does not honor the Son does not honor the Father who sent him. I tell you, anyone who hears my word and believes him who sent me has eternal life, and does not come under judgment/

condemnation, but has passed from death to life. Very truly, I tell you, the hour is coming, and is now here, when the dead will hear the voice of the Son of God, and those who hear will live. For just as the Father has life in himself, so he has granted the Son also to have life in himself; and he has given him authority to execute judgment, because he is the Son of Man. Do not be astonished at this, for the hour is coming when all who are in the graves will hear his voice, and will come out—those who have done good, to the resurrection of life, and those who have done evil, to the resurrection of condemnation. (John 5:19–29)

I have quoted this passage in its entirely because of its extraordinary richness, and because it illustrates the balance John tries to hold in this matter. Although John clearly seeks to make Jesus' ministry itself a time of judgment, he maintains, and thereby reveals the force of, the dominant belief in the future judgment of God carried out through Jesus Christ. The authority to exercise judgment is connected to a sharing in the life of God. And because Jesus shares that life and authority fully, John regards a decision made for or against him by humans as a decision for or against God. The future judgment by the Son of Man, therefore, will simply reveal the judgment that comes as a result of the judgment made by humans themselves with regard to the Son of Man.

The confession that Jesus will come again to judge the living and the dead, I have shown, derives directly from the experience of his resurrection and enthronement at God's right hand, where he shares fully in God's life and authority. This conviction, I have also tried to show, is widely attested in the New Testament writings. This central and critical conviction can and must be distinguished from the several scenarios offered by the New Testament writings that imagine *how* that future coming and judging will occur.

There are three reasons why we must distinguish the conviction from the scenario. First, no one can know the future, not even the writers of the New Testament. The mystery of God's working in the world remains a mystery, as Paul reminds us, even when it is disclosed (Rom 16:25; 1 Cor 15:51). Jesus himself confesses concerning the return of the Son of Man that "about that day or hour no one knows, neither the angels in heaven, nor the Son, but only the Father" (Mark 13:32). All statements made in the New Testament about the future are based on an interpretation of present reality, expressed by the symbols of that age.

Second, the variety of scenarios presented by the New Testament itself argues against choosing any one of them as definitive. As with the stories of the resurrection, they combine conviction and imagination to communicate a vision of the future that corresponds to the truth about the present. Third, it is necessary to avoid confusing ideas about the end-time (eschatology) and judgment. They are distinct though related, so that it is possible for John, in the long passage I have quoted, to describe judgment without necessarily thinking it would take place at the end of time.

The New Testament offers a variety of scenarios. It may be helpful to review some of these, precisely because present-day Christians are unaware of how various they are. Paul, for example, can speak about the world's groaning in anticipation of the future revelation of the children of God (Rom 8:18–24) without referring to the end-time, judgment, or the Son of Man. Likewise, he can speak about "the end" as Jesus handing over the kingdom to his Father, which involves the destruction of all his enemies and the subjection of all reality so that "God will be all in all" (1 Cor 15:24–28), without alluding to a "coming of Jesus" or "judgment." Similarly, he can speak about being "with the Lord [Jesus]" either in connection with the arrival or (second) coming of the Lord (1 Thess 4:17) or apart from it (2 Cor 5:7; Phil 1:23).

Paul does offer two vivid scenarios that do not entirely agree. In 1 Thessalonians, Paul refers several times to the arrival or (second) coming of "our Lord Jesus," using a term widely used for the visits of Greek potentates to cities (1 Thess 2:19; 3:13; 4:15; 5:23; see also Matt 24:3, 27, 37, 39). In his portrayal of this "coming," he uses apocalyptic symbolism—there is a cry of command, an archangel's call, God's trumpet, and clouds. He uses this symbolism to ensure his readers that both the dead and the living will take part in this triumph. They should therefore not grieve for those who have died (4:13–17). Paul says that this will happen suddenly, when least expected, like a thief in the night (5:1–3).

In this description, Paul says nothing about judgment or punishment. Indeed, the function of Jesus' return is "to rescue us from the wrath that is coming" (1 Thess 1:10). This scenario reminds us of Hebrews 9:28: "Christ, having been offered once to bear the sins of many, will appear a second time, not to deal with sin, but to save those who are eagerly awaiting him" (see also 2 Tim 4:17).

In his second letter to the Thessalonians, in contrast, Paul speaks of the arrival or (second) coming of "our Lord Jesus Christ," with a different emphasis. Now, in response to those who are in a panic because they think the Lord has already come (2:2), he provides some unmistakable signs that must precede this arrival. Now not the salvation of the elect, but the punishment of the opponents occupies center place (2:3–11). Rather than a happy reunion in the clouds, we have the Lord Jesus resisting the lawless one who rebels against him, "destroying him with the breath of his mouth, annihilating him by the manifestation of his coming" (2:8). In this scene, Jesus is less the assessor of human deeds (Rom 2:16) than the one who intervenes as champion on the side of the oppressed.

In neither of these scenarios does Paul use the term "Son of Man" or explicitly state that the second coming of Jesus is for judgment—despite the fact, as I have shown, that he clearly thinks that we all must stand before the judgment seat of Christ (2 Cor 5:10).

The Synoptic Gospels, in turn, provide (with some internal variations) a scenario of "the things that are to happen" (Mark 13:4) that draws in some considerable measure from the apocalyptic vision of Daniel 7. In Mark, the coming of the Son of Man does not explicitly involve either judgment or punishment and focuses (like 1 Thessalonians) on the saving of the elect from tribulation. Mark 13 includes the persecution of the faithful (13:9–13), wars and cosmic disturbances (13:6–8), and the claims of false messiahs (13:14–22). These precede the saving of the elect (13:20).

The climax of this scenario is when "they will see the Son of Man coming in clouds with great power and glory. Then he will send out the angels, and gather his elect from the four winds, from the ends of earth to the ends of heaven" (Mark 13:26–27). The passage promises that these things will happen "before this generation passes away" (13:30), but also without warning, so there is the need to be watchful (13:32–37).

Luke's version edits Mark considerably, distinguishing the time of the early persecution of the church (Luke 21:12–19) from the destruction of the Temple that ushers in the age of the Gentiles (21:20–24) and from all the cosmic signs, and leads to the vision of "the Son of Man coming in a cloud with power and great glory" (21:27) that announces the coming of the kingdom of God (21:31). But as with Paul and Mark, Luke does not offer a scene of judgment. Neither does he speak here of a saving of the elect or the punishment of the wicked.

It is Matthew who massively expanded the scenario of the end-time and connected it to the final judgment by the Son of Man. In his version of Jesus' apocalyptic discourse (Matt 24), Matthew includes all of the elements found in Mark, including the salvation of the elect summoned with a loud trumpet by an angel (24:31; see 1 Thess), as a result of the appearance of the Son of Man on the clouds of heaven. But Matthew includes the idea of judgment by comparing that time to the days of Noah (24:36–41) and including the parable of the wicked household manager (24:45–51), followed by two further parables of judgment connected to the second coming: the parables of the wise and foolish virgins (25:1–13) and of the talents (25:14–30).

These prepare for Matthew's final and most powerful picture of the end-time, "when the Son of Man comes in his glory, and all the angels with him, then he will sit on the throne of his glory" (25:31). Matthew presents Jesus as the judge who welcomes into the kingdom those who have welcomed the little ones and so have welcomed him, and dismisses those who in refusing the little ones have refused him (25:32–45), so that "these will go into eternal punishment, but the righteous into eternal life" (25:46). In Matthew, then, we find the fullest expression in the Gospels of the conviction that not only will Jesus come again, but come as judge of the living and the dead.

By far the most complex and difficult scenario is presented by the Book of Revelation, which tells of the visions of John concerning "what soon must take place" (Rev 1:1). As in other writings of the type called "apocalyptic," the elaborate symbolism of visions, numbers, beasts, angels, and the like actually serves a simple understanding of history as a battle between the forces of good and evil, with God siding with good against evil.

In Revelation, however, the fundamental victory has already been won by the "lamb who was slain but lives," namely, Jesus

(5:1–14). He rules powerfully in heaven as "Lord of lords and King of kings" (19:16). With the risen Jesus in heaven are the saints who have proven faithful to God, and who worship eternally around the throne of God (7:13, 17). The complex visions of "what is going to happen" on earth show how God's victory, though difficult, is inevitable.

In Revelation, God is not the dispassionate judge but the one who fights on the side of the elect for the extermination of evil (and the evil ones). The final sequence shows the binding of Satan for a thousand years, which is followed by the triumph of those who had died for Jesus and who, in this first resurrection, reign with God and the Lamb on earth for a thousand years (20:1–6). But Satan is released and causes more trouble, before being utterly consumed (20:7–10). Then John provides a vision of final judgment:

> Then I saw a great white throne and the one who sat on it; the earth and the heaven fled from his presence, and no place was found for them. And I saw the dead, great and small, standing before the throne, and books were opened. Also another book was opened, the book of life. And the dead were judged according to their works, as recorded in the books. (20:11–12)

After this judgment comes John's vision of "a new heaven and a new earth," when the heavenly Jerusalem descends to earth and God dwells among humans, making everything new (21:1–8).

Despite its powerful poetry, its complexity and detail, its self-description as prophecy (22:7), the Book of Revelation is, like all the other scenarios of the end-time offered by the New Testament, an effort to imagine what cannot be known or adequately expressed, even imaginatively. Though some treat it as a special key, it enjoys no more authority than the witnesses of Paul or the Gospels. It stands with them as a witness to a conviction, based on the experience of the resurrection of Jesus, that God's judgment over the world will be accomplished and that judgment will be carried out in and through Jesus Christ the Lord.

Not surprisingly, perhaps no proposition in the creed so polarizes contemporary Christians as this one. We see the flourishing of millenarian Christianity, usually married to fundamentalism. It regards the Book of Revelation as the canon within the canon, the writing that is supremely and uniquely normative for today because it speaks of "what will come." Millenarians read it as a cryptogram predicting the present and analyze current events as harbingers of Armageddon. And they fret about the rapture. We also find Christians who emphatically reject such an apocalyptic—and in their view, fanatic—version of Christianity, but do not appreciate the importance of the conviction that God judges the world in Christ. They maintain an Enlightenment conviction that judgement is bad for religion.

I find both poles to be wrong. Millenarians are wrong because they have confused the Christian conviction and hope with one imagined vision of that conviction and hope. Anti-millenarians are wrong, because in rejecting that false identification, they have also given up on the conviction and hope.

What has brought about this polarization? Why do some Christians embrace an apocalyptic vision of the future, while others reject any idea that Jesus will "come again in glory to judge"?

Millenarianism appeals to the marginalized, those whose expectations of power, possessions, or prestige have been disappointed—the relatively deprived who take their deprivation absolutely. Apocalyptic visions appeal to them because these visions let their hostility and resentment find a religiously acceptable release in a God who does the work of judgment for them.

But if this is the case, why does apocalyptic Christianity flourish today among Americans who are often financially prosperous? Because material prosperity is not all that matters: millenarian Christians today are culturally and intellectually marginalized. They explicitly uphold a vision of the future—including a literal and physical return of Jesus, a rapture into heaven, and a thousand-year reign of the Messiah on earth—that is scorned by the modern world, including cultured and intellectually advanced Christians. For apocalyptic Christians, an unswerving devotion to the Book of Revelation is the test case of loyalty to scriptural inspiration and truth over against the corrosive effects of the Enlightenment among other Christians.

How can we account for the rejection of the conviction that Jesus will come to judge the living and the dead among sophisticated Christians? One factor is the revulsion felt by modern people at all forms of fanaticism in religion, and millenarians have tended to fanaticism ever since the Montanists of the second century. Another is the contemporary preference for a "God of Love" rather than a "God of Justice" (as though there could be one without the other). The late twentieth century perfected the dogma that all deviance was a matter of sickness rather than sin, and preferred a "God of infinite forgiveness" and "unconditional love," who would not judge or punish even the incorrigible.

A third factor is the widespread collapse of any expectation concerning "the world to come." A great final court at which Jesus assigns some to eternal life and others to eternal punishment is simply unimaginable for most modern people. If they cannot accept the possibility of the resurrection of the just, the condemnation of the reprobate to eternal punishment is unthinkable. How can we believe in a God who is "less just" and "less loving" than we are?

A fourth factor is the sense of dismay at the triumph of evil in the world. We are scarcely the first generation to experience the cognitive dissonance between belief in an all-powerful God who works for the good and the experience of the constant and inexorable triumph of wickedness. Apocalyptic literature is itself one ancient response to this dissonance, relieving it by showing God's triumph as coming in the future. But our generation is one for which that dissonance is particularly sharp because of our awareness of systems of corruption and criminality that have led to the destruction of the innocent in numbers difficult to compute.

Underlying all these factors is a more fundamental one, which is the combined loss of the strong sense of God as creator and the strong understanding of the resurrection of Jesus. Not only must the extravagant fantasies of millenarianism be rejected, if Christianity is defined "within the bounds of reason" as modern people prefer, but all traditional Christian eschatology. First, if God brings the world into being at every moment and sustains it by his power, then at every moment, the human heart is called into question by God, and is asked, "Whose creature are you? To whom do you belong?" If God is not creator in this sense, then God is not judge. But modern Christians think of God as part of the cosmic process, not its creator. Second, if Jesus has been exalted to God's right hand as sovereign Lord and as "life-giving Spirit" (1 Cor 15:45), he is the one who can and will judge the living and the dead. But if Jesus is not alive in this sense, he cannot judge the living and the dead.

With such misunderstanding at both poles, it is particularly important to remember that the creed's propositions can be understood as what I have called "critical theological concepts." They state *that* something is the case, not *how* it is the case. This insistence prevents our distorting other truths. Christians who profess that Jesus "will come to judge the living and the dead" must begin, therefore, by acknowledging that they are as much in the dark concerning humanity's future as anyone else. They have no direct information about heaven or hell (much less any hypothetical intermediate states) and have no better evidence for their existence than those who deny them. They have no privileged access to a divine timetable or a set scenario of the end-time, and are free to deny—on the basis of Scripture!—that there is any such timetable or set scenario.

So what does this phrase of the creed, understood as a critical theological concept, tell us? The profession of Jesus as judge does not state how God through Christ will restore right relations in the world (that is, bring about justice), but it does state that God in Christ knows what those relations are and is powerfully at work to make them right.

It states further that God is our judge here and now. We are opaque to each other, but we are all transparent to the God who makes us and to the Lord Jesus who shares God's life. As Hebrews says, "Before him no creature is hidden, but all are naked and laid bare to the eyes of the one to whom we must render an account" (4:13).

This is a truth both frightening and comforting. We do not know each other fully and do not even know ourselves truly, but we are known fully and truly by the one who creates all that is. Even when I am most alone, I am transparent to my creator. Indeed, Paul speaks of grace in terms of "being known by God" (1 Cor 8:3; Gal 4:9), rather than of knowing God. It is God's presence to us that gives us the freedom to be ourselves, rather than the prisoner of others' perceptions of us and demands upon us.

And it is because we are open to the gaze of God that we can afford to be honest with ourselves. We can admit to ourselves the truth that is already known to the only one who truly counts. And finally, only because God is judge do our interior intentions matter.

Sincerity and purity of heart mean something only if, as Jesus assures us, "your father in heaven sees in secret" (Matt 6:4, 5, 18).

On the other hand, the denial of God as judge leads to the distortion of other truths. If Jesus will not "come again in glory to judge," we must assume sole responsibility for doing justice in the world. If there is no heaven or hell to balance the scales of this-worldly iniquity and suffering, we must balance them. Unfortunately, humans lack the capacity to do justice fully and balance the scales. Unlike God we do not see all things at once and see them truly. Our knowledge of any situation is partial and always biased. We do not even know our own hearts truly, and are even less able to judge the hearts of others. We are forced to judge by "appearances," and appearances are often deceiving. In short, we take on a divine responsibility without the divine power to fulfill that responsibility.

A second distortion occurs in our inner life. If God is not judge—if the creator and the resurrected Lord Jesus do not know us at every moment—we need not strive for purity of heart, for sincerity in intention, for the prayer of silence. If we are not seen by God, but only by public opinion, we can feign any number of politically correct postures while having hearts that speak in quite a different way. We can protest racism and in our hearts detest persons of other races. We can march in favor of feminism and internally despise women. We can argue loudly for social justice and begrudge every moment or morsel shared with another. Hypocrisy is indeed the tribute vice pays to virtue. If only appearances count, why not wear the disguise? Likewise, why have sincerity of intention if I alone know it? Why not do the right thing for the wrong reason? Above all, why should we ever pray in secret—the prayer of silence that is essential for transformation in the spirit—unless the "Father who sees in secret will reward" us (Matt 6:4)?

HIS KINGDOM

It is no surprise to find the God of Israel understood as the supreme king among the gods and over the earth, for no other political image could so well capture the Lord's total power over creation and history, together with the Lord's ability to have and execute a will for his own people as well as all other creatures. And it is no surprise that the rule of the exalted Lord would be called "the kingdom."

But it is not an image that pleases some present-day sensibilities. A fair number of Christians seek to expunge such language, particularly through alternative translations. They prefer "God's Dominion" or "the Realm of God," and rather than "king" they want "sovereign" (who could be either male or female).

Many object to kingship language because it uses male terms, and I have given extensive attention to those criticisms earlier, when speaking about God as Father and as all-powerful. In this case, seeking to remove gender gets one only halfway, since some of the texts speak about the kingdom of Christ, and he is inescapably male. The cost of removing all kingship language is significant, for with the elimination of the "king" goes the meaning of ascent and exaltation and glorification and enthronement and crown, all the splendid symbolism by which other ages and cultures could mark the difference between ruler and ruled. Moreover, monarchical language is deeply appropriate to speak of a single will directing all reality and demanding the allegiance of every mind and heart, precisely for the same reason that it is repellant to many of us as a form of human politics. There is a real though limited value in seeking to level out the differences among humans. There is something appallingly banal about seeking to reduce the King of the Universe to Citizen God.

Scripture has no such difficulties with imagining God in terms of the most powerful position that a human could occupy. For the Psalmist,

> The Lord is a great God, and a great king over all the gods, for in his hand are the limits of the earth, and the heights of the mountains are his. His is the sea, and he himself made it. And his hands made the dry land. Come, bow down and worship before him, let us cry out before the Lord who made us, because he himself is our God and we are his people. (LXX Ps 94:3–6)

God is king over all pretend rulers (all "the gods") because God is the creator of all things, which calls especially for recognition from those whom God has created as his own people. Thus, the Psalmist can say, "the Lord is a great king over all the earth" (LXX Ps 46:2) and "the king of all the earth is God" (LXX Ps 46:7) and also include the prayerful recognition "my king and my God" (LXX Ps 83:3; 144:1; see also Ps 5:2; 28:10; 43:4; 67:24). So also the prophets can speak of God as "the Lord our King" (Isa 6:5; 33:22) and as "a great king" whose "name is known among the nations" (Mic 1:14).

The proclamation of "the kingdom of God," building on the tradition of Yahweh's rule over all creation, is fundamental to Jesus' mission as depicted in the Gospels. Mark uses the expression some eighteen times, Matthew, his equivalent expression ("kingdom of the heavens") some forty-nine times, and Luke, some forty times. Jesus proclaims the breaking into history of God's effective power and rule (Mark 1:15) over creation, and particularly God's claim on human allegiance. The kingdom is not a geographical place; it is rather a relationship of power, in which God and creature are properly aligned. God's power to rule is manifest in Jesus' ministry through his powerful deeds of healing and liberation (see Luke 11:20). The meaning of that power is poetically interpreted by Jesus' parables (see especially Mark 4:11, 26, 30, and Matt 13:11, 19, 24, 31, 33, 38, 41, 43, 44, 45, 47, 52).

The term is used less frequently though still consistently in the other New Testament writings. Although John uses the term only twice (see only John 3:3, 5; 18:36), the Book of Acts traces the preaching of the kingdom of God from Jesus (1:4), through Peter (8:12), to Paul (14:22; 19:8; 20:25; 28:23, 31). The phrase "kingdom of God" appears in Paul's letters with some frequency (Rom 14:7; 1 Cor 4:20; 6:9, 10; 15:24; Gal 5:21; Col 4:11; 1 Thess 2:12; 2 Thess 1:5). 2 Peter 1:11 speaks of "the eternal kingdom of our Lord," and Revelation 12:10 of "the kingdom of our God."

Several passages in Paul also speak of God's rule as one that is exercised as well by the Son in virtue of his resurrection. Ephesians 5:5 speaks of "the kingdom of Christ and God," and Colossians 1:3 speaks even more simply of "the kingdom of his beloved Son." Similarly, in 2 Timothy, Paul says that he bears witness "in the presence of God and of Christ Jesus, who is coming to judge the living and the dead, and by his appearance and by his kingdom" (4:1; see also 4:18).

As we have seen, that Jesus participates in God's rule over creation as a result of his resurrection is the corollary of his "exaltation," "glorification," "ascension," and "enthronement" at God's right hand (see especially the use of Ps 110:1), as well as the designation of Jesus as "Lord" (in this context, equivalent to "king"). In contrast to the title of Lord, however, the title of king is rarely assigned to Jesus, except in the Gospels of John and Matthew and the Book of Revelation. But when read in light of the resurrection experience, the Gospel parable that speaks of a man who goes away to claim a kingdom (Luke 19:11–27)

certainly takes on added resonance, especially when Jesus also be-
stows a kingdom on the twelve (Luke 22:29–30) "that the father
has given to me." Likewise, in the perspective of the resurrection
and exaltation of Jesus, the greeting of Jesus as "the king" at his
entry into Jerusalem has a deeper meaning (Matt 21:5; Luke
19:38). Likewise, the title under which Jesus is executed and re-
viled—"King of the Jews"—means more than it seemed to at the
time (Mark 15:2, 9, 12, 18, 26, 32; Luke 23:2, 3, 37, 38; Matt 27:11,
29, 37, 42). Only the reader can know that Jesus has by his resurrection entered into "his kingdom that will have no end" prophe-
sied to Mary (Luke 1:33).

The Gospels of John and Matthew particularly develop the
image of Jesus as king. In John's Gospel, Nathaniel applies the title "King of Israel" to Jesus in 1:49. John has the people greet
Jesus as king at his entry and then ties the title to the prophetic
statement in Zechariah 9:9 (John 12:13, 15). And he greatly expands the discussion of Jesus' kingship in the scenes of Jesus before Pilate (18:33–39) and of his crucifixion (19:3–21). With
deep, dramatic irony, John has Pilate seat Jesus on the judgment
seat and then proclaim to the crowd, "Behold your king," to
which they respond, "We have no king but Caesar" (John
19:13–15). John further has Jesus say, in response to Pilate's question whether he was a king,

> My kingdom is not from this world. If my kingdom were
> from this world, my followers would be fighting to keep
> me from being handed over to the Jews. But as it is, my
> kingdom is not from here. Pilate asked him, So you are a
> king? Jesus answered, You say that I am a king. For this I
> was born, and for this I came into the world, to testify to
> the truth. Everyone who belongs to the truth listens to my
> voice. (John 18:36–37)

In Matthew's Gospel, Jesus says to Peter, "I give to you the keys of the kingdom of heaven" (16:19) and then refers to himself as the Son of Man coming in his kingdom (16:28). In his portrayal of the final judgment, Matthew speaks of "the Son of Man coming in his glory, and all his angels with him, then he will sit on the throne of his glory" (25:31), and in that passage, he twice refers to the Son of Man as "the king" (25:34, 40). That story concludes, as we know, with the king welcoming the righteous into "eternal life" (25:46).

Finally, in his version of Jesus' bestowing ruling authority to the twelve (see Luke 22:29–30), Matthew speaks of Jesus as king without using the term:

> Amen I say to you who are following me, that in the regeneration, when the Son of Man will sit upon the throne of his glory, you also will sit upon twelve thrones, judging the twelve tribes of Israel. (Matt 19:28)

Outside the Gospels, Jesus is called king explicitly only in the Book of Revelation. He is called "Ruler of the kings of the earth" (1:5; see also 15:3). The Lamb (Jesus) who makes war on the seven kings who oppose God's rule is called, in Revelation 17:14, "the Lord of lords and King of kings" (see also 19:16; 22:3).

SHALL HAVE NO END

The creed states that "his Kingdom shall have no end," that is, his kingdom is eternal. This conviction would seem to follow logically from the fact that the kingdom is God's own rule over creation, the rule that Jesus assumes because of his enthronement (Ps 110:1), which is by definition eternal.

The creed is specific on the point, however, because of a concern raised by Scripture itself. In Paul's long discussion of the resurrection in his first letter to the Corinthians, he envisages God's triumph occurring in a sequence that might give support to those already inclined to regard the Son as less than fully equal to the Father. Paul says,

> But now Christ has been raised, the first-fruits of those who have fallen asleep. For since death was through a human being, a resurrection from the dead is also through a human being. For just as all die in Adam, so also in Christ all will be made alive. But each in its own order: Christ as first-fruits, then those who belong to Christ in his coming, and then the end, when he hands over the kingdom to the God and Father, when he has destroyed every Rule and every Authority and Power. For it is necessary for him to rule, "until he put all his enemies beneath his feet." The last enemy is death. For "he has put all things under his feet." But when it says that "all things are made subject," clearly this is apart from the one who subjected all things to him. But when everything is subject to him, then the Son also will be subject to the one who subjects all things to him, so that God will be all in all. (1 Cor 15:20–28)

This is certainly not an easy passage to understand. As I have suggested earlier, whatever vision Paul might have had of the future, it cannot be taken as more than an imaginative portrayal based on his conviction about the Christians' present experience (the power of Jesus' resurrection), his reading of the Scripture (in this case, Ps 110:1 and Ps 8:7, just as in Heb 1:13 and 2:5), his sense of the fitness of things, and his concern to address the confusion or error of his readers.

In the present case, Paul is responding to those who are denying that there is a resurrection of the dead (15:12). Though scholars still debate this point, they seem to have been denying a
bodily resurrection. They believed, I think, that since Christ has
been resurrected, and their minds have been transformed by his
presence, there is no further need of a "resurrection." They are
already, as Paul notes sardonically earlier in the letter, "already
filled, already rich, already ruling!" (4:8).

He wants therefore to show them two things. The first is that
they cannot yet be ruling because the kingdom of God has not yet
been completely established. Sin and death are still "powers and
authorities" that must be conquered (15:53–56). They are only at
the first stage, Christ's being raised, but the second stage, his coming, has not yet occurred. And this is his second point. The reason
there is as yet no evidence for a bodily resurrection apart from
Christ's is that it hasn't yet happened. That will happen when he
comes again.

As he tries to make these points, Paul also addresses the apparent scriptural conflict between Psalm 8, which speaks of God
having made everything subject to a "Son of Man," and Psalm
110:1, which speaks of "the Lord" telling "my Lord" that he
should sit at his right hand "until I place your enemies as a footstool beneath your feet." Paul uses Pslam 110:1 to correct three
possible misimpressions that might be gained from Psalm 8:7.

First, the subjection spoken of in Psalm 8 is future rather
than past, since the enemies are still out there: death and sin still
have to be utterly destroyed. Second, "all things" in Psalm 8:7
means the "enemies" that Psalm 110 tells us God will place under "the Lord's" feet. Third, Psalm 8 cannot mean that the Son
supplants the Father. Rather, the Son will hand the kingdom to
the God and Father. God remains the one who is all in all.

In light of the Arian controversy, which as we recall denied the full divinity of the Son, the Nicene theologians were under-standably concerned, lest this complex passage from Paul be read in a way that so emphasizes the Son's subordination to the Father that he appears to be only a creature. Thus, they emphasize in the creed that *his* kingdom has no end. Just as Paul had used Psalm 110 to correct a possible misreading of Psalm 8, so did they want the rest of the New Testament's evidence about the eternal king-dom of the Son to clarify Paul's statement, to assert that the Son of God continues to share in God's eternal rule forever.

Our problem as we profess these words is having confidence that they are true—in any sense. This claim brings to a head all the difficulties that Christians have tried to resolve for centuries about the delay in Jesus' coming again, the continuing reign of injustice and sin in the world, and the apparent absence, indiffer-ence, or impotence of God in face of all this. What sense does it make to profess a rule that has no end, if within our actual experi-ence, it never seems to have had a beginning?

The problem is most acute, naturally, for those who expect God's kingdom to be realized in the social or political perfection (or at least radical improvement) of the world, and who expect Jesus' proclamation of that rule to begin such a reformation. Those whose hope in Jesus is directed only to his historical human work have no real kingdom to celebrate, for Jesus' ministry and witness did not noticeably change the structures of society accord-ing to the measure of justice.

Traditional Christians, who have placed their hope for God's rule in the transformation of human freedom into a glad obedi-ence of the creator—a service to be realized visibly in the com-munity of the church—may feel almost the same way. How little evidence there seems to be of lives changed. How often the church seems to betray its own identity as the place in the world where the rule of God is supposed to be so real that it can stand as a witness of the world's own possibility, a sacrament of what the world might eventually be.

Creedal Christians must acknowledge here above all how paradoxical, even absurd, our confession of the creed seems, even to us. If Jesus is not even fully "my Lord," or in any manifest way "our Lord," then how can we proclaim him as "Lord of lords and King of kings"? Is our profession, then, simply a stubborn resistance to the truth about our lives? Is it a willful lie or self-deception? Is it an example of delusion, to proclaim that a kingdom has no end when by the evidence it does not even have any existence?

Or is the profession here, as elsewhere, itself a challenge to enact what it says? Is it a witness that we bring against our own failure to live by God's rule? Is it a statement, like the one that says God is creator, whose truth is so difficult actually to imagine and embody that we must repeat it to ourselves even with gritted teeth, alone and together, in the hope that we can glimpse and obey a truth that has grasped us even if we have not grasped it?

This experience of dissonance draws us to consider more closely the next sections of the creed, which deal respectively with the Holy Spirit and the church. For if there is an actual and present rule of God in the world, then it must be found, not in the conquest of visible enemies, but in the triumph of love and life, however halting and partial, over sin and death. And this is the work of the Spirit. And it is the calling of the church.

Chapter Seven

WE BELIEVE . . . IN THE
HOLY SPIRIT

The Holy Spirit is, from our perspective, the link between the risen Christ and the church, the means by which we experience the power of the resurrected one and are being transformed into his likeness. With the understanding of the Holy Spirit not only as a power but a person, we finally come to appreciate the richness of the inner life of God that has been revealed to humans and into which the baptized have been initiated, the life of the triune God.

It is fitting, then, that the creed should pause over the nature and work of the Spirit before turning to its statements on the church. For unless what it says about the Holy Spirit is true, then the church is simply another organization among others, rather than the sacrament of God's presence in the world. Depending, indeed, on how seriously the church has taken the role and power of the Holy Spirit, it has functioned more as a legal system or more like a living organism.

The expansion of the church's profession of the Holy Spirit

marks the difference between all earlier creeds and the Nicene-Constantinopolitan Creed of 381, which is essentially the version recited in the liturgy today by Christians (this is the version given in full at the end of chap. 1). Earlier versions of the creed had been content with the simple affirmation "we believe in the Holy Spirit" or, even more simply, "and in the Holy Spirit."

The expansion resulted from the continuation of the Arian controversy, which became even more radical and bitter following the rejection of the Arians at the Nicene Council in 325. The Holy Spirit was a convenient point of attack for those whose main target was the divinity of the Son. If the Spirit that worked through the Son and is at work in Christians is only a creature and not God, then the Son is not God either.

The problem for those who crafted the creed was that the profession of the Holy Spirit was not self-evident from Scripture. Gregory of Nazianzus asks starkly, "Is the Spirit God? Most certainly. Well, then, is he consubstantial [i.e., one in being]? Yes, if He is God" (*Oration* 31, 10). But he then explains how the understanding of the Spirit developed slowly:

> The Old Testament proclaimed the Father clearly, but the Son more darkly; the New Testament plainly revealed the Son, but only indicated the deity of the Holy Spirit. Now the Holy Spirit lives among us and makes the manifestation of himself more certain to us; for it was not safe, so long as the divinity of the Father was unrecognized, to proclaim openly that of the Son; and so long as this was still not accepted, to impose the burden of the Spirit, if so bold a phrase may be allowed. (*Oration* 31, 26)

Gregory recognizes not only that God's revelation to humans takes place over time and takes time to be understood, but also that in the case of the Holy Spirit, present experience is critical to that understanding. It is not only what Scripture says about the Spirit, in other words, but also how the Spirit of truth itself "guides us into all the truth" (John 16:13), that enables us to profess the Spirit more fully than those before us.

Gregory's insight comes from the heart of Christianity's core conviction about the living God. God's revelation is not something given only in the past, nor is it something that can be adequately contained by any human words, including those of sacred Scripture, as important as its witnesses and interpretations of God's revealing activity are. Rather, the living God continues to reveal himself through creation and the continuing experience of the Holy Spirit.

As it has always been, the Holy Spirit serves as the symbol for God's reaching humans, whether through creation, prophetic spokespersons, Jesus the Son of God, or the movements of grace within the believing community, for that grace also is always the gift of the Holy Spirit. Humans continue to experience God in the world, and because of this experience of God, our appreciation of the work of the Holy Spirit must inevitably continue to grow beyond the hints provided by the New Testament.

Corresponding to this appreciation for the openness of revelation, to be sure, is the conviction that the truth toward which the Spirit leads us does not reject God's earlier revelation but rather deepens and extends it. As John's Gospel has Jesus say of "the Spirit of truth,"

I have said these things while I am still with you. But the Advocate [*parakletos*], the Holy Spirit, whom the Father will send in my name, will teach you everything, and remind you of all that I have said to you. [John 14:26; see also 16:13–15]

WE BELIEVE . . . IN THE HOLY SPIRIT

By beginning this section in precisely the same way as the sections that speak of the Father and the Son, the framers of the creed already signal that the Holy Spirit is to be thought of in the same manner as Father and Son. In some sense, as we shall see, the first three statements, that the Spirit is "Lord and Giver of Life," that the Spirit "proceeds from the Father [and the Son]," and that the Spirit "is worshiped and glorified with the Father and Son," seek to secure that equality of status.

Such clarification is necessary because the language of the New Testament about the Spirit is itself ambiguous or, perhaps better, describes the mystery in several dimensions. As with other elements of the creed, the New Testament nowhere provides a comprehensive and precise teaching on the Holy Spirit. The Nicene theologians therefore drew as best they could from these diverse texts, guided as they were by the continuing experience of the same Spirit in the church, to state those things on which the witnesses seem to agree. The full testimony of the New Testament witnesses—as well as the experience of grace within the church—is required to establish the point that when Christians speak of the Holy Spirit they are not speaking only about a power, but also about a person.

The New Testament presents several daunting difficulties to those searching in it for the identity of the Holy Spirit. The two words making up the term, for example, do not always appear together. Does every reference to "spirit" mean the "Holy Spirit"? Clearly not, yet there are some hard cases that might be decided either way (see, e.g., James 4:5). And sometimes the New Testament does speak of "spirit" while meaning "Holy Spirit." Does every mention of "holiness" or "holy" imply the work of the

Holy Spirit? Perhaps, but one must proceed cautiously and not assume so in every case (see 1 Thess 3:13).

In previous chapters, I have spoken of the term "Holy Spirit" as the experiential correlative to the conviction that Jesus is resurrected and exalted to God's right hand, expressed most succinctly by Paul in 1 Corinthians 12:3, "No one can say, 'Jesus is Lord,' except by [or in] the Holy Spirit." The resurrection touched the followers of Jesus with power.

The term "spirit" distinguishes the sort of power meant. The first believers were not suddenly given military, economic, political, or other material forms of power, but had been touched and transformed in their own spirits—that is, in their capacities for knowing and loving—and from this transformation derived new capacities to embody that spiritual power. Because their spirits were changed, they recognized the power of change as itself spirit.

The term "holy" distinguishes the source of the spirit. This transforming experience came from outside themselves as a transcendent presence. It is only God the creator of humanity who can fundamentally transform humans, as LXX Psalm 50:12–13 suggests: "Create a pure heart in me, O God, and put a new and right spirit within me; do not cast me away from your presence, and do not take your Holy Spirit away from me."

A wide range of passages therefore speaks of the Holy Spirit primarily as the *power* at work in humans. We are not surprised to find this focus especially in the earliest writings that emerge out of and try to express the experience of the resurrection. In Paul, the Holy Spirit is a power (Rom 15:13, 19; 1 Cor 12:4; 1 Thess 1:5–6; 2 Tim 1:7) that dwells in Christians (Rom 8:9, 11; 1 Cor 3:16, 19; 2 Tim 1:14) and gives them life (Rom 8:11; 3:25; Gal 3:25) as a first-fruits (Rom 8:23) or seal (Eph 1:13) or pledge (2 Cor 1:22) of a future glory (2 Cor 4:16–5:5).

At first glance, speaking of the Holy Spirit as a present and active transforming power seems to dominate Paul's language (see also Rom 1:4; 2:29; 5:5; 8:2; 9:1; 14:17; 15:16; 1 Cor 2:4; 7:40; 12:3, 13; 14:2, 15, 16; 2 Cor 12:18; Gal 3:2, 4, 14; 5:16; Eph 2:18, 22; 3:5, 16; 4:3, 4, 23; 5:18; 6:18; Phil 1:27; 2:1; 1 Thess 5:19; 2 Thess 2:13; 1 Tim 3:16; Tit 3:5), as also other early nonnarrative writings (Heb 6:4; 9:14; 1 Pet 1:12; 1 John 3:24; 4:1–2; Jude 20; Rev 4:2).

At the same time, the earliest Christian writings, from the very beginning, use language about this transforming power that suggests the presence of a *person*. From the very first days, Christians spoke of the Spirit as something more than an impersonal energy or force, by speaking of the Spirit as knowing and willing in ways that only persons can do.

Thus, Paul speaks of being led by the Spirit (Rom 8:14; Gal 5:18), of the Spirit bearing witness (Rom 8:16), coming to assistance (Rom 8:26), praying (Rom 8:26), showing love (Rom 15:30), searching (1 Cor 2:10), knowing (1 Cor 2:11), teaching (1 Cor 2:13), giving gifts (1 Cor 12:7), deciding (1 Cor 12:11), providing a word of wisdom (1 Cor 12:8–9), sharing fellowship (2 Cor 13:13; Phil 2:1), and speaking (1 Tim 4:1). Hebrews refers to the Spirit "saying" (3:7) and "making clear" (9:8) and "testifying" (10:15). 1 Peter 1:11 speaks of the Holy Spirit "making known," and 2 Peter speaks of the Holy Spirit "leading" (1:21). In 1 John 5:6 and 5:8, the Spirit "testifies," and Revelation repeatedly has the Spirit "speaking to the churches" (2:7, 11, 17, 29; 3:6, 13, 22).

The later writings also speak of the Holy Spirit in a similarly complex way, as a power and a person. In the Synoptic Gospels, the Holy Spirit appears as a power that comes upon Jesus in his baptism (Mark 1:8; Matt 3:11; Luke 3:16, 22) and works through him (Matt 4:1; 12:18, 28; Luke 4:1, 14; 10:21). In Luke's Gospel particularly, the Holy Spirit serves as the power that enables people to speak prophetically (Luke 1:15, 17, 80; 2:25, 23), even Jesus himself (4:18). The Holy Spirit descends on Mary in the conception of Jesus (Matt 1:18–20; Luke 1:35).

In each of the Gospels, the Holy Spirit also appears personal, as when the Spirit "drove" Jesus out into the desert to be tempted (Mark 1:12), or when Simeon "has revealed to him" by the Holy Spirit that he would see the Lord's Messiah (Luke 2:26) and was "guided by the Holy Spirit" into the temple (Luke 2:27), or when Jesus himself is "led" by the Spirit (Luke 4:1). Jesus promises his followers that when they are brought to trial, they should not be anxious about what to say, because "the Spirit of your Father will be speaking in you" (Matt 10:20; Mark 13:11).

The Acts of the Apostles (the second volume of Luke's Gospel) is often regarded as "the Book of the Holy Spirit" because the Spirit is mentioned so often and is so important to the story. On one side, the Spirit is the "power from on high" that Jesus promises his followers (1: 2, 5, 8) and that comes upon them at Pentecost as the spirit of prophecy (2:17–18, 33, 38; see 21:4). The Holy Spirit is powerfully active in the proclamation and deeds of the first witnesses (4:8, 25, 31; 6:3, 5, 10; 7:55; 8:15, 17, 18, 19), including Paul (9:17; 13:4, 9, 52; 19:2, 6). And the overwhelming outpouring of the Holy Spirit on Gentiles signals their acceptance by God and impels the community to baptize them as well and include them in the people without requiring circumcision (10:38, 44, 45, 47; 11:15, 16, 24, 28; 15:8; 19:2, 6).

On the other side, the Holy Spirit acts as a person or character within the story. Just as the Holy Spirit spoke in the past through David (1:16; 4:25) and Isaiah (28:25), so those who are "filled with the Holy Spirit" speak "just as the Holy Spirit was giving them to declare" (2:4). The Holy Spirit "witnesses" through the apostles (5:32), even to those who "lie to the Holy Spirit" (5:3) or "resist the Holy Spirit" (7:51). The Spirit speaks to Philip (8:39), to Peter (10:19; 11:12), and to the church (13:2), and "testifies" to Paul in every city (20:23). The Spirit appoints supervisors for the church in Ephesus (20:28) and directs Paul's movements in his ministry (16:6, 7). The Holy Spirit even "agrees with" the decision of the apostolic council to include the Gentiles without circumcision (15:28–29).

The distinct personal identity of the Holy Spirit in these earliest writings could hardly have been clear, precisely because the Spirit's role in mediating God's presence through the resurrection of Jesus could be—had to be—described in so many ways. The Spirit was the spirit of the Son *and* of the Father.

Thus, Paul refers to the "spirit of adoption" by which we become children of God through Christ (Rom 8:15) and, consistent with this, speaks also of "the Spirit of Christ" (Rom 8:9), "the Spirit of his [God's] Son" (Gal 4:6), and the "Spirit of Jesus Christ" (Phil 1:19). At the same time, he speaks of "the Spirit of the one who raised Jesus from the dead," which can refer only to the Father (Rom 8:11) and, consistent with this, refers to the "Spirit of God" (Phil 3:3; 1 Thess 4:8), the "Spirit from God" (1 Cor 2:12), and the "Spirit of the Living God" (2 Cor 3:3).

Other early literature is similarly ambiguous. 1 Peter speaks of "the Spirit of Christ" in 1:11 and "the Spirit of God" in 4:14. 1 John 4:2–3 speaks of the "Spirit from God" and "Spirit of God," as the one that properly confesses Jesus. The language of the earliest Christian writings, in short, appears to give little attention to the Spirit's distinct identity. What is important to them is that the Spirit touches us personally with the personal presence of God through the resurrection of Jesus.

LORD AND GIVER OF LIFE

This conviction is expressed by the two designations that find their way into the creed, "Lord" and "Giver of life." These titles serve to encompass both aspects of the Spirit's identity and work in the New Testament. And indeed they are often found together, as these writings try to convey the nature and meaning of the Holy Spirit's presence.

In a previous chapter, I examined the New Testament's broadly held conviction that the gift given humans by God through Christ could be described as "eternal life," by which was meant a share in God's own life through the resurrection of Jesus. Only God who creates life can be "Giver of life" (see LXX 2 Kings 5:7; Neh 9:6; Job 36:6; Ps 70:20). Paul calls God "the God who gives life to the dead" (Rom 4:17) and says that "He who raised Christ Jesus from the dead will also give life to your mortal bodies" (Rom 8:11). Even the law given by God could not "give life" in this sense (Gal 3:6).

As only God can give life, it is striking how this gift of life is attributed to the work of the Holy Spirit. Paul tells the Galatians that if they "live by the Spirit," they ought also to be led by the Spirit (Gal 5:25). In 1 Corinthians 15:22 and 15:36, Paul speaks how those who have died "in Christ" will be "given life," and in 1 Corinthians 15:45 he makes an even more dramatic statement. Drawing on the creation story in Genesis (Gen 2:7), he says, "Thus also it stands written that the first human Adam became a living soul, but the last Adam became a life-giving Spirit." Here the power of God to give life, the resurrected status of Jesus, and the work of the Holy Spirit are all drawn indissolubly together (see also 1 Pet 3:18).

The same convergence of the terms "Spirit," "Lord," and

"life-giving" is found also in 2 Corinthians. Having said that "the letter kills but the Spirit gives life" (3:6), Paul develops a contrast between the glory of God's presence that was only temporary in the revelation of Moses and the glory that shines on the face of the resurrected Christ (see 2 Cor 4:6):

> Indeed, to this very day, whenever Moses is read, a veil lies over their minds. But when one turns to the Lord, the veil is removed. Now the Lord is the Spirit. Where there is the Spirit of the Lord, freedom. And we all, gazing with unveiled face at the glory of the Lord, are being transformed from glory to glory, just as from Lord who is Spirit. (2 Cor 3:16–18)

In the earliest of the New Testament writings, then, the title "Lord" points to the intimate connection between the Spirit experienced by Christians (both in the beginning and now) and the Lord God who creates all things, and the Lord Jesus who sits at the Father's right hand. To say the Spirit is "Lord" is to say that the Spirit is God. In the same way, the title "Giver of life" ascribes to the Spirit the power that can rightly be ascribed only to God and that Christians have experienced in the transformation of their existence by the Spirit that touches them because of the resurrection of Jesus. To say that the Spirit is "Giver of life" is to say that the Spirit is God.

The later writings, particularly the Gospels, continue this way of speaking of the Spirit as both a power and a person, and as both Lord and life-giver. Their treatments broaden and deepen, but do not fundamentally change, those of the earlier writings. In John's Gospel, the Spirit appears primarily as a power in 1:32, 33; 3:5–6; 7:39, and 20:22, but in others as a person. Thus, one can be born "out of the Spirit" (3:8), the "Spirit breathes where it wills"

(3:8), and the Spirit gives (3:34). God is defined as Spirit in 4:24. In John 5:21, the evangelist draws an absolute connection between the power to give life found in Father and in the Son: "Just as the Father raises the dead and gives life, so also the Son gives life to whom he wishes." But then in 6:63, John has Jesus declare, "The Spirit is the One who gives life," adding, "the words I speak to you are spirit and are life."

Distinctive to John is calling the Holy Spirit the Paraclete. The term can mean either advocate or comforter, and in John the Spirit that will come to Jesus' followers after his glorification (John 7:39) will play both roles. At his last meal with his followers, Jesus tells them that he must return to the Father, but that he will not leave them alone:

> I will ask the Father and he will give you another advocate to be with you forever. This is the spirit of truth, whom the world cannot receive because it neither sees him nor knows him. You know him because he abides with you and he will be in you. (John 14:16–17)

As advocate and comforter, the Holy Spirit will, John has Jesus say, "teach you everything and remind you of all that I have said to you" (John 14:26) and "testify on my behalf" (John 15:26). The Spirit who comes to humans also represents Jesus and is the means by which Jesus also "remains with" and is "in them" (John 14:26).

The personal character of the Holy Spirit and its equality with Father and Son is nowhere more impressively displayed than in the final commission given by the resurrected Jesus to his followers in Matthew 28:20:

> All authority in heaven and earth has been given to me. Go therefore and make disciples of all nations, baptizing

them in the name of the Father and of the Son and of the
Holy Spirit, and teaching them to observe everything that
I have commanded you. And see, I am with you always, to
the end of the age.

Here the Father, Son, and Holy Spirit are both distinguished and
united in a single "name" that is invoked upon those who enter
the people of God through baptism. (Matthew's text is not, as
some have claimed, a late invention. It reflects a long-standing instinct, as shown by Paul's spontaneous farewell to the Corinthian
congregation at the end of his second letter to them: "The grace
of the Lord Jesus Christ, the Love of God, and the Fellowship of
the Holy Spirit, be with all of you" [2 Cor 13:13].)

Acts, as we have seen, wants to express both that the Holy
Spirit is the power and person that transforms the lives of believers in the Lord and that this power comes from, and indeed is, a
manifestation of the same God who created and saved them (is
the giver of life). For Luke, the Father and Son are together the
cause of the Spirit that humans receive. The Father is the ultimate source and the resurrected and exalted Jesus the proximate
source.

The Spirit that has been poured out on the first followers,
Peter argues, comes from the one they had rejected:

This Jesus God raised up, and of that all of us are witnesses. Being therefore exalted at the right hand of God,
and having received from the Father the promise of the
Holy Spirit, he has poured out this that you both see and
hear. (Acts 2:33)

The New Testament witnesses individually and as a whole
give magnificent support to the designation of the Holy Spirit as

Lord and as life-giver. If these same texts do not make the Spirit's relation to the Father and Son precisely clear, the reason is not that the Spirit lacks such relations. It is rather that the nature of those relations, as they exist within God and as they are shown to us, necessarily remain obscure, both because of the superabundance of the life they celebrate and our very limited capacity to understand any relationships at all, even between humans. Nevertheless, the creed tries to clarify and explain the relation in the next lines.

WHO PROCEEDS FROM THE FATHER AND THE SON

This short statement has generated more controversy among Christians of the past than any other part of the creed, and was one of the causes—at least, one of the explicit causes—of the schism between Catholic and Orthodox Christians that became final in 1054. Its ability to create controversy is the more remarkable, since few Christians today have any idea what it means, or why anyone would care about it.

I will argue in the last chapter that frugality in belief is a virtue and that the creed is generally virtuous that way. But this statement is the exception. It is not needed. The other statements about the Spirit are sufficient. By going a step too far in the direction of precision, the creed—in my judgment—overstepped what humans strictly can say about the inner life of God and provided the occasion for theological hairsplitting and therefore for division.

The controversy arose not at the Council of Constantinople, but considerably later. The creed originally had "the one who is coming out of the Father," the version that is still used in the Orthodox tradition.

There is nothing magical about the term "coming out" in itself. It is used in the New Testament for "going out" from one place to another (see Matt 3:5; Acts 9:28; John 5:29) and for words "coming out" of a mouth (Luke 4:22; Eph 4:29; see also Rev 1:16; 9:18; 11:5; 19:15). But the creed clearly alludes to Jesus' words about the Paraclete in John 15:26, the spirit of truth "who is coming out from the Father."

The creed's shapers were trying to state what Scripture stated and to reaffirm in another way the divine character of the Spirit experienced by humans. No more than the Son is the Spirit a creature: as the son is "begotten" by the Father, so does the Spirit "come out of" the Father. The key, however, is the term "out of." The Son and Spirit are not made by God, but are "out of" God, and are therefore themselves divine.

Some believers fully committed to the Spirit's divinity, however, thought the full testimony of Scripture pointed toward what is sometimes called a "double procession" of the Spirit. The testimony of the New Testament to the Spirit is richly ambiguous, and a considerable amount of evidence can be amassed in favor of the position that the Son as much as the Father is the origin of the Spirit. The Holy Spirit is variously called "the Spirit of the Son" (Gal 4:6), "the Spirit of Christ" (Rom 8:9), and "the Spirit of Jesus Christ" (Phil 1:19). Even the passages of John that speak of the Spirit coming out of the Father can be read as including the Son (e.g., John 16:4). Christian theologians assumed that the way the persons of the trinity are revealed in the experience of salvation by humans—called the "economy of salvation"—truly points to the life of God in itself. Therefore, some ancient theologians supported the idea of a "double procession" of the Holy Spirit from the Father and the Son. This position was held most explicitly by theologians writing in Latin (Ambrose, Jerome, Augustine) and some writing in Greek (like Cyril of Alexandria), but was explicitly rejected by some Greek-speaking theologians such as Theodore of Mopsuestia and Theodoret.

The Latin phrase *filioque* ("and the Son") was apparently added to the Nicene-Constantinopolitan Creed at the Third Council of Toledo in 589. When the creed began to be chanted at Mass in Charlemagne's version of the Holy Roman Empire after 800, the phrase entered into the bitter political rivalry between the Byzantine Church (centered in the New Rome of Constantinople) and the Catholic Church (centered in Rome and allied with the upstart Frankish version of the empire). The introduction of this version of the creed by Frankish monks in Jerusalem in 807 made an already bad situation worse.

The Patriarch of Constantinople Photius, who had other reasons for disliking Rome, condemned the addition around 864 as contrary to the teachings of the fathers of the church. From that time forward, the *filioque* has been a chief complaint of the Orthodox against the Catholics, not only because they think it wrong, but because it shows the insensitivity and arrogance of the West. Beginning with the so-called Reunion Councils held at Lyons in 1274 and Florence in 1439, all efforts to heal the division have failed—perhaps because this breach is all the greater for being based on cultural and linguistic alienation even more than on doctrine.

Is there any substance to the dispute? Some, but not much, and not enough to justify the centuries-long division between Christians, all of whom profess everything else in the creed in common! The East can argue that there must be a single fount of divinity in the trinity, otherwise the oneness of God might be obscured. The West can argue that everything is common to the Father and Son (remember "of one being") and therefore the procession of the Holy Spirit must also be common to both Father and Son. But that's about it as far as substance is concerned. The difference is at best a nuance, at most an emphasis on one set of testimonies in Scripture against another set of testimonies (often appearing, as I have shown, in the same writings).

But taken as a whole, the *filioque* controversy is a scandal that brings creedal Christianity as such into disrepute. It provides the opponents of creeds with all the ammunition they desire. Here we have a great and bitter battle, all the more savage because it is between family members and over such a minor point. Here we see theology at its worst, as a form of word-chopping with little real contact with living faith. Here we see the unholy alliance between belief and power politics, supporting the suspicion that all belief is simply a matter of power and politics. Here we see disputants insisting on being "right" even at the expense of being "unrighteous," condemning and rejecting each other on a matter that ought to allow diversity and mutual respect.

Having said that, I happen to think that the phrase "and the Son" is fully in tune with the scriptural testimony taken as a whole. I am not displeased to recite the creed with my community with those words included. But I think of it in the way Paul thought about eating meat when offense might be given to others.

First, just as "the kingdom of God is not a matter of eating and drinking" (Rom 14:17), neither is robust and true Christian faith a matter of getting the processions of the trinity correct—if "procession" is even the best way to describe the relations of the Father and Son and Spirit! Second, Paul says, "if your brother is being injured by what you eat, you are no longer walking in love. Do not let what you eat cause the ruin of one for whom Christ died" (Rom 14:15), and "if food is a cause of my brother's falling, I will never eat meat" (1 Cor 8:13). If my fellow Christian is offended by *filioque*, then I have no need to say it ever again.

WITH THE FATHER AND SON HE IS
WORSHIPED AND GLORIFIED

The point that the creed wished to make through the language of procession is here made more powerfully and emphatically through the language of worship: the Holy Spirit is not a creature but is God, and, as God, is to receive from humans precisely the same homage as the Father and Son.

God alone is worthy of worship. The statement that the Holy Spirit "is worshiped" means "is to be worshiped" or "deserves to be worshiped." Thus, in Jesus' temptation, Satan offers Jesus dominion if he will "fall down and worship me," and Jesus responds by quoting Deuteronomy 6:13, "You shall worship the Lord your God; him alone shall you serve" (Matt 4:10; Luke 4:8). Note how "worship" expresses and is a form of "service." It follows that all language in the New Testament about "being led by" or "obeying" or "living according to" the Spirit refers to service of the Spirit that is equivalent to the worship of the Spirit.

The inclusion of this term in the creed is an example of the growth of perception within the church because of its continuing experience, for the New Testament itself does not use the language of worship in connection with the Holy Spirit. Indeed, the New Testament generally restricts its use of worship to God (1 Cor 14:25; Rev 22:9) and divine pretenders (Rev 13:4, 8, 12, 15). The risen Lord receives such homage (Matt 28:9; Luke 24:52; see also Matt 2:2, 8, 11). But the New Testament says nothing explicitly about the Spirit being worshiped.

What the creed states is therefore derived from what Scripture says otherwise about the identity and work of the Spirit. It is a theological inference, supported most, perhaps, by the passage in John in which Jesus discusses true worship with the Samaritan woman. In that exchange, Jesus shifts the topic from the rivalry between Samaritan and Jewish places of worship to the kind of worship God requires:

> The hour is coming and now is, when the true worshipers will worship the Father in spirit and truth. And the Father seeks such worshipers of him. God is Spirit and those worshiping him must worship in spirit and truth. (John 4:23–24)

Given the identification later in the Gospel of the Paraclete and Holy Spirit as "the Spirit of Truth" (14:17), it was natural to read this passage as referring to the Holy Spirit. It is still some distance, to be sure, from worshiping in spirit to worshiping the Spirit, but one can see how John's language helps in making that journey.

If God alone is worthy of being worshiped, God alone is worthy of being glorified. In ordinary Greek usage, the term *doxa* can mean either "opinion" or "glory." The connection is clear when "glory" means something close to "reputation" or "honor" (see Matt 4:8; Luke 12:27; 14:10; John 12:43; Rom 2:7, 10; 3:7; 2 Cor 6:8; 1 Thess 2:6).

In the Septuagint, however, the terms *doxa* and *doxazein* ("to glorify") take on a deeper resonance, because they are very often used to translate the Hebrew term *kabōd*. In English, this is usually rendered as "glory," but in many instances, it retains its etymological sense of "weight" or "presence."

The *kabōd Yahweh*—"glory of the Lord"—in such passages means much more than "the Lord's reputation"! It points to the presence and power of the Lord. When *doxa* is used in such passages, therefore, it takes on some of the same nuance (see Exod 16:7, 16; 24:16; 40:35; Lev 9:6; Deut 5:24; LXX Ps 18:1; 28:2; 56:5).

Similarly, the verb *doxazein* is used to translate the Hebrew form of *kbd* that means to recognize the presence and power of the Lord (Lev 10:3; Ps 14:4; 21:23; 49:15, 23; 85:9; 90:15; Isa 66:5). Thus, it is impossible to translate the majority of New Testament passages that contain *doxa* or *doxazein* in connection with God as though they referred merely to opinion or reputation. They mean that, to be sure, but they also in many cases carry the deeper resonance drawn from the Septuagint (see Acts 7:2, 55).

The majority of New Testament passages, indeed, use "glory" in clear connection with the presence and power of God. Thus, in Romans 9:4, Paul speaks of "the glory" as one of the gifts of God to Israel. Similarly, he says that idolators have "exchanged the glory of the immortal God" for creatures (Rom 1:23), and all humans have "fallen short of the glory of God" (Rom 3:23), except the faithful Abraham who "gave God glory"—that is, acknowledged him as powerful to bring life out of his and Sarah's moribund bodies (Rom 4:20). It is through the "glory of the Father" that Jesus is raised from the dead (Rom 6:4), and "glory" is used in similar ways throughout Paul's letters (see Rom 5:2; 15:7; 1 Cor 2:7–8; 11:7; 15:40; 2 Cor 1:20; 3:7–11, 18; 4:4–6, 15, 17; Eph 1:17–18; 3:13, 16; Phil 2:11; 4:19; Col 1:11, 27; 3:4; 1 Thess 2:12; 2 Thess 1:9; 2:14; 1 Tim 1:11; Tit 2:13) and other early writings (Heb 1:3; 1 Pet 4:11, 13; 5:1, 10; Rev 15:8; 21:11, 23).

To "glorify God" in the New Testament means more than to praise God. It means to acknowledge God's presence and power and its claim upon humans (see Matt 5:16; 9:8; 15:31; Mark 2:12; Luke 2:20; 5:25–26; 7:16; 13:13; 17:15; 18:43; 23:47; Rom 1:21; 15:6, 9; 1 Cor 6:20; 2 Cor 9:13; Gal 1:24; 1 Pet 2:12; 4:16; Rev 15:4). When God is "glorified through Jesus," it means that God's presence and power are made manifest through Jesus (1 Pet 4:11), a theme developed particularly in the Gospel of John, where what Jesus does "glorifies God" (13:31; 14:13; 15:8; 17:1, 4) and at the same time "glorifies" Jesus as the incarnate presence and power of God among humans (1:14; 2:11; 7:39; 8:54; 11:4; 12:16, 23, 28; 13:31; 17:1, 5).

But the closest the New Testament comes to connecting the Holy Spirit and glorification is the statement in John 14:16 that the Paraclete "will glorify me." Thus, when it says "and glorified," the creed extrapolates beyond the explicit scriptural evidence for the nature and role of the Holy Spirit. It does so on the basis of believers' continuing experience of the Spirit, especially their growing recognition that the grace that comes to them in the gift of the Holy Spirit is in reality a share in the divine life, and therefore a participation in God's glory. They came to appreciate that they can "boast in the hope of the glory of God" because "God's love has been poured into our hearts through the Holy Spirit that has been given to us" (Rom 5:2–5). They came to believe that through the transforming work of the Spirit (2 Cor 3:17–18), their pains and affliction were preparing them "for an eternal weight of glory beyond all measure" (2 Cor 4:17).

To recognize the Holy Spirit through worship, therefore, and to give the Holy Spirit glory is to acknowledge that in the work of the Holy Spirit in Christ and in us, we see the work of God.

HE SPOKE THROUGH THE PROPHETS

The final statement made about the Holy Spirit is really the basis of the others. It is in the way God has revealed Godself through the work of the Holy Spirit among humans that we have been able to discern in the Spirit another "person" of God. This is the reason we say "we believe in the Holy Spirit in the same way we profess our belief in the Father and the Son."

The Spirit is the one who has spoken through the prophets.

The assertion is brief but also remarkably suggestive. In some sense, everything else that is stated by the creed relies on the truthfulness of this affirmation, for if in the speech of humans—including what is said not just in words but also in actions and lives—God has not truly disclosed God's "word" or "will" or "self," then the entire notion of divine revelation is empty, and everything we think we have learned from it a delusion.

Like its older and younger siblings, Judaism and Islam, Christianity is fundamentally a prophetic religion. The prophet is not first of all someone who predicts the future, but one who speaks for God. The prophet speaks to other humans for God and from God's perspective. The prophet's speech—even when a matter of bodily action—is therefore designated "God's Word." The ancient prophets of Israel set the pattern. They are able to discern in the ordinary social and political life around them the meaning it has to God.

Prophets are people who hear God's Word in the words people speak or refuse to speak to each other. Prophets are people who see patterns of a deeper meaning in the gestures and actions that everyone can see but not everyone can interpret. And prophets speak that interpretation in behalf of God: "Thus says the Lord" (Amos 1:6; 2:1; 3:12). Because prophets characteristically see and hear differently, they are also characteristically at odds with their fellows, who often reject the prophets and their message (sometimes violently).

What is most remarkable about these prophetic religions is that they seriously maintain that some humans are capable of seeing and hearing at such a deeper level, and, most stunning, that when they speak and act, God is somehow speaking and acting through them. Their human words do not simply speak "about" God; they express God's Word. Because of the prophets, God's presence and power in creation do not remain merely implicit; they are made explicit through the most distinctive human capacity, the capacity for language.

To believe in the reality of prophecy is by implication to believe certain critical truths both about God and about humans. It supposes the understanding of God as creator that we examined in chapter 3 and the understanding of God as Spirit that we have examined throughout.

This belief in prophecy assumes, first, that the God who creates the world at every moment can be seen—better, can be disclosed—through creation and through human events and intentions. More than this, prophecy assumes that the creator God seeks communication with creatures, and is able to use the perceptions and words of humans to make explicit the meaning implicit in the patterns of creation and human life. To put it another way, prophecy assumes that God has created humans with the capacity to see and hear the world from a perspective that is God's, that humans are created in God's image and have in their very makeup the capacity to communicate with God and to speak truly of God.

The belief in prophecy assumes, second, that God communicates with humans and humans with each other in the name of God, through the capacities that we identify as those of *spirit*. God can be everywhere present to creation because God is Spirit. God can reach into the interior of all things because God is Spirit. From the other side, humans can "see" and "hear" through those capacities of knowing and loving that make them embodied spirit. Thus, it is appropriate that the "person" of God at work in prophecy be called the "Holy Spirit."

The preceding helps us understand the relation of the words "spoke through the prophets" to the text of Scripture. The creedal statement provides a rule for reading Scripture, in three ways. First, it clarifies that in all those who are truly prophets, the

Holy Spirit has spoken. Thus, we are to understand the Holy Spirit to be at work in Moses and all the Old Testament prophets after him, even when Scripture itself does not state that they spoke "in the Spirit." Conversely, in all those through whom the Holy Spirit has spoken in word and action, we are to acknowledge the presence of prophecy. It is appropriate in this sense to think of Jesus as a "prophet like Moses" (Luke 4:16–18; 7:16; 24:19, 27; Acts 3:21; 7:37), and to think also of the witnesses who proclaimed Jesus as prophets (Acts 2:17–21).

Second, the creed corrects any remaining Marcionite tendency within Christianity (see chaps. 1 and 2) that would make a fundamental distinction between the revelation of God in the Old Testament and in the New Testament. The same Holy Spirit is at work through the prophets of Israel and in Jesus and his apostles, not to replace error with truth, but to give an ever more explicit expression of truth. The revelation of God in creation, covenant, and incarnation is a continuum. When Christians declare Jesus to be the Word of God incarnate, they are declaring him to be the ultimate and full expression of prophecy.

Third, the creed directs us to perceive Scripture itself as prophetic. When Paul says, "all Scripture is inspired by God" (2 Tim 3:16), he expresses a broadly shared conviction about the writings of the Old Testament. Because they are "God-breathed," the Scriptures are able to "instruct [us] for salvation through the faith that is in Jesus Christ" (2 Tim 3:15). In the writings of the New Testament itself, the texts of the Old Testament are "prophetic" above all because, when read in light of the experience of the crucified and raised Messiah Jesus, they in turn illuminate the identity and role of Jesus (see Acts 2:16, 3:18, 21, 24; 10:43; 26:22; 28:23; Rom 1:2; 3:21; 16:26; Heb 1:1; 1 Pet 1:10).

Christians interpreted Jesus through the writings, and the writings through Jesus (see Acts 8:32, 35; 17:2, 11; 18:28; Rom 1:2;

15:4; 1 Cor 15:3–4; Gal 3:8; 4:30; 1 Pet 2:6), precisely because they were "prophetic writings" (Rom 16:26; 2 Pet 1:20). Thus, the Gospel narratives in various ways show how the "words of the prophets" find their true meaning in the events of Jesus' ministry, death, and resurrection (Matt 1:22; 2:5; 8:17; 13:35; 27:9; Mark 1:2; Luke 3:4; 4:17; 24:27, 44; John 1:23, 45; 12:38).

Further, to regard the Scriptures as prophetic means to read them as speaking for God to every age, so that the texts of Scripture always remain open to new significance as God continues to act in the world. Thus, the first Christians did not restrict the relevance of the prophets to the life of Jesus, but saw them as applying directly to the experiences in which they were involved, as also pertaining to the salvation through the faith that is in Jesus Christ. So Acts declares, "The Holy Spirit rightly spoke through Isaiah the prophet," about the continuing resistance to the gospel by Paul's compatriots in Rome (Acts 28:25). So James of Jerusalem said, "the words of the prophets agree with this thing," about the decision by the early church to include Gentiles in fellowship without circumcision (Acts 15:15).

The New Testament's own use of the Scriptures of the Old Testament, in short, provides us with the best example of how to read both the Old and New Testaments. It is not enough to discover what they meant in their historical context, as though they were simply human compositions. It is necessary also to be open to their prophetic voice, which can speak to every age and help every age discern the work of the Living God in the present.

The same Holy Spirit that breathes through those texts breathes in human hearts and minds as they read and, more important, continues as the breath of the ever-creating God (Gen 1:1) who is always bringing a new creation into existence. Reading Scripture as prophecy means reading for the Spirit, looking not for information about the past but transformation in the present. It requires the discipline and sacrifice of being attentive not only to the texts but to the way we live.

As the phrase "spoke through the prophets" guides our reading of Scripture, so it also provides a rule of faith for our lives today. Because the Holy Spirit is the breath of the Living God, the Spirit's work continues today. When discussing the first Christian experience of the resurrection, I emphasized the importance of the symbol "Holy Spirit" as a means of expressing the presence of Jesus' personal, transcendent, and transforming power among believers, a power that persists and can be felt. Perhaps the greatest loss Christianity has suffered in its long history is the loss of that ongoing sense of the resurrection experience and, with it, an appreciation of the Holy Spirit as an ever active agent of change, for the reshaping of human minds and hearts and the energizing of communities.

Such language is, I readily grant, simply nonsense to those, even among Christians, who view reality from the perspective of Modernity we discussed in the Introduction. Talk of the Holy Spirit, and Pentecostal or Charismatic Christianity, seems to them a way of talking about ghosts and angels in a more acceptable fashion—a slippage into superstition—or an invitation to fanaticism and sectarianism. Open the door to the Holy Spirit and soon you'll find people speaking in tongues when the bishop is present, or prophesying in the middle of Mass, or healing people without the AMA's permission. And once people start doing all that, they'll end up in some millennial cult with nothing to drink but poisoned Kool-Aid. Even if these things don't occur, Modern Christians reject Pentecostal or Charismatic Christianity because it seems too much concerned with personal experience and transformation, and too little concerned with the improvement of the human lot through social reform.

Charismatic Christianity has sometimes fulfilled these stereotypes. Its communities sometimes become inward-looking sects, hostile to "the world" outside. Some members pursue only their own salvation with no concern for the vulnerable and marginal. The script Paul penned in his letter to the Galatians—beginning in the spirit and ending in the flesh—is performed with numbing (and uninspired) regularity, and aspirations for inspiration are not always healthy for folk already psychologically troubled. To be fair, however, the faults of Charismatic Christianity are not necessarily more deadly than those of comatose custom and modern skepticism. And if history shows that "spirit" and sect too often go together, it also suggests that if there were more Spirit, generally there would be less need for sect.

But this simple point must be made emphatically: Charismatic (and Pentecostal) Christianity has grasped the essential message of the New Testament more profoundly than any of its politer and better-spoken neighbors. The New Testament proclaims as good news that God's Holy Spirit has been released on all flesh through the resurrection of Jesus Christ from the dead and his exaltation to God's right hand, and that this Holy Spirit is both present to humans and powerfully able to change their lives. The gift that Charismatic Christianity constantly offers to otherwise forgetful or alienated Christians is the witness to this reality: God's Holy Spirit continues to shape saints and raise up prophets in our world.

What is it that Charismatic Christianity has seen so vividly? We can assess the New Testament evidence in reverse order. Luke perceives and portrays the earliest Christian movement as a "Charismatic Christianity" that is essentially prophetic in character. The Spirit poured out at Pentecost is the spirit of prophecy (Acts 2:17–21). Luke wants his readers to see the deeds and preaching of Jesus' followers as the continuation of Jesus' own prophetic work in the world, now as "the prophet whom God has raised up" through resurrection (Acts 3:22; 7:37).

In addition to designating certain members of the church as "prophets" (Acts 11:27; 13:1; 15:32; 21:9, 10), Luke describes those who proclaim Jesus in prophetic terms: they are full of the Holy Spirit (4:8; 5:32; 6:3; 7:55; 11:24; 13:9), work signs and wonders among the people (4:30; 6:8; 8:6; 14:3; 15:12) as Moses (7:36) and Jesus (2:22) had done; they speak boldly (4:13; 13:46; 28:31) and bear witness (2:32; 10:41; 13:31; 22:20); and they proclaim as "God's Word" (4:29; 8:14; 13:5) the good news about Jesus (5:42; 8:4, 12, 25, 40; 11:20; 13:32; 14:7; 15:35). Their message and their manner of life threaten the established religious and political powers. Among the people, some accept and some reject them, but resistance to them is resistance to God's Holy Spirit (5:3, 9, 32).

Is Luke simply romanticizing the beginnings from the perspective of a later generation? The evidence from Paul and other early writings suggests he is not. We have observed earlier how Paul speaks of the first believers all being baptized "into one Spirit" and even "being given one Spirit to drink" (1 Cor 12:13). Among the "gifts that come from the one Spirit" (1 Cor 12:4) are speaking with tongues in the Spirit (14:2) and praying or singing in the Spirit (14:14–15), but Paul gives a special place to the "spirits of the prophets" within the assembly (14:32).

Paul prefers prophecy to speaking in tongues (1 Cor 14:1), because tongues-speaking only builds up the one speaking, whereas prophecy testifies to the entire assembly and "builds it up" in faith (14:4, 17). It is prophecy that can challenge outsiders and unbelievers to recognize the presence of the Living God in the community of faith (1 Cor 14:20–25). Paul therefore places "prophets" as those with the second most important gift in the community after the apostles themselves (1 Cor 12:28–29; Eph 4:11).

Even more impressively, the Book of Revelation shows us an

understanding of the church as essentially a prophetic community. John sees the church as a community of saints and servants,
whose prophetic role is carried out by their bearing witness to
Jesus. Like the prophets of the Old Testament, they testify to
God's truth and judgment in an explicitly hostile world. Revelation uses the title "prophet" eight times (10:7; 11:10, 18; 16:6;
18:20, 24; 22:6, 9), the verb "to prophesy" twice (10:11; 11:13),
and the noun "prophecy" seven times (1:3; 11:6; 19:10; 22:7, 10,
18, 19). It uses this prophetic language with its other main terms
for believers in this book, such as "saints" (16:6; see 18:11, 24),
"servants" (see 10:17; 11:18; 22:9, and especially 19:10), and "witness" (22:18; 19:10). To be any of these is to be a prophet.

It is significant that Revelation applies these terms equally to
those struggling on earth against the powers of idolatry and corruption and oppression, to those now victorious in heaven, and to
Jesus himself (1:5; 3:14; 19:11). As in Acts, we find a continuity of
prophetic witness between Jesus and those who speak and act
faithfully in his name. In 19:10, the angel says, "the witness of
Jesus is the Spirit of prophecy," and in 22:6, God is called "The
Lord . . . of the spirits of the prophets." In this prophetic book, the
Spirit shapes the saints and servants of the Lord into the
prophetic spokespersons of God in the world in order to continue
the witness *of* Jesus by witnessing *to* Jesus.

The clear testimony of these three New Testament witnesses
(Acts, Paul, Revelation) is that the spirit of prophecy did not end
with Jesus, and that the Holy Spirit given to Jesus' followers because of his resurrection and enthronement is a prophetic spirit
that enables them to speak and act boldly in witness to God, both
individually and corporately. The New Testament therefore gives
us reason to think that "spoke through the prophets" can be
amended to read "speaks through the prophets."

Three conclusions follow from this simple adjustment. The

first is that the church's discernment of the Spirit must include listening to the voices of prophets from within, who are raised up by God in every age to challenge the church to greater integrity, and by so challenging also to build up the church. The second is that the church's mission is less that of winning adherents (success = growth) than it is of bearing faithful—prophetic— witness to the world of the reality of God's claim upon the world (success = fidelity).

The third is that God's Holy Spirit can speak through the prophets in any time and place. God's Holy Spirit can raise up prophets from the unlikeliest prospects, as often (perhaps more often) outside the church than inside it. The church therefore has the responsibility to discern the word of God as it is written "by prophets on the subway walls" and in all those movements of protest and reform by which the genuine freedom of humans is advanced.

Because the church serves the Living God rather than its own precedents, it must discern prophecy not only from within but also from without, and hasten to obey when such prophecy is truer to the good news in Jesus than the church's own tradition. Recent history has demonstrated that the church often needs to learn its prophetic task from outsiders. Protests against human slavery were sharper and more insistent outside churches than in them. Because the church finally did listen, and Christians were led by the Spirit to perceive the evil of slavery—even though Scripture clearly allowed its practice—slavery is no longer defended as an option for Christians. The movement to recognize the full human rights of women did not by any means arise within the church but outside it, and the church remains one of the places where sexism can flourish.

The Holy Spirit that is poured out on believers is not only a spirit of prophecy that enables them to bear witness (Acts

2:14–21) but also a "spirit of holiness" (Rom 1:4) that transforms their existence. Holiness or sanctity (both words translate the same Greek word) is the goal of Christian life. The mature Christian is the saint, the holy person. To be sure, the term "holy" is appropriate in the proper sense only to God. It designates the absolute otherness of God. God is utterly different from the world and from anything in the world, cannot be defined by any human idea, cannot be measured by any worldly standard, cannot be controlled by any human desire.

How astonishing, then, to hear placed in God's mouth this statement: "Be ye holy as I am holy" (Lev 11:44), restated by Paul in 1 Thessalonians 4:3. Scripture proposes that what God is, God wills that we should become. But since we are not God, and cannot be different *from* the world in the way that God is, we must be different *within* the world.

Debates over the question of how Christians are called to be different within the world constitute the confused field of Christian ethics. But it is clear that to be holy is not essentially a matter of observing a set of rules that separates Christians from others in terms of diet or ritual or even morality. Nor is it only or primarily a matter of creating social policies and practices. In the classic Christian understanding of holiness, it is the transformation of human persons by the Spirit of God. It is not a matter of what we intend or decide or do, but of our response to God's gift. The Spirit enables both the gift and the response. As Paul says, "God has not called us for uncleanness, but in holiness. Therefore whoever disregards this, disregards not man but God, who gives his Holy Spirit to you" (1 Thess 4:7–8).

The power by which God transforms humans is the Holy Spirit. Christian spirituality is therefore not a matter of cultivating some dimension of the human spirit, but a matter of obedient response to the Spirit of God. From the very start, Christians have been convinced that "the grace of our Lord Jesus Christ" by which they are saved (Acts 15:11; Rom 5:15; Eph 2:5) is more than simply God's "favor" shown them, but is truly the "gift" of a share in God's own life through the Spirit that comes to them from the Father and the Son (see Rom 5:5).

The process of transformation in holiness, therefore, is the process by which God creates a space for God's own freedom within the human heart through the work of the Holy Spirit: "Now the Lord is the Spirit. And where the Spirit of the Lord is, there is freedom. And we all, gazing on the glory of the Lord with unveiled faces, are being transformed into the same image, from glory to glory, just as from the Lord who is Spirit" (2 Cor 3:17–18).

We have a model for a life transformed through the Holy Spirit in Jesus. Paul tells the Galatians that if they "live by the Spirit," then they ought also to "walk by the Spirit" (Gal 5:25), and explains this a few verses later by telling them to "bear one another's burdens, and so fulfill the pattern of the Messiah" (or: "law of Christ," 6:2). The pattern of the human Jesus' own char-acter—the way he "loved me and gave himself for me" (Gal 2:20b)—is to be the pattern of the Spirit's transformation of hu-man existence: "I have been crucified with Christ; it is no longer I who live but Christ who lives in me; and the life I now live in the flesh I live by the faith of the Son of God" (Gal 2:20a). Paul therefore speaks of "putting on the Lord Jesus" (Rom 13:14) and of "putting on the new person which is being renewed in knowl-edge after the image of its creator . . . Christ, who is all in all" (Col 3:10–11).

The process of sanctification to which Christians are called (1 Thess 4:3; 1 Cor 1:2) is therefore a matter of growing into con-formity to the "mind of Christ" (1 Cor 2:16; Phil 2:5). The "mind of Christ" is not merely a matter of knowing about Christ or mechanically imitating Jesus' human life. Christians living in this time and place cannot act as Jesus did in his time and place. They cannot simply repeat his specific deeds and words. They are called rather to use the "mind of Christ": to translate into the circumstances of their lives the same attitudes and dispositions, the same pattern of radical obedience toward God and radical self-giving to others, that formed the character of the human Jesus.

To have the mind of Christ means learning to embody the mind of Jesus in a manner of life that is at once fully our own and fully the work of the Holy Spirit. In Paul's summary: "Present your bodies as a living sacrifice, holy and acceptable to God, which is your spiritual worship. Do not be conformed to this world but be transformed by the renewal of your mind, so that you may test what is the will of God, what is good and acceptable and perfect" (Rom 12:1–2).

The spirit of prophecy and the spirit of holiness are not different spirits but the same Holy Spirit of God. But if this Holy Spirit is not displayed in the actual lives of those claiming to be Christian, how can anyone (including the Christians themselves) take seriously the Christian claim that God is creator, that Jesus is Lord, and that the Holy Spirit gives life? If the church closes its ears to the voice of prophets from within, if the church does not challenge the world through its own prophetic manner of life, if the church ignores or rejects the prophets raised up outside the church, how can skeptics take seriously the claim that the Holy Spirit speaks through the prophets? If nothing in Christians' lives offers concrete and convincing evidence that God is creator, that Jesus is savior, and that the Spirit sanctifies, what other evidence can Christians offer?

In this statement as in others, the creed does more than declare what Christians believe. It challenges those who recite the creed week by week to live as though that which they recite is true. The creed is itself an instrument of prophecy.

THE LIFE OF THE TRIUNE GOD

When speaking of God, we have seen throughout our reflections, we must remember the infinite distance between the human words we must use and the God of whom they are trying to speak. We humans can speak of God only indirectly and by way of metaphor. Even then, our every affirmation must be countered by a negation. When we say that God is creator, for example, we must also deny that God creates in any manner familiar to us from human workmanship. Our calling God "Father" must always bear with it the negation that God is not father in the manner of human fathers.

The great temptation of theologians—and anyone reading this book is thinking as a theologian—is to suppose that because we have words to say, we have captured the reality. The dramatic and disastrous consequences of such arrogance are revealed by the *filioque* debacle. Parties on either side of the debate moved all too confidently from the expressive but ambiguous language of Scripture to assuming that they could dissect the relations within the life of God and describe them with precision.

Theology is a dangerous craft, and theologians ought to have emblazoned on their consciousness a reminder from the greatest Christian theologian. Paul makes allusion to equally great predecessors (Isaiah and Job) when, after trying to figure out what the "mystery" of God means with respect to Jews and Gentiles, he cries out:

O the depth of the riches and wisdom and knowledge of God! How unsearchable are his judgments, and how inscrutable his ways. For who has known the mind of the Lord? Or who has been his counselor? Or who has given a gift to him to receive a gift in return? For from him and through him and in him are all things. To him be the glory forever. Amen. (Rom 11:33–36)

That is the theologian's proper perspective, and proper goal, and proper prayer!

God is not available to us for examination. We do not know God from the inside. We are not God's equals. All we are comes from him. Paul asks the Corinthians in another context, "What do you have that you did not receive? And if you received it, why do you boast as though it were not a gift?" (1 Cor 4:7). The theologian is not one who examines the "mystery" of God as though it were the blueprint for a building, whose systems lie open for inspection to the professional eye.

The theologian is rather one who has been caught up—somehow—in an intricate drama as one of its very minor characters—caught up halfway through the play, told only snippets of what has already transpired, and asked to play a role for a scene or two before departing stage right, still not knowing how the play turns out, much less who wrote it or for what reason. The gifted theologian may perhaps be given a small speaking part—and may perhaps, by hazarding a line of dialogue (an aside between members of the crowd, to be sure, far from the main action), add something small to the drama. Or not. It is good for the theologian to know the theologian's place, since theologians are always tempted to take center stage.

We do not know much at all. We have not so much come to know God as we have had the experience of coming to be known by God (Gal 4:9). And yet, we do affirm—and the creed is one of the prime ways in which we make the affirmation—that in this contact, we have also learned something of the one who has created us, sustained us, saved us, and sanctified us. We affirm that the way God has shown God to be in our experience of the world and of Jesus Christ and of the transforming power of the Spirit provides us some hint of who God truly is.

We affirm, we trust, that God has been truthful in God's self-revelation, and that the "faces" of God that we have learned through our experience, and that we have tried to express, however poorly, in our language—first of all in the language of Scripture—show us something of God's own life. From God's work in creation, salvation, and sanctification, we learn something, we think, about the one who creates, saves, and sanctifies. We think. But we think carefully, as students who know their place but barely know their subject.

At this point in our reflection on the creed, then, it is appropriate to ask about the implications of meeting God as Father and as Son and as Holy Spirit, these three "persons" through whom the same God has been revealed to us. Encountering someone as friend, then as lover, then as partner and comforter, we naturally are moved to reflect on the ways in which these "faces" are not just roles played to suit the circumstances, or masks worn in order to deceive, but dimensions of the other's inner life that were called to outward expression in their relation with us. It is in such fashion that we, by analogy, try to move carefully from the celebration of the life into which God has caught us up to an appreciation of God's own life.

The first and most obvious realization is that Christian monotheism is not the same as the monotheism espoused by Judaism and Islam. Christians maintain as firmly as they do that there is but one source for all reality who is not to be confused with the world, that this one source is the world's creator and judge and savior, the one from whom all things come and toward whom all things are directed. But by speaking of Son and Spirit as coequal to the Father, Christianity has—in the view of Jews and Muslims—compromised pure monotheism and slipped toward a form of polytheism. In the early period of conflict between Judaism and Christianity, Jewish critics insisted that Christians held to "two powers in heaven," namely, the Father and the Son. And Islamic critics likewise accused Christians of "giving partners to Allah."

But Christians believe that God has revealed a richer inner life that enables us to think of the one God in a new way. In light of what they consider God's own self-disclosure, Christians think of the oneness of God not only in terms of singleness (as do Judaism and Islam) but also in terms of unity. What the mystery of the trinity discloses is not a mathematical problem (how can one be three?) but the mystery of life given and shared. The trinity is the mystery of God's own life as life given and received and shared in a never-diminished abundance of being. The trinity shows us God as community.

Against all assertions that revelation must fit within the bounds of reason—if a triune God offends human logic, for example, then the language of Scripture must be made to point toward a humanly intelligible God—orthodox Christianity asserts another premise: that reason seeks out the logic embedded in God's revelation. If the experience of our hearts and the language of Scripture demand a more complex apprehension of the God we worship, then our thought must follow.

This is not a matter of importing polytheism into monotheism. It is rather a matter of paying attention to the way in which God has been experienced. Once more, the ineluctably experiential character of the Christian faith is at the heart of trinitarian confession. We proclaim God as triune because that is how we have experienced God, indeed how God has been revealed to us. Let reason follow, and make what sense of things it can.

We can begin to imagine God's inner life through the communitarian life that God has shared with us. God's creation of the world at every moment now appears not as an arbitrary gesture, but as the overflowing of divine energy that seeks embodied expression and response. The overflowing love between human spouses that seeks expression in bearing children who can be loved and who can respond in love is a pale imitation of God's creativity.

We can now see God's gift of self through the "sending forth" of a Son who, in turn, "loved [us] and gave himself for [us]" (Gal 2:20) as the external expression of the same self-giving that exists always between Father and Son and Spirit. It is life given so that life can grow. Mutuality in giving leads not to the diminishment of any but the enhancement of all. In the same way, in the life-giving Spirit who bonds us together in love (Eph 4:2), we catch a glimpse of the exchange of love within the life of God.

Imagining God in communitarian terms (a trinity of life) also enables us to think of other aspects of revelation—and therefore our life in the Spirit—in a richer manner. Take, for example, the notion of humans as "created in the image of God" (Gen 1:27). In light of the trinity of life in God, we are able to appreciate not only the plural pronoun for God used in the Genesis text—"Let us make Man in our Image" (1:26)—but also the plural recipient of that image: "God created humans in his image, in the image of God he created *them*, male and female he created them" (Gen 1:27). God's image, it follows, is found not best in individual humans, but in humans as they are related to each other.

When Paul speaks of being transformed into the image of Christ, who is the image of the unseen God (Col 1:15), he does so in communitarian terms: "we" are being so changed (2 Cor 3:17–18; 4:4–6; Col 3:10–17) within a community of love and exchange enlivened by the Holy Spirit of God. Thus, we are able to imagine the Christian community in ways that reflect the life of the trinity, in which diversity and unity are not opposites but mutually positive dimensions of life together, and in which equality of worth and subordination of function are not incompatible but complementary.

These are only two ways in which the richness of the trinitarian life can begin, in some small part, to become ours. There is no end to the ways in which our minds can grow into a deeper appreciation of the triune God who continues to touch and transform us, for there is no end to God.

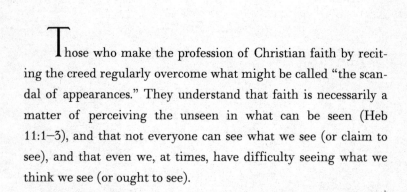

ONE, HOLY, CATHOLIC, AND APOSTOLIC CHURCH

Those who make the profession of Christian faith by reciting the creed regularly overcome what might be called "the scandal of appearances." They understand that faith is necessarily a matter of perceiving the unseen in what can be seen (Heb 11:1–3), and that not everyone can see what we see (or claim to see), and that even we, at times, have difficulty seeing what we think we see (or ought to see).

The confession of God as creator requires that we overcome the apparent reality that the world is random or meaningless. The confession of God as judge demands transcending the apparent reality that evil always proves triumphant. The confession of God as savior means getting past several such stumbling blocks: that humans are not worth such infinite concern, that God could not enter a material world and our bodily lives, and that God would not save a broken humanity through the broken body of a crucified messiah.

The confession that God is sanctifier demands that we see beyond the inescapable evidence that we are still untransformed and unsanctified. Those who regularly and devoutly recite the words of the creed speaking of Father, Son, and Spirit are adept at asserting truths that seem contradicted by most of the available evidence.

The section of the creed that speaks of the church as one, holy, catholic, and apostolic demands an equal or even greater capacity to overcome the scandal of appearances. Christians confess that this church—the word used by the New Testament simply means "assembly" in secular Greek—this gathering of frail human beings, is the triune God's chosen instrument for the work of transforming the world. The very structure of the creed implies that the invisible God who is creator and judge, the risen Christ who is enthroned with the Father, and the Holy Spirit who sanctifies humans work through and in the life of a community that is, in Nietzsche's phrase, "human, all too human!"

The creed states that God is not only active in the lives of individual humans, or in the great movements of history, but most visibly and powerfully in the all-too-obviously physical, institutional, complex, messy fact of a specific human community. The profession of the church as part of the necessary statement of Christian belief is, clearly, both a critical and a scandalous proposition.

The church is a critical theological concept. We do not claim a complete or adequate understanding of God's intentions in calling the church into existence, but we affirm that the denial of the church leads to a distortion of authentic Christian life, in which something essential is lost. And, as with the other paradoxical propositions in the creed, we believe that the confession that the church plays an essential role in God's work more fully fits with the testimony of Scripture than does its theoretical or practical denial.

What might we say positively about the church as a critical theological concept? The church is, in a real sense, the continuation of the incarnation, the embodied presence of the resurrected Jesus through the power of the Holy Spirit. When Paul speaks of "the body of Christ," he means that the gathering of the faithful in the Spirit is the place in the world where the raised Messiah finds the means of expression in the world. The church is ideally God's laboratory for communal life before God, the model that the world can see and imitate as the basis for its own rebirth as God's creation. Only within this body of Christ can the pattern of "life for others" that Paul understands as the enactment of the "mind of Christ," the "bearing of one another's burdens" that Paul calls "the law of Christ," find full expression, for only a community of faith and love provides the possibility for such mutual self-donation. When, therefore, Paul refers to the church as the place where the mystery of God is being revealed, he means that it is the sacrament of the world's possibility.

Only as a people, as a visible "assembly of God," can humans adequately express and represent the true nature of God as it has been revealed through Father, Son, and Holy Spirit. We have learned to know and to praise a triune God, whose life is defined in terms of mutual emptying out and sharing in a constant and fruitful exchange. God seeks among humans a community that shows forth the meaning of such life in reciprocal and life-giving relationships. And in the way the trinity's life itself seeks expression and embodiment in creation, so the church is called to express and embody its rich mutuality of life in service of creation.

If all this is true, what is lost by denying it? The denial of the church as the instrument of God's revelation is (among other things) the denial of the classic Christian understanding of salvation. Christian salvation does not pertain only to individuals. It is not given so that some people might be transformed and others not, or some go to heaven and others go to hell. In Scripture, salvation is understood in communal terms. God seeks the salvation of a people, and seeks their salvation *as* a people.

In a very real sense, the expression "outside the church there is no salvation" is true to the New Testament. This is because, for the New Testament, salvation is not so much a matter of one's eternal destiny as it is a matter of belonging to a people within which God's own life is powerfully at work. The answer to the question "Are you saved?" is not "Yes, I am going to heaven," but "Yes, I am among the people whom God is saving." Because of this, the focus of Christian attention ought to be neither the headlines (as though salvation were a matter of changing social structures) nor our navels (as though salvation were a matter of cultivating my private spirituality), but the arena of our life together as a people, for it is in this arena that God is "working out [our] salvation" (Phil 2:12–13).

But we must admit that if denying the church is a mistake, it is a reasonable mistake to be made. As a corporate body, an institution, and a community that has passed through two thousand years of history, the church is a large stumbling block to faith. If the condition of the empirical world makes us question whether there is a creator, and if the resistance of the flesh makes us doubt the power of the Spirit, and if the continuance of sin and evil makes us skeptical of the reality of God's rule through the resurrected Christ, the church has all too often been the prime evidence supporting these questions.

The church through the ages has been driven by the fleshly passions of lust, avarice, malice, and pride. It has sinned against God and humans and, in its willful refusal to acknowledge God's prophetic voice, has also sinned against the Holy Spirit, not only in the bad old days but very much also in these days. And the church has even been an instrument, whether consciously or because it has been besotted by its own needs and privileges, in the doing of evil.

It is no surprise, then, that the practices and even the very existence of the church as an organization have seemed to Christianity's critics a compelling reason to reject Christianity's claims. The classic distinction between the "good Jesus" and the "evil church" enables critics to affirm what they perceive to be generous and humane in the words and deeds of Jesus without subscribing to the pinched and oppressive doctrines and rituals of those who claim to represent Jesus. Even within the Christian tradition, theologians from Marcion to Karl Barth have claimed the eternal and the pure and the good in the message of Jesus as the genuine essence of faith, while rejecting, or only grudgingly acknowledging, the community whose organized structure as a religion seems to betray that essence.

Two manifestations of this discontent with the church as an organized body are two alternative ideas of salvation that have arisen within Christianity, exemplified in the ancient movement called Gnosticism and the modern movement called liberation theology. The discontent and protest they represent, and the different answers they offer, appeared in a variety of forms in the church's long history, appearing now as monastic or mendicant movements, now as revolutionary cells or even combatants.

In Gnosticism, the church as a body represented precisely what Jesus' saving words called humans to transcend. It served the form, but not the substance or spirit, of the Christian life. At best, the church was the gathering place of rational people who might, with some prodding, themselves become "enlightened ones" whose deeper knowledge of the truth freed them from bondage both to body and to community. At worst, the church exemplified the "mud people" whose lack of brains—and therefore lack of potential for transformation—was shown precisely by their devotion to the rituals and doctrines and leadership that came from those notoriously inept followers of Jesus, the apostles. In either case, the most genuine form of Christian existence was apart from or parasitic upon the public and institutionalized church, whose usefulness consisted only in its ability to provide a seedbed of converts and a useful contrast to the higher life.

Liberation theology has also found the hierarchical and sacramental church to be a scandal: the church of bishops and priests and cathedrals and schools is too wealthy, too self-preoccupied, too inefficient, too corrupt, and too often controlled by the "powers and principalities" that sponsor oppression. How can it be an effective instrument of righteousness, how can such a church represent the kingdom of God and of his Christ, when it is so obviously a creature of the kingdom of this world? Instead, Christianity must throw itself into battle for the liberation of humans from oppressive social systems.

Who can deny the force of these powerful resistance movements within Christianity? Who can deny the power of the Gnostic complaint that the church has often served the form rather than the substance of Christian life, and that it has preferred precedent and prestige to the moral and spiritual transformation of its members? Who can deny the sting of the liberationist charge that the church has often represented just those patterns of repression and oppression that reveal not the rule of God but the rule of Satan? Who can deny the fact that at times the church has seemed to prefer any friendly totalitarian system to any movement of liberation, and that the church has sometimes actually colluded in the extermination of cultures and peoples as part of its reprehensible liaison with kings and princes and entrepreneurs and adventurers?

Those of us who can admit all this and nevertheless remain as loyal if critical members of this church must have both a high tolerance for paradox and some rational grounds for not fleeing so compromised and corrupt a community. I think there are two such grounds: the logic of the church's story and the testimony of Scripture. They are the reason we can rationally hold a critical loyalty to the church.

The first rational ground for remaining loyal not only to the idea but also the reality of the church is the logic of the story that the creed tells. From the beginning to the end of the story, God's Holy Spirit seeks to express itself in body. Creation itself is the first instance, as the invisible God finds expression in the coming-to-be of visible reality at every moment, not least in those creatures in whom God seeks to find reflected God's own image. The pattern of God's seeking to express God's Word through human bodies finds its complete expression in the incarnation. In Jesus, the "fullness of God dwells bodily" (Col 2:9).

In this reading of the creed's story, then, the church is the logical—and perhaps even necessary—way in which God continues to find expression. The existence of the church is fitting for those of us who read the story this way. Indeed, if the triune God did not find its life in a community of faith and love—were there no church—there would be cause to wonder what the first part of the story might have meant. The issue for us is whether the church, whose existence is so fitting, can or does live up to its awesome call to embody the life of God in the world.

The second rational basis for a critical loyalty to the church is that such an attitude much better fits the full testimony of Scripture than does claiming to accept Jesus but not the community living in his name. The testimony is unmistakable. Both the Old and New Testaments testify to God's desire to form a people of God's own on earth. They reject the notion of a purely spiritual rule of God that requires no embodied expression.

One cannot read the Old Testament except as the story of

God's effort to shape a distinctive people among the nations of the earth, a people that is so dedicated to the doing of God's will that it can serve as a "light to the Gentiles," that is, precisely as a sign of what they also might become if they too should turn to the Lord of Israel and live by the Lord's commandments (Isa 49:1–7). God called and nurtured this unlikely people not for its own sake but for the sake of revealing in the world God's glory, showing all other humans how the power and presence of the Lord can transform humans—not least from the destructive patterns of individualism that grow from the disordered drives of sin, to the constructive patterns of life lived together in fidelity and compassion (Deut 4:5–7).

One cannot read the New Testament except as the story of the establishing and nurturing of precisely the same sort of community as a temple of the living God, now not on the basis of a revealed law but on the basis of the power of the Holy Spirit. We find no Christians in the New Testament except as members of a community called a church. We find no exhortations directed to individual Christians, as though transformation were merely a matter of personal virtue. The New Testament always speaks to the attitudes, dispositions, and practices of communities. Its writings are always, explicitly or implicitly, addressed to a public assembly of believers.

The two testaments themselves are aware of the problem we are addressing. The community God calls to represent God's presence on earth has always been a profoundly ambiguous witness. The prophets constantly denounced the people for giving in to the temptations of idolatry and for preferring riches, pleasures, kings, foreign powers, and even false prophecy to being God's loyal people. The prophets testify that God's people require chastening when they fail, as they do over and over, to represent God faithfully by their words and especially by their deeds.

The New Testament likewise bears abundant testimony to the ways in which, from the earliest days of the church, its witness was threatened from within by corruption and dissension. Many of its letters would never have been composed had the earliest communities not been so prone to destroying the gift they had been given, through rivalry, dissension, corrupt behavior, even idolatry.

The church has never been a pure or perfect instrument. Yet we confess, nevertheless, that it has been a chosen instrument, whose exalted calling may be betrayed by its members yet somehow also manages to survive the ways in which "the name of God is blasphemed among the Gentiles because of them" (Isa 52:5; Rom 2:24).

In declaring the church "one, holy, catholic, and apostolic," the creed states the four classic "marks of the church," which express the ideal character of God's people. Since the marks are in fact ideals, the church always falls short of all of them. Indeed, the four marks tend to pull in different directions, creating inevitable tensions, most notably between unity and holiness. Various manifestations of the church have tended to prefer some marks over others. In this brief discussion, I will touch on the scriptural basis for each of the four marks, as well as the stress for actual life in the church that pursuit of the ideal entails.

ONE

That the church is "one" can be taken in two senses—as a way of claiming uniqueness and as a statement of its ideal unity. First, it might be claimed that there is but a single church, just as there is but one God. God has chosen from the world's peoples a community that will make explicit in its teaching and life the hope for God that is implicit in the best strivings of all people everywhere. But this claim can be applied in two radically different ways.

On one hand, it can easily be turned from a sense of witness to the world into a claim of privilege. On this basis, the church can claim to have replaced Israel as "God's elect people"—and has done so. It can disqualify the spiritual teachings of other religions on the basis of exclusive possession of spiritual truth—and does so. And rival versions of the church can and do fight bitterly against each other to represent the "one" church of Christ worthy of that name. Although there is a certain truth to the ideal of a single church, it is an ideal that, when claimed as a reality, can become dangerous.

On the other hand, it is possible to apply this claim in another fashion. It is possible to consider that everywhere people "call on the name of the Lord" (1 Cor 1:2; Rom 10:13) with faith and love, there is the reality of the church. This does not "spiritualize" the church—as though authentic Christianity bypassed all material forms of expression—but rather envisions a genuine ideal toward which every diverse expression of the church points.

The second way to understand "one" is not as a claim—implicit or explicit—set against other claims, but rather as an ideal concerning the life of the church from within: the church is one because it lives a life of real unity. In Luke's idealized portrait of the first community of believers in Jerusalem, the note of unity is struck with particular insistence: "all who believed were together and had all things in common" (Acts 2:44), and "the whole group of those who believed were of one heart and soul, and no one claimed private ownership of any possessions, but everything they owned was held in common" (Acts 4:32).

The ideal of the church as united is expressed classically by Paul, when he exhorts his readers to:

make every effort to maintain the unity of the Spirit in
the bond of peace. There is one body and one Spirit, just
as you were called to the one hope of your calling, one
Lord, one faith, one baptism, one God and Father of all,
who is above all and through all and in all. (Eph 4:3–6)

Within this unity, Paul then adds, there is also diversity: "but
each of us was given grace according to the measure of Christ's
gift ... the gifts he gave were that some would be apostles, some
prophets, some evangelists, some pastors and teachers, to equip
the saints for the work of ministry, for building up the body of
Christ" (Eph 4:7–12; see also 1 Cor 12:4–11). Paul also allows for
a diversity of practice in matters that are not critical to the identity of the community. Since "the kingdom of God does not consist in food and drink," for example (Rom 14:17), he explicitly
encourages diversity in matters of diet and even of the observance of special days when individuals' consciences lead them to
such diversity (Rom 14:1–23; see 1 Cor 8:1–13). At the same time,
Paul did not allow diversity in perceptions and dispositions and
behaviors utterly incompatible with the life of the Spirit, and demands that such forms of deviance be excluded from the church
(see 1 Cor 5:1–6:20; 10:21–22; Rom 16:17–18; Gal 4:30; 2 Thess
3:14; 1 Tim 1:20; Tit 3:10–11).

Paul sees, in other words, that unity is not the same thing as
uniformity. Indeed, the unity of the Spirit allows and even requires diversity. The diversity within the community is analogous
to the trinity of persons within the one God. Paul says that to
have the "fellowship of the Spirit," his readers are not required
each to see things exactly the same way, but rather that each
should have the same "way of thinking" that was in Christ Jesus,
which Paul spells out in this fashion: that each member look not

only to one's own interest but even more to the interests of the others (Phil 2:1–4).

Though Christians have confessed the church as one for many centuries, it has never achieved the balance Paul describes. It has wavered between the extremes of uniformity and deviance. At one extreme is uniformity. Unity is understood completely in terms of sameness, not only in belief and morals, but also in ritual and thought, with a corresponding instinct to suppress otherness. A genuine member of the community conforms in every respect to the dominant ethos of the community. Difference is equated with defiance, diversity with deviance. At the other extreme is deviance. Not every form of diversity within the believing community is legitimate. Some forms of otherness do threaten the essential unity of the faith.

What do we do to seek the ideal of the church as "one"? Everyone can agree in theory with Augustine's dictum, "in essentials, unity; in nonessentials, freedom; and in all things, charity." The difficulty is in the execution, for one person's "nonessential" is another's "essential," and charity quickly goes out the window.

The community of faith needs genuine and mutual discernment concerning its shared life. Discernment, in turn, requires loyalty to what all agree is essential, the encouragement of diverse gifts that build rather than diminish the community, and the willingness to exercise charity through a "hermeneutics of generosity" one toward another.

HOLY

The second classic mark of the church is that it is "holy." We spoke of this at the end of the last chapter, and will develop that discussion here. God's command "Be ye holy as I am holy" (Lev 11:44–45) is addressed to the people Israel as a whole. As God's holiness denotes his "otherness" from all created things, so is Israel to witness to the Lord by remaining "other" within creation. The ritual laws of Israel—the organization even of time and space in accord with the will of the one Lord—express bodily and visibly that the nation is defined utterly by its commitment to this Lord.

The ideal of holiness is carried into the New Testament. Paul tells the Thessalonians that God wills their sanctification or holiness (1 Thess 4:3, 7), which means not simply the behavior of individuals but the character of the community as such (1 Cor 1:2; 6:11; Eph 5:26; 1 Thess 3:13; 5:23). Indeed, the title "the saints" applies to ordinary members of the church rather than an elite class within the church (Rom 1:7; 1 Cor 6:1–2; 14:33; 2 Cor 1:1; Eph 1:1; Phil 1:1; Col 1:4; 1 Thess 5:27; 1 Tim 5:10).

Paul also recognizes the tension between the fact that his readers "have been sanctified" through the gift of the Holy Spirit and baptism (1 Cor 1:2; 6:11; Eph 5:6) and the fact that they are "called to be holy"—meaning that they are not now all they might be—through a process of personal and communal transformation (1 Cor 1:2; 2 Cor 7:1; 1 Thess 3:13; 4:3). As the dwelling place of the Spirit that is Holy, the church can conceive of itself as a holy temple of God, but must also express that holiness in its behavior (1 Cor 6:19–20).

Like ancient Israel, then, the church is called to be different within the world, to stand in witness to the world of the truth about God through the way in which it is "other" than the world. Christians have from the first grasped one aspect of this witness firmly. They have understood that personal transformation through the Holy Spirit means a growing conformity to the image of Jesus Christ, so that "those who live by the Spirit are also led by the Spirit" (Gal 5:25), so that "the mind of Christ" (1 Cor 2:16) and the "law of Christ" (Gal 6:2) progressively become the pattern for the mind and heart of the believer.

Becoming a saint has classically been understood as a deeper incorporation into the story of Jesus, so that believers might increasingly and ever more spontaneously share the faith of Jesus in God and express Jesus' self-sacrificial love toward others. Insofar as the church remains a community in which such transformation is possible, it retains something of its essential purpose.

But the holiness of the church means something more than that it is a community within which individual saints can grow. It means that the church as a corporate entity, as an institution, must also be witness to the presence and power of the risen Lord Jesus in the world. To be a sacrament of the world's possibility, the church must embody a difference from the world that is visible and imitable. Christians have always grasped the idea but have frequently disagreed on the implications for behavior.

Should the church's otherness consist in its organizational structure, or in a distinctive diet, or in countercultural clothing? Or should its difference from the world be found in its practices, both ritual and moral? Most Christians have said no to the first set of options and yes to the second set: the church must challenge the world on the basis of its worship and moral practice.

Agreement on this point, however, has led in turn to debate and often discord and division over which forms of worship and which moral practices should characterize the church as holy. From Paul's struggles with the Corinthian and Galatian churches forward, Christians have struggled to discern, with any degree of unanimity, which practices are consonant with the life of the Holy Spirit and which practices are contrary to the Spirit, which practices are essential practices for all Christians and which are optional expressions of the Spirit (see 1 Cor 12–14; Gal 4–6).

Thus, the impulse toward holiness in the church has tended toward disunity. The attempt to meet the second mark of the church means a failure to meet the first—as I said, they tend to pull in different directions. Holiness is identified with some specific practice that then becomes the measure of authentic Christianity (Paul shows how speaking in tongues was made such a "sign of the spiritual person" in Corinth [1 Cor 14]). Some insist that holiness is a matter of observing certain holy days, while others insist that not observing such days is the true sign of holiness. Some Christians insist that obedience to the Pope is a betrayal of the obedience of faith that is owed only to the gospel, others that obedience to the Pope is the perfect expression of obedience to the gospel. Some Christians separate from others (or drive others out) over the time and style of baptism, the nature of the Eucharist, the need (or not) of bishops, how Scripture is to be read, who is to be ordained, and many other "essentials."

From the Montanists and Marcionites to the Hutterites, holiness has been a principle of division in the Body of Christ to the degree that some practice or other has been made the supreme defining element of holiness, and holiness has been made the exclusive mark of the church's authenticity. It can fairly be said, I think, that Christians have not yet succeeded in understanding holiness as a way of living in unity, and understanding that unity as encompassing diverse understandings of holiness rather than only one.

CATHOLIC

The third classic mark of the church is that it is catholic. Before examining the term, it may be helpful to make the (I hope obvious) point that the creed does not say that the church is "Roman Catholic." That term is, indeed, oxymoronic. It combines the element of universality with a highly particular adjective. The Roman Catholic tradition (the reader will remember it is my own) may believe the Roman tradition is all-encompassing, but that is simply mistaken.

The term in Greek means "throughout the whole." As applied in the creed to the ideal church, it means both a universality of extent and an inclusiveness that embraces differences within a larger unity.

First, the catholic church is the one that exists everywhere, rather than simply in one place. Implicitly, then, catholicity asserts the general over the particular in any argument about the nature of the church. Thus, in his arguments against the North African sectarians the Donatists, Saint Augustine constantly held before them the fact that the truth as represented by his party was the truth for all other Christians throughout the empire.

Second, the ideal of catholicity also implies inclusiveness. A sect may include only males or females, or whites or blacks, or rich or poor, or Democrats or Republicans. We know, in fact, that many Christian denominations in America can be defined in just such terms of exclusivity; they are more notable for whom they exclude than for whom they include. But the ideal church should be one that embraces differences within a larger unity.

The ideal of inclusion was voiced by Jesus' call to the outcast and his offer of table fellowship to sinners. The church of the first generation extended it by the decision to include Gentiles without requiring that they be circumcised and observe the Mosaic Law.

And it was expressed programmatically by Paul in Galatians 3:28: "As many of you as were baptized into Christ have clothed yourself with Christ. There is no longer Jew or Greek, there is no longer slave or free, there is no longer male and female; for all of you are one in Christ Jesus" (see also 1 Cor 12:13; Col 3:11). Paul here names the three great status markers in antiquity by which humans were not merely distinguished but "put in their place" as well: ethnicity, class, and gender. (From Paul's language elsewhere, it is certain that he would also include the distinction between "rich and poor" [see, e.g., 2 Cor 8:9]).

Note that Paul does not obliterate the distinctions, as his lengthy discussion of the three pairings in 1 Corinthians 7 makes clear. But he makes the distinctions opportunities for expressing unity (being "one in Christ") through reciprocal gift-giving, rather than the means by which some are excluded or suppressed. It is entirely appropriate that the church expand the ideal of catholicity as it understands more about the distinctions that separate humans. For example, as we learn, through the power of the Holy Spirit, more about the ways in which humans are created, even the gender distinction between male and female seems inadequate. The church needs to seek ways of expressing its hospitality to those whom God has called but who do not fit comfortably within our accustomed categories.

The church's catholicity must embrace cultural differences. The church cannot be simply a European church or an American church: in Christ there can be no Asian or African, American or European. If catholicity is diminished whenever a church is (in fact as well as principle) all-male or all-free, it is also diminished when the church speaks within only one cultural language.

In his letter to the Ephesians, Paul argues that the church is *essentially* a place where differences are reconciled. The "dividing wall" of hostility that separated Jew and Greek expressed the alienation of humans from God. The reconciliation between God and humans achieved through the death and resurrection of Jesus must also be expressed by reconciliation between humans:

> But now in Christ Jesus you who were once far off have
> been brought near by the blood of Christ. For he is our
> peace; in his flesh he has made both groups into one and
> has broken down the dividing wall, that is, the hostility
> between us. He has abolished the law with its command-
> ments and ordinances, that he might create in himself
> one new humanity in place of the two, thus making
> peace, and might reconcile both groups to God in one
> body through the cross, thus putting to death that hostil-
> ity through it. (Eph 2:13–16)

That, says Paul, is Jesus' work of reconciliation (see also 2 Cor
5:16–21). And what is the church's mission? To embody this reconciliation in its own manner of life. Paul continues that through
Jesus everyone has access "in the one Spirit to the Father." Thus,
the Ephesians:

> are no longer strangers and aliens, but you are citizens
> with the saints and also members of the household of
> God, built upon the foundation of the apostles and
> prophets, with Christ Jesus himself as the cornerstone. In
> him the whole structure is joined together and grows
> into a holy temple in the Lord, in whom you are being
> built up together into a dwelling place for God. (Eph
> 2:17–22)

The world constructed by humans is a place of rivalry and
competition and murder and war. It is a place of envy and pride
based on the distinctions people use to define themselves by exclusion. Paul suggests that the church's entire mission is to provide an alternative way of life, one measured by the "new

human" who is Jesus, and one that grows through inclusion and reciprocity rather than through exclusion.

The corollary of this is that if the church fails to be a community of reconciliation, it has failed its essential mission. For Paul in the letter to the Ephesians, indeed, the church would have no more reason to exist. Note that, in this respect, to be catholic is to be holy. If the church is truly a place were differences do not separate but find reconciliation, then the church is "other" than the world in a real and challenging manner. It does become the sacrament of the world's possibility, the sign of what the world can be.

Against this ideal—the deepest meaning of the third mark of the church—the profound human tendency to gather with the like-minded, and therefore to form "the church" on the basis of similarity rather than difference, is difficult to overcome. Even with the power of the Holy Spirit, the catholic ideal is seldom accomplished.

Even when a particular community is fortunate enough to have reconciled within it races, genders, and the other differences that divide humans, it is all too often the case that the church divides just as eagerly on the basis of one ideology or another, so that even within a congregation there are pockets of "holiness" where the true church is thought to be found. Is the hostility between "traditionalist" and "liberal," after all, any less a rupture of the reconciling community than that between slave and free, or Jew and Greek?

At the same time, it is also important to recognize that a "cheap catholicity" is also destructive. The church must seek to reconcile all humans, but it cannot let go of its ideal of holiness and reconcile itself to patterns of sin and idolatry. A catholicity that is simply a lack of standards is not worth much, nor is a catholicity that simply accepts the standards of the larger society. Neither of these truly reconcile.

Genuine reconciliation, and authentic catholicity, comes at a cost. It demands the honest recognition of differences, as well as the recognition that, to us at least, the differences matter a great deal. And then it demands the hard and slow work, guided by the Holy Spirit, to find ways of relativizing the differences that we would like to see as absolute and turn them into opportunities to enrich the life of God within the community. This work is not quick or easy.

APOSTOLIC

The fourth classic mark of the ideal church is apostolic: the ideal church is identifiable as the church of the apostles. This claim can be taken in a more conservative, historical sense, as well as in a more radical, prophetic sense.

The conservative sense has been important since the battle over Christian identity in the mid-second century. Against Gnostics who claimed to have a continuing revelation superior to that given to Jesus' original apostles, Irenaeus and Tertullian made historical continuity with the lives of the apostles—above all in teaching and morals—an essential mark of the authentic church. Such continuity could be demonstrated institutionally, moreover, by tracing the line of episcopal succession from the time of the apostles. The apostolic tradition—meaning not just the Scriptures but the traditions and interpretations of the continuing church— is the original and authentic form of Christianity derived from Jesus himself.

The question is asked of every innovation whether it finds any precedent in the tradition as it derives from the Christian beginnings. The legitimacy of this move is obvious: many innovations, like Gnosticism, are in accord with neither the letter nor

the spirit of the New Testament, which could be most reliably de-
termined by consulting the tradition. The danger of the move is
also clear: in the name of tradition and precedent, it is possible to
challenge and disqualify movements of the Spirit by which God
seeks to lead the church to a greater maturity.

The radical, prophetic sense of "apostolic" is therefore
equally important. The church in every age must be measured by
the standard of the apostolic age as witnessed not by the later tradition but by direct appeal to the writings of the New Testament.
Placing the contemporary church against the one depicted in the
Acts of the Apostles makes clear how much the prophetic witness
of the church has been compromised by its many strategies of
adaptation and survival over the centuries. This is the sense of the
word employed by reformers like Martin Luther, who combatted
the excrescences of medieval Catholicism by appealing to the
teaching and practice of the New Testament. Where in the New
Testament do we find Pope or cardinals? Where do we find
mandatory celibacy? Where do we find indulgences, or even pur-
gatory? Where do we find the office of the Inquisition? These are
powerful questions. Equally needed is the prophetic call to a sim-
pler and more radical "New Testament" lifestyle by Christians, a
rejection of wealth and power and prestige in favor of poverty
and lowly service, a life directed by the Holy Spirit more than by
papal decretals.

The legitimacy of this move is obvious: the mark of apostolic-
ity is a necessary ferment of renewal, as the church is always
prone to identify its tradition with the truth, rather than seek the
truth that God reveals at every moment through the working of
the Holy Spirit in the lives of people. Its danger is perhaps less
clear than the danger of the conservative understanding, but is no
less real: a call for return to the simplicity of the New Testament
days can have as its corollary a denial of the legitimacy of any

form of development in doctrine, morals, or institution. The prophetic voice can all too easily be just as reflexively hostile to institution and authority as authority and institution are reflexively hostile to the voice of prophecy.

ONE, HOLY, CATHOLIC, AND APOSTOLIC

The four marks of the church describe an ideal that the church has never and will never fully realize. The church of Jesus Christ is necessarily—and not only accidentally—a place of tension and conflict as well as a place of reconciliation. The church consists of free human beings whose experience leads them to think differently, even about shared ideals. Tension and conflict are thus natural to human communities, and they arise as much from the work of the Holy Spirit driving Christians to energetic creativity as they do from spiritual inertia and sloth.

The tension created by difference within the church challenges it to grow to greater maturity, to find ways of becoming more catholic, holy, and apostolic as one community. It demands discernment on the part of all, and the willingness to work together toward a consensus (if only temporary) concerning what is essential and what is not essential.

The stress created by difference and disagreement within the church also threatens its survival as a community, as it struggles to find a way to include everyone in principle and exclude no one in principle, different as they are, so long as they live by the faith and love of the Lord Jesus. The greatest threat and challenge to the church is not its sheer survival or even its success in winning adherents, but its ability to sustain life together with integrity.

A commitment to the church as an actual rather than an ideal community of faith therefore has as its corollary a willingness to suffer patiently the stresses that life among members always entails. Those who choose to remain loyal—loyal, one hopes, critically—to the actual rather than the ideal church need four qualities. First, they must cultivate the ability to live within tension rather than flee it, recognizing that tension is a sign of life rather than death. Second, they must cultivate discernment as the one gift of the Spirit that is given to all and whose exercise is required from all. Third, they must begin to think and act to make the marks of the church work together, not against each other, seeking unity as a mode of catholicity, seeking holiness as a way of being apostolic.

Finally, they must embrace the awed humility of the man who has somehow been chosen as husband by a splendid woman, knowing that they are constantly messing up, but knowing as well that they are sharing in a life greater than any they could have imagined or achieved on their own. We have not chosen each other but have been chosen, not for our own purposes, but for another's.

WE CONFESS ONE BAPTISM

The creed uses a different word to introduce each of the last two statements. Everything so far has been governed by the "we believe" with which the creed begins. Those saying the creed thus commit themselves not only with their minds but with their hearts to the one God, the one Lord Jesus Christ, the Holy Spirit, and even the church, as the human instrument God has chosen to continue the revelation of the triune life. Now the creed uses the verb "confess" for our acknowledgment of baptism and the forgiveness of sins, because our confession of these realities is important but does not call for the same commitment. They are what we "confess" to be the case in the inner life of the church.

In baptism, we meet the visible, public, particular, and very much embodied nature of the church. Christians do not become Christians through an interior self-realization, or through fulfilling enough course credits, or through filling out an application for membership, but through a process of public initiation, and one that is profoundly humbling.

The one to be initiated undergoes a public bath administered by others. Everyone who stands at the Eucharist each Sunday and recites this creed, therefore, must acknowledge a fundamental dependence on others. We are all not only children of God, but in a real and physical sense also children of the church. Sometime in our life we were loved enough that someone sought for us the gift of eternal life, and sponsored us for baptism.

Baptism is the ritual of initiation that imprints the fundamental pattern of Christian life on the believer. The efficacy of baptism does not depend on the holiness of the minister but only on the faith of the church as a whole and the faithfulness of God. The symbolism of baptism, from the time of Christian origins to the present, points to the several dimensions of this life.

For adults who received baptism at the Easter vigil, it symbolized a sharing in Jesus' "passing over" from death to life. The act of washing itself symbolizes purification, and the forgiveness of sins (1 Cor 6:9–11; Eph 5:26), as well as the bath of rebirth, regeneration, or resurrection (see John 3:5–8; 1 Pet 1:3, 23; Tit 3:5; Rom 6:1–11). The taking off of old clothing and the putting on of new clothing symbolizes the leaving behind of the old self and the taking on of a new identity, one created according to the image of Christ (Gal 3:27; Col 3:10–11).

The lighted candles used in baptism symbolize the illumination of the mind and heart through the light that is Christ (see Eph 5:14) as "the glory of God shining on the face of Christ" (2 Cor 4:6). Finally, the breathing of the Spirit symbolizes our adoption as children of God (Gal 4:6–7), who are called to be "conformed to the image of his Son, so that he might be the first-born of many children" (Rom 8:29).

The path of Christian discipleship and spirituality is therefore marked out by this pattern of initiation. Not only individual Christians but the church as a whole are marked out as a community whose life demands moving constantly and progressively, from slavery to freedom, from fear to boldness, from death to life, from darkness to light, from selfishness to generous love, in the pattern of the living Lord Jesus and as guided by the Holy Spirit. Growth in the Spirit does not mean learning new revelations or adding new practices, but understanding ever more deeply and enacting ever more consistently the gift that has been given us by God: "As you therefore have received Christ Jesus the Lord, continue to live your lives in him, rooted and built up in him and established in the faith, just as you were taught, abounding in thanksgiving" (Col 2:6–7).

Such growth in insight and practice requires of us that we ever more surely and steadily "put on the Lord Jesus Christ" (Rom 13:14), and have "the mind of Christ" (1 Cor 2:16), "fulfill the law of Christ" (Gal 6:2), and "learn obedience from what we suffer" as he did (Heb 5:8), until "all of us come to the unity of the faith and of the knowledge of the Son of God, to maturity, to the measure of the full stature of Christ" (Eph 4:13).

Why does the creed specify that baptism is "one"? Partly, perhaps, to echo the language of Paul in Ephesians, "There is one body and one Spirit, just as you were called to the one hope of your calling, one Lord, one faith, one baptism, one God and Father of all, who is above all and through all and in all" (Eph 4:4–5). But also, certainly, it is to assert something about the character of the church: one baptism strikes the notes of unity and catholicity.

Wherever there are Christians, there is baptism. Whether it is celebrated before throngs at the Easter vigil or in a lonely hospital room, whether with the running water of a river or the blessed water of a font or a bloody puddle of water in war, baptism is the same. It is the one (and only) sacrament we all partake, the one ritual we all agree is necessary. And despite all our differences about the manner and timing of baptism, we all agree that it is given "for the forgiveness of sins" and that it decisively moves us from the world into the church of Jesus Christ. For this very reason, baptism is also "one" in that it is not to be repeated.

Because baptism is one, we do not need a later "baptism in the Spirit" that makes one "born again" or releases the gifts of the Holy Spirit. The story of Acts, in fact, suggests that these visible manifestations of the Spirit could result from the laying on of hands after baptism (Acts 8:16–23; see also 19:6), but the bulk of the Acts story closely connects the bestowal of the Holy Spirit with baptism itself, either as its result (Acts 2:37–42; 19:3–6) or as its impetus (Acts 10:44–48; 11:15–16). Elsewhere in the New Testament the Holy Spirit is abundantly and powerfully available for the transformation of their lives to all the baptized (see, e.g., Rom 6:1–11; 8:1–39).

Paul, indeed, insists that nothing fundamentally adds to the status given to the baptized as adopted children of God. This is the burden of his argument in Galatians and Colossians, where he finds himself fighting against the deeply human instinct to compete, even in matters religious. Almost everywhere in the religious life of antiquity (and today) multiple initiations mark the stages of progress and maturity, with each initiation conferring higher status within the group.

In Galatians, Paul sees that those who seek to impose circumcision as a ritual of initiation after baptism, which will presumably give greater maturity, are actually seeking to "indulge the flesh" (6:12–13) by introducing a note of rivalry and competition into the life of the Spirit (5:16–21). He insists that those who are baptized into Christ are all one, and that there is no longer Jew or Greek, slave or free, male and female (3:28). But if circumcision gives higher status and can only be practiced by males, Christianity would be a religion in which males could always have higher status simply because they are males. The fundamental egalitarian nature of the church as a community of faith embracing all humans would be destroyed. Paul insists, then, that baptism is sufficient, and that the attempt to seek "more" is actually to deny the gift that had already been given (5:1–3).

In the church at Colossae, as well, Paul confronted those who sought to "disqualify" others by insisting that baptism must be supplemented by circumcision, ascetical practices, and even mystical experience, to reach a greater "maturity" (read: status) within the church (Col 2:16–19). In response, Paul defines maturity not in terms of adding experiences but of deepening, of growing in insight into the mystery of the gift that has been given (Col 2:2–15) and in the moral practice based on the image of Christ (Col 3:1–17).

We don't know if Paul convinced the Galatians and Colossians, but we do know that eventually the human instinct for distinction overtook Christianity. Eventually, confirmation became the sacrament of "maturation." Ordination brought still greater status. Later, priesthood stood as the climax of six lesser ranks of clerical status, and the entry into the "higher" ranks of monsignors and bishops and archbishops and cardinals and Pope.

The church has never entirely lost sight of its conviction that "one baptism" creates a radical equality among all the faithful, and that a priest (or pastor) is not "more Christian" than a layperson, nor is the Pope in any fundamental way of more significance (except in terms of responsibility and the call to service) than the director of education at Sacred Heart Parish, nor is the crusade evangelist closer to God as an evangelist than the child in the third row at First Baptist.

But the church has certainly not cultivated that insight, and has indeed often acted as though the clergy were the real Christians and the great body of the "merely baptized" were a passive and helpless audience for the truths and services provided by the professionals. The simple statement of the creed challenges this tendency, and reminds all the faithful who recite it not only that all the baptized are equal in the sight of the Lord, but that they are also all equally responsible for the body of Christ—and equally responsible to him.

FOR THE FORGIVENESS OF SINS

The creed links the one baptism directly to the forgiveness of sins by a phrase that can mean both purpose and result: baptism is given for the purpose of forgiving sins, it leads to the forgiveness of sins, and it generates the practice of forgiving sins. The connection between baptism and the forgiveness of sins is firmly grounded in the witness of the New Testament. In the Gospels, John offers baptism for the repentance of Israel and the forgiveness of the people's sins (Mark 1:4; Luke 1:77; 3:3). Jesus himself expresses the good news from God through the forgiveness of sins (Matt 9:2, 5; 12:21; 26:28; Mark 2:5–10; Luke 5:20–24; 7:47–49; John 1:29; 8:1–11), and commissions his followers to continue the proclamation of the forgiveness of sins (Luke 24:47; John 20:23).

The Book of Acts tells us that baptism became for the earliest church the ritual medium for expressing this forgiveness. At Pentecost, Peter exhorts the crowd, "Repent, and be baptized every one of you in the name of Jesus Christ, so that your sins may be forgiven; and you will receive the gift of the Holy Spirit" (Acts 2:38). Paul reports that after his encounter with the risen Jesus, he is told by Ananias, "Get up, be baptized, and have your sins washed away, calling on his name" (Acts 22:16; see also 3:19; 5:31; 10:43; 13:38). Paul says of Jesus that "in him we have redemption, the forgiveness of sins" (Col 1:14; see Eph 1:7), and also connects the liberation from sins to the Christian experience of baptism (see Rom 6:1–8:3; 1 Cor 6:9–11; Eph 5:25–27).

. In the next chapter I will comment on the blessed spareness of the creed on any number of points. This is an example. It offers no theory of sin, just as it proposes no theory of salvation. But just as it asserts that God entered human existence "for us . . . and for our salvation," so it affirms that in baptism this salvation is expressed by "the forgiveness of sins." If baptism is the ritual initiation into the life of the community of salvation, and if baptism is given for the forgiveness of sins, then forgiveness of sins must mean more than the mere cancellation of a debt in the past. It must mean, as well, a lifting of the weight of sinful attitude and disposition that drags us downward.

Baptism into the Christian community therefore means initiation into a community enlivened by the forgiveness of sins and called to the practice of forgiveness. The church is (at least potentially) a place of healthy realism about sin in a world that does not recognize it as such. Many among us have virtually abandoned the notion of personal sin, treating it as a pathology due to genes or environment, but certainly not the result of free choice. We are not sinners needing forgiveness. We are simply people who have somehow gotten sick. We are basically fine once we get free of unhealthy influences.

Alternatively, we sin not because we are selfish and self-seeking to the neglect and even harm of others, but because we have not nurtured our own best potentials, because we have neglected our own dreams and allowed others to make excessive demands on our attention and energy. We must therefore "forgive ourselves" in order to move toward that state of health which is uncomplicated and constant self-preoccupation.

Alternatively, we have been massively sinned against, and our traumas are so many and so profound that forgiveness is impossible. The remainder of our life must be spent in recovery, the key moment of which is the assigning of appropriate blame. I am so exhausted by recovering from the sins committed against me that I don't have the energy to be a sinner myself.

Compared with these views (and corresponding lifestyles), how clean and crisp is the message of the good news, which begins with the recognition that we all need to repent, because we are all sinners. What a remarkably positive appreciation of human dignity is the recognition that we are not merely the result of others' decisions or social pressures or even underdeveloped evolution, but are free creatures! We are responsible for our actions. We are therefore also responsible for the harm we do to ourselves and other people.

We are, to put it simply, guilty of sin. Guilt is not a feeling but a rational estimation of human responsibility. Guilt is not a block to self-esteem but a step toward self-honesty. Guilt does not cover us in shame but opens us to forgiveness. What a proper understanding of the order of the universe it is to acknowledge that we need, not our own forgiveness, but God's forgiveness. What a sober and sane realization of the embodied and social character of human existence it is to know that we need the forgiveness of others. And what a fitting thing it is that—as the Lord's own prayer tells us—as we ask God for forgiveness, so are we obliged also to practice forgiveness toward others (Matt 6:12; Luke 11:4).

The creed tells us that the church, therefore, is at least this: a community that recognizes that it is sinful and stands in need of God's forgiveness, and a community that seeks to embody the practice of forgiveness as a sign to the world (see James 5:13–18). But the difficulty of the practice of forgiveness should not be underestimated. We may think that we are forgiving, when all we are doing is denying that we have hurt or been hurt by sin. We may think we are forgiving when we have only grown weary of the fear and anger generated by hurt, and have accommodated ourselves to the presence of sin in ourselves or others. We may think we are forgiving when we are only acquiescing in sin against ourselves or against others.

We learn the true nature of forgiveness from the way in which God forgives us. Because God knows us completely, God is also able to see that we are not totally identified with our sinful behavior, even if we think of ourselves as defined by sin. God is able to see and to summon a self that we perhaps are not able to see. God calls into being that which is as yet only potential within us, namely a self that is not a sinner. In this sense, God forgives *us* rather than the sin. The sinful self is allowed to die. The self that can live to righteousness is raised by God. When we are able to trust that God so forgives us, we are able then to "turn" or "convert" to the self that God sees and calls into being, and can ourselves activate the self that lives again to righteousness.

We can learn how to forgive each other from the way in which God forgives us. We can cultivate the habit of seeing in others a self that is not defined by their sin. We can seek that self and call it into being, encouraging the growth of that larger self that is capable of living in communion. And as we learn this discipline of genuine forgiveness, we also grow larger—both because we are forgiven in turn and because we increasingly see our neighbors as God perceives them.

But let us also always be aware that we are not God, and cannot forgive as God forgives. We do not see the other truly and completely. There are hurts that we are not able, either individually or communally, to get around or grow past—to forgive or accept forgiveness for. And it is precisely in this humble condition of inadequacy and failure and even sin that we most truly implore the merciful God to forgive us, so that we might someday approach forgiving others as, we trust, God now already forgives them.

WE LOOK FORWARD TO THE RESURRECTION OF THE DEAD AND THE LIFE OF THE WORLD TO COME

For its last statement, the creed uses a term other than "believe" and "confess." In Greek, it means "expect," and the translation "look forward to" captures the active sense of anticipation in the original. With this proposition, the creed completes its story. We have already declared that Christ "will come again with glory to judge the living and the dead. His Kingdom shall have no end." Now the creed states a conviction not only about the work of God—its main, almost exclusive focus throughout—but also about the hope that pertains to us.

The two phrases "resurrection of the dead" and "life of the world to come" are closely entwined in origin and meaning. The notion of a "world/age" to come (the word "world" means both at once) develops within apocalyptic and Pharisaic Judaism together with the expectation of a resurrection of the dead. The earliest explicit witness to the resurrection in Scripture comes in 2 Maccabees. A Jewish mother and her seven sons are commanded by the king Antiochus IV to eat pork in violation of God's law, and when they refuse, they are executed in the most grisly fashion, from oldest son to youngest, while their mother watches. Each young man declares the conviction that enables him to endure such tortures. As the eldest says, "You are depriving us of this present life, but the King of the world will raise us up to live again forever. It is for his laws that we are dying" (2 Macc 7:9).

The hope of a future age in which the righteous might live, then, emerges out of the cognitive dissonance created by the experience of death in witness to Torah. Why the cognitive dissonance? Because Deuteronomy promised that fidelity to the Law would lead to long life on the land, but these young men died at the hand of foreign oppressors precisely because of their loyalty to the Law. Belief in a future age and resurrection maintains God's promise in the face of such contradictory evidence.

The promise is now understood not in terms of longevity, but in terms of eternal life with God. Justice is not denied, only delayed, the reward for faithfulness given not now but later. The psychological benefit of this apocalyptic vision is obvious. But is it also true? Do we have here only an example of disappointed human hopes changed into expectations from the divine because disappointment is unbearable?

The short answer is that we don't know whether it is true, as concerns us; and as concerns Jesus, we have only the evidence of our experience, as ambiguous as that often is. But we can also recognize that belief in the resurrection represents a genuine deepening in the faith of Israel. This hope rises to the level of Qoheleth and Job, each of whom, in his fashion, considered the easy equation of Deuteronomy between righteousness and human success—long life, safety on the land, prosperity, many children—suspect in light of actual human experience.

The Maccabean martyrdoms drew out of Israel's own deepest experience and conviction a perception of God as King of the World that transcended Deuteronomy's categories altogether. If God is truly the one God of all creation, God is simply not limited by space and time and therefore can do what we cannot, including bringing the dead to life. The Maccabean mother says to her sons as they face their deaths:

> I do not know how you came into existence in my womb; it was not I who gave you the breath of life, nor was it I who set in order the elements of which each of you is composed. Therefore, since it is the Creator of the universe who shapes each man's beginning, as he brings about the origin of everything, he, in his mercy, will give you back both breath and life, because you now disregard yourselves for the sake of his law. (2 Macc 7:22–23)

From the start, Christianity has shared with classical Judaism this belief in the resurrection and the future life. In the Synoptic Gospels, Jesus scorns the position of the Sadducees, the Jewish sect that denied the resurrection of the dead (Mark 12:18–27; Matt 22:23–33; Luke 20:27–36). In John's Gospel, Jesus says of the future resurrection:

> The hour is coming, and is now here, when the dead will hear the voice of the Son of God, and those who hear will live ... the hour is coming when all who are in their graves will hear his voice and will come out—those who have done good to the resurrection of life, and those who

have done evil, to the resurrection of condemnation. (John 5:25–29)

According to the Acts of the Apostles, the proclamation of the resurrection went hand in hand with the proclamation of Christ (4:2, 33; 17:18, 32). In his defense speeches, Paul declares repeatedly that he stands trial because he witnesses to the "hope of Israel," which he identifies as the resurrection from the dead (see Acts 23:6; 24:15, 21; 26:23). The letter to the Hebrews lists "the resurrection of the dead and eternal judgment" as among those "elementary teachings concerning Christ" that ought to be assumed for those who wish to move on to more mature considerations (6:2). The Book of Revelation envisages both a first and a final resurrection as part of God's triumph over evil (20:1–15).

When speaking of the resurrection and enthronement of the Lord Jesus, we saw how Paul, in particular, connected what happened in Jesus to what is now happening in believers, and their hope concerning the future. In 2 Timothy, Paul expresses that future hope in this way: "if we have died with him, we will also live with him; if we endure, we will also reign with him" (2:11–12). Thus, when he seeks to reassure the Thessalonians who are grieving "like those with no hope" at the death of their loved ones (1 Thess 4:13), he assures them that those who have died will "rise first" (1 Thess 4:16). He bases this assurance on the resurrection of Jesus: "For since we believe that Jesus died and rose again, even so, through Jesus, God will bring with him those who have died" (1 Thess 4:14).

When Paul seeks to rebut those in Corinth who appear to be denying a general resurrection of the dead, he does so by referring to the good news of Jesus' resurrection by which they are being saved: "Now if Christ is proclaimed as raised from the dead, how can some of you say there is no resurrection of the dead?"

(1 Cor 15:12). He insists that what happened in Jesus will happen also to us: "But in fact Christ has been raised from the dead, the first-fruits of those who have died ... all will be made alive in Christ, but each in his own order, first Christ the first-fruits, then, at his coming, those who belong to Christ" (1 Cor 15:20–23).

Though rooted in Christian experience, this last claim of the creed is one of the easiest targets of Enlightenment criticism. If truth must be measured by the evidence of history, all claims about the future must be simply wishful thinking, a form of fantasy. And if the value of religion within the bounds of reason is its capacity to support the moral life, as the modern mind insists, the claims fare no better. Too avid a collective eschatology can be blamed for fomenting social fanaticism (see the Radical Reformation), and too serious an individual eschatology can be blamed for encouraging social passivity (the "pie in the sky by and by" critique).

Half agreeing with the Enlightenment and embarrassed by the extreme forms of eschatology, most contemporary Christians are strung along a long and confused spectrum of positions, none especially convincing or attractive. At one end are those who insist that one of the New Testament's visions of the future is in fact a literal prediction of the end-time. At the other end are those who translate all Christian expectation of the end into a this-worldly hope for the alteration of social, economic, and political structures through the revolutionary participation of the righteous.

Between these extremes are the vast majority of Christians who are simply confused. They may recite the words of the creed, but they have little sense of expectation for God's triumph. At best, they look for some version of the profoundly individualistic "four last things": death, judgment, heaven, hell. Three of these create fear, and the hope connected with the fourth (heaven) is vague. Not a few Christians simply identify the future life with the immortality of the soul, and some even consider reincarnation to be compatible with Christian faith.

Jesus' response to the Sadducees can be turned against each of these positions: they understand neither the Scripture nor the power of God (Mark 12:24). The scriptural base of each position is weak or nonexistent. The millenarian version of Christianity grounds itself in the apparently pious adherence to the witness of the Book of Revelation, but this version is actually impious. First, it elevates one witness in the New Testament and ignores the others, and second, it literalizes the metaphorical language of Revelation itself, reducing its powerful prophetic protest against idolatry to the level of a cosmic train schedule.

The liberation version has even less scriptural support. Even with its passionate appeal to social justice, it represents a return to the Deuteronomic vision and fails to reckon with the implications for hope of a crucified and raised Lord Jesus.

Remarkably, the "four last things" version of eschatology actually has the strongest support in the New Testament, but it ignores all the passages that speak of the future resurrection and judgment and world to come in common, rather than individual, terms. This is why Christians holding this view can so easily make it fit with belief in the immortality of the soul or even reincarnation.

None of these views understands the power of God as it has been revealed in creation, Scripture, and the experience of the death and resurrection of the Lord Jesus Christ. Each of them reduces what Paul calls a "mystery" (1 Cor 15:51) to a set of problems: how to align visions with historical events, how to remedy social ills, how to find room for so many bodies! Each of them represents a loss of a robust sense of God as creator. For at its end the creed returns to its beginning, with the affirmation of God's infinite power to create, in this case to create life from death. We remember how Paul connects the power to raise the dead and the power to create. Speaking of Abraham, he says,

> In the presence of the God in whom he believed, who gives life to the dead and calls into existence the things that do not exist, hoping against hope, he believed that he would become the father of many nations . . . he did not weaken in faith when he considered his own body, which was already as good as dead [for he was about a hundred years old] or when he considered the barrenness [literally, the deadness] of Sarah's womb. No distrust made him waver concerning the promise of God, but he grew strong in his faith as he gave glory to God. (Rom 4:17–20)

The power of God to create from nothing, says Paul, is more than sufficient to raise the dead to life. And he goes further, connecting the birth of Isaac from the "dead" Abraham and Sarah to the resurrection of Jesus, so that the words "It was reckoned to him as righteousness" (Gen 15:6) applied not only to Abraham, but also "to us who believe in him who raised Jesus our Lord from the dead" (Rom 4:24).

For Paul, and for all Christians who have managed to see reality through the eyes of Paul and the other New Testament witnesses, if one grasps what is claimed by calling God "Father almighty, maker of all things visible and invisible," it is just as easy (and rational) to accept God's capacity to raise one human being (Jesus) from the dead as accepting God's capacity to give a child to elderly parents. If God did this, God can be expected to raise all humans from the dead.

By no means does this suggest, however, that human beings can understand adequately any aspect of God's creative power, least of all his power to bring resurrection and a future life. To affirm that God creates the world does not mean we have an authorized theory of how God creates. To claim the truth of the resurrection and enthronement of Jesus does not mean that we can declaim on the manner of his resurrection and exaltation. We know even less about how God will raise the dead and lead the righteous to eternal life. At least the evidence for creation lies all about us, and the evidence for the resurrection can be found within our hearts. But none of us can project the future.

This is why Paul responds vigorously with "you fool!" to some in Corinth who ask, "How are the dead raised? With what kind of body do they come?" (1 Cor 15:35–36). In the discussion that then follows, Paul argues that we cannot know what the resurrected body will be like on the basis of our knowledge of the body we now have, any more than we could know from the shape of a seed the character of a tree. The mortal body that is sown in dishonor will be raised in honor: what Paul means is that it will somehow partake in the glorious life of God (1 Cor 15:37–49). But how can any of us, including Paul, guess what that might mean?

What Paul is certain of is that there is an infinite distance between God the creator and all creatures, even those created in the image of his Son: "flesh and blood cannot inherit the kingdom of God, nor does the perishable inherit the imperishable" (1 Cor 15:50). This in turn means that "we will all be changed" (15:51). Beyond this, Paul does not want to venture, nor should we. With him, rather, we should conclude, "Thanks be to God, who gives us the victory through our Lord Jesus Christ" (15:57), and explore the implications for our lives of such a hope. As Paul tells us, "Be steadfast, immovable, always excelling in the work of the Lord, because you know in the Lord your labor is not in vain" (1 Cor 15:58).

What we "look forward to," then, is the full revelation of God's power as creator and as ruler of the world. God seeks to share the fullness of life through creation and re-creation. We do not hope simply for some kind of survival after death, as the logical consequence of having an "immortal soul," or (even sadder) the perpetual repetition of mortal life through reincarnation. Survival is not salvation. Persistence in mortality is not glorification.

We hope that as embodied creatures, and as God's people, we shall in the end reach the full sharing in God's own life that Jesus, "the pioneer and perfecter of faith," has achieved (Heb 12:2), that we might find full conformity to the body of Christ. As Paul says, "Our citizenship is in heaven, and it is from there that we are expecting a savior, the Lord Jesus Christ. He will transform the body of our humiliation, that it might be conformed to the body of his glory, by the power that also enables him to make all things subject to himself" (Phil 3:20–21).

This final proposition of the creed serves as a rule of faith for the way we conduct our lives as Christians. We live as those aware that God's work in the world is not yet finished, that the transformation of humanity itself and of creation is not yet complete, and that each of us and all of us still face judgment and resurrection. Specifically, we know that the body has a future in the new creation. Just as God has honored the human body through creation in the image of God and then through the incarnation and resurrection of Jesus, so God will honor the body through its glorification. This means that Christians must regard the body as a significant instrument for God's work.

Because of the resurrection, we can use the body in certain ways that otherwise would be foolish. Martyrdom as a witness to God's will in the face of corruption, tyranny, and idolatry is the obvious example, but so is virginity as a life of witness to God's power to generate new life apart from biological processes. A life of poverty in service to the needs of others makes little sense if we go around only once and this is all the life we can ever have. As Paul says, "If for this life only we have hoped in Christ, we are of all people most to be pitied" (1 Cor 15:19). But if we have been caught up in the life of a God whose entire nature is the sharing of life, we can also gladly dispose of ourselves with a generosity that the crabbed and narrow calculus of self-interest can never imagine.

Because the resurrection offers the body an honorable future in the new creation, we must engage the structures of this world to move them toward the new creation—in a manner that likewise appears foolish. Salvation does not consist in the improvement of political and economic systems. But the hope of a blessed resurrection—especially when preceded by a judgment based on the terms suggested by Matthew 25—certainly demands of us a passionate commitment to the social and political body, as well as to clothing the bodies of those who are naked and visiting the bodies of those who are sick or in prison. Not least are the social structures and processes of the church to be engaged, so that the embodied witness to the truth of God might have integrity.

No less does our embodied participation in God's life demand an ecological awareness and commitment to the "body" that is the earth. It is a horrible distortion of Christian eschatology to act as if only humans mattered. Humans were created in God's image to tend the earth in a manner that gives glory to God (Gen 1:26–31). Treating all other creatures and the earth itself as given only to serve the needs and desires of humans is a form of blasphemy. We do not know how God will bring about a "new heaven and a new earth," in which "the first heaven and the first earth have passed away, and the sea was no more" (Rev 21:1), but we can be sure that those who look with hope for a blessed resurrection will not pillage and pollute God's creation.

If we truly look for the resurrection of the dead and the life of the world to come, how we dispose of our body matters. We will be judged on the way in which we have lived as embodied creatures. Yet we remember that the world remains God's. We are not the judges of the world, God is. We live, therefore, in a spirit of freedom and detachment. How we act determines our future, but it does not altogether determine the world's future. Indeed, precisely the fact that we can dispose of the body in only one way at each moment reminds us both of the seriousness of our choices and our ultimate inability to predict or control the consequences. I can do only one thing at a time: I can fast or feast, march or watch, say yes or no to my neighbor. And I can never know whether I did the right thing.

We live, therefore, not in certainty but in hope. The present moment—the only moment in which we can act—is not a period of emptiness before the final act. The present is a time of transformation of our selves and of our world, which God is accomplishing in and through our mortal bodies even now. Our Christian hope, therefore, is less a promise for the future than a perception of the present as shaped by the one who calls into life that which is not, who raises Jesus from the dead, and who can also raise our mortal bodies into a fellowship with the Living God.

AMEN

The creed ends with the ancient Hebrew word "Amen." Amen usually concludes a prayer, and often a prayer said by someone else, and means: "may it be in the manner you have spoken." It declares our agreement and confirmation. Those reciting the creed say amen to their own profession. They mean, "May we actually agree with these words we have said, may they actually be true, and may our lives be ones that actually express these truths in a consistent and compelling way."

But we who recite the creed also know that we fail to agree with the words of our common faith in so many ways, that we waver every day as to whether they are true, and that we always fall short of expressing their truth consistently and compellingly. And so we say our amen, as Paul taught us, through Jesus Christ: "For the Son of God, Jesus Christ, whom we proclaimed among you, Silvanus and Timothy and I, was not 'yes and no,' but in him it is always 'yes.' For in him every one of God's promises is a 'yes.' For this reason it is through him that we say the 'Amen' to the glory of God. But it is God who establishes us with you in Christ and has anointed us by putting his seal on us and giving us his Spirit in our hearts as a pledge" (2 Cor 1:19–22).

Chapter Nine

CREEDAL CHRISTIANITY

Everything up to this point has been introduction. To those who have little awareness of what Christians say they believe, and to those Christians who remain uncertain either about what the church believes or how much they believe it, I have tried to give some sense of where the creed came from, what it does, and what it means. Now I want to make an argument on behalf of the creed. I propose that Christianity would be healthier and have greater integrity if it paid more attention to the Nicene Creed.

THE CREED AS DEFINITION: BOUNDARIES NOT BARRIERS

The church today desperately needs a clear and communal sense of identity: What does it mean to be a Christian? The answers tend toward one of two extremes. We have seen this repeatedly as we examined the ways in which statements of the creed are interpreted. At one end are those with clear, unyielding boundaries, by which they define true Christianity. At the other are those who have dropped almost all boundaries, and have conformed themselves to the Modern or Enlightenment mind. The first extreme includes Evangelical and Pentecostal Protestants as well as a considerable number of Roman Catholics unhappy about the post–Vatican II church. The second extreme includes mainline Protestants and those Roman Catholics committed to *aggiornamento*.

Some groups within Christianity have remarkably clear boundaries. They know exactly who they are, how they are different from others, and what they demand of their members. They insist on the "literal" meaning of Scripture and on "classic Christian teaching." Even though they are often as individualistic in their piety as other forms of Christianity, they expect conformity to the group in matters of doctrine and behavior. They are also the forms of Christianity that are growing fastest in number and influence.

Unfortunately, these Christian groups tend to confuse the accidental with the essential. They tend to make some single element of belief or of morals the litmus test of membership and indeed of true Christianity. For some, it is the literal inspiration and inerrancy of Scripture; for others, baptism in the Spirit; for others, recognition of papal authority; for many, the condemnation of homosexuality and the canonization of the nuclear family; for many, a politics that calls itself conservative but is often reactionary. Failure to agree means exclusion. Such forms of Christianity flourish because they actually demand something of their members and they satisfy the human hunger for clarity and certainty.

They are also fundamentally sectarian, because they define

themselves as much by what they oppose as what they affirm. They exemplify the classical definition of heresy as the elevation of one truth to the distortion of other truths. What each of them opposes in one way or another is the entire world shaped by Modernity. The Enlightenment is the great enemy.

These groups pay a remarkable amount of attention to some small point of self-definition, compared to the attention they give to the heart of the gospel. Worse, they are often preoccupied with external signs of conformity but neglect the evidence of abuse and corruption around them. The classic example is their public opposition to sexual immorality accompanied by their blindness toward economic injustice. And because they set their boundaries by what is nonessential rather than what is essential, they repel those outside (and some of those within) who despair at their consistent habit of straining the gnat while swallowing the camel.

At the other extreme, some groups lack any real sense of boundaries. They do not answer the question "What does it mean to be a Christian?" clearly, and offer little sense of what is demanded of the individual Christian. They have explicitly or implicitly assimilated to the world of Modernity, have resisted the creation of strong boundaries in favor of an openness to the world, and have aligned themselves politically with the forces of change within culture rather than with the forces of resistance. They define Christianity in terms of acceptance and inclusion, and regard boundaries as barriers.

This extreme also has its inconsistencies. It is, in a sense, as sectarian or heretically selective as the first. It attacks the other style of Christianity for identifying Christianity with reactionary politics, but is itself just as committed to liberal politics. It bemoans the narrowness of a literalistic reading of Scripture in service of doctrine, but is just as committed to a literalistic reading of the Bible in service of history. It condemns the other extreme's narrow-minded, exclusionary style of life, not recognizing in such condemnation another form of narrow-minded exclusiveness. It mocks the periodic appearance of charlatans among the ranks of Evangelical leaders, but seems incapable of recognizing the charlatans among its own leaders.

Its most significant heresy, however, is its exaggerated and distorted commitment to individual liberty at the expense of communal integrity. If each Christian decides what Christianity means and which of its norms are truly norms, the church has then become a club that one can join on one's own terms.

Perhaps the most remarkable evidence for Christianity's confusion—at both extremes—is the fact that since the time of the Enlightenment, the longest-running of all Christological heresies has deeply infiltrated the church with scarcely any protest or controversy, much less the calling of a council of bishops to clarify and defend the faith of the church. I mean the replacement of the Christ of faith with the so-called historical Jesus.

Please note that I am not speaking of the historical study of Jesus and the Gospels. I speak of the repudiation of the church's faith in the resurrected Lord and the replacement of that faith with a Jesus reconstructed solely on the basis of what history can reliably tell us, as measured by the methods of the modern critical historian. This view has become so widespread and has received so little opposition—especially in liberal forms of Christianity—that in some circles it is regarded as the best available theology rather than as a dreadful distortion of the truth of the gospel.

I submit that the question of the nature and work of Jesus Christ is central to the identity of Christianity. If the significance of Jesus is simply his words and deeds in first-century Palestine (to the extent that we can know them), the very existence of the church is a mistake. If Jesus is not the powerful risen Lord through whom we approach God, the entire life of the church is a lie. It is the complete *inattention* to this question that is most startling to anyone with any sense of history.

How can greater attention to the creed help the church establish boundaries of self-definition that are not barriers? How does the creed help the church set its boundaries where they ought to be? I think it does this first by simply functioning as a clear and communal statement of the community's faith. The creed is clear, it is not ambiguous or complicated. It can be understood and affirmed by children as well as by adults. And it is communal: each Christian understands the propositions of the creed distinctively, to be sure—a necessary and blessed corollary of freedom!—but each affirms this specific set of propositions as the community's faith.

Second, the creed challenges every member of the community and places demands on them. The creed expresses what and how the church believes more and better than I do. Therefore it calls me to a level of belief and practice that is now beyond me. I do not belong to a club, but to a people that demands of me commitment and growth.

Third, the creed is not a set of abstract convictions, but a rule of faith with a clear and coherent internal logic. It is therefore possible to determine from the creed which behaviors conform to this logic and which do not. It is both an instrument of discernment and a set of interrelated principles for the shaping of a coherent community life.

Fourth, the creed invites Christians into reflection on what is truly essential to Christian life. By its very structure, the creed encourages a large vision of the entire story, seen in its entirety, rather than a narrow focus on one point or another. The creed cultivates a consciousness of what Christians have in common rather than a consciousness of what separates them.

Fifth, the creed identifies itself as one instrument of Christian identity among others. The creed tells us to seek the truth of God in "all things visible and invisible," and in the incarnate and risen Lord Jesus, and in the Scripture, and in the work of the Holy Spirit, and in the church. The creed opens possibilities for Christians of all sorts to grow together within a framework of their essential and shared commitment.

THE CREED AS PROFESSION OF FAITH: PROPHECY TO THE WORLD

The point of having strong boundaries of self-definition is not that all Christians should think and act exactly alike, still less that the church develop those sharp edges that make for successful marketing. The point, rather, is to ensure that the church be able to speak a prophetic word clearly to the world. How can the church be a sacrament of the world's possibility—a sign of what the world can be—if it does not clearly grasp or convincingly express the essential truths by which it claims to live? If Christians do not know the character of God and God's work, how should the world?

Time and again in this book, I have noted the ways in which the creed expresses a view of reality that is profoundly countercultural, not in some small point of style or other, but in its whole perception of the world and how humans are to act in the world. To the degree that Christians have failed to grasp or to live by this vision of reality, they fail to challenge the world.

The world ignores as quirky and weird the high boundaries some Christians base on nonessential points and cannot even see the eroded boundaries of other Christians who seek above all things to make Christianity acceptable to the larger world. But the more Christians can truly claim and live by the creed's countercultural perceptions, the more powerfully can their profession of faith also be prophetic in both meanings of the word: they identify God's presence and power within creation, and thereby also call into question those cultural and intellectual forces that deny God's presence and power.

Creedal Christians are able to offer a world desperate for significance and direction a unique vision of the world's origin, meaning, and destiny. It has become a commonplace to observe that the post-modern condition is one in which there is no universal unifying interpretation of reality—no secure and shared truth—only a collection of competing claims. This nihilism is not the odd idea of philosophical types. It is the modus operandi of the marketplace. Indeed, if there is one universal, unifying interpretation in the world, it is some form of social Darwinism that reduces human life to the brutal competition to survive. The most widely used language in the world today is commerce, the most practiced form of politics is war. The best vision the world offers—evolution, through competition—has no apparent goal or point, and certainly no concern for the weak and vulnerable who will lose out in any such competition.

The savage battle for economic supremacy is leading the earth rapidly toward ecological exhaustion, and has already led to the economic slavery of countless millions, not alone in the third world but equally (if with more things) in the first. Even as this happens at an ever quicker pace, the omnipresent and increasingly omnipotent media camouflages the naked reality with the fig leaves of distraction and entertainment, while the corrupting nihilism of advertising reduces everything to the level of commodity.

In such a world—and it is ours—the creed offers an account of the world's true origin and destiny, and therefore its meaning, that is available nowhere else. The creed tells the world a truth about itself that the world does not know. The power of the Christian myth, found in its clearest and most compelling form in the creed rather than in Scripture, should not be underestimated, especially in a world whose *best* alternative is an endless and pointless evolution.

Simply to *have* an account of the world with a beginning, climax, and end is a rare possession in the contemporary world. To have such an account that enlarges the vision of reality and enables humans to live more humanely within the world is to have a gift worth sharing. But if Christians themselves do not know, or cannot remember, or do not really believe their own myth, what do they have to offer the world?

Where else in today's world can humans hear a humane and healing word, or encounter an alternative vision of reality actually being enacted? Who can tell the world's true story—who can tell *the world* its true story—better than those shaped by Christianity's creed? Christians can say that "all things visible and invisible" come from a God who is all-powerful and a Father, and gives humans the world as a garden for them to tend with awe, not as a playground willfully to pillage. They can speak of a God who has created humans in a divine image, and therefore of intrinsic and profound worth for their own sake, rather than as disposable and interchangeable parts of a social machine to be manipulated for the benefit of the powerful.

They worship as Son of God the one who entered their own history and lifted them up to a share in God's own life, and are therefore able to think of the human body and even time itself as revealing something of God's life. They know the Son of God suffered and died, and therefore know, even while fighting the powers of evil, that suffering, especially for the sake of others, can transform reality. They can speak not of the evolution of the species through mechanisms occurring quite apart from their freedom, but of the transformation of persons through a Holy Spirit that cannot take place apart from their freedom.

They can envision a society that is grounded not in rivalry, envy, and competition but in mutual sharing and edification, because they are members of a church that seeks to be at once holy and one and catholic and apostolic. They take moral integrity with utter seriousness, knowing that they are to be—are being—judged by a God who sees into their hearts, not by a media that is easily fooled. They place their hopes for the future in God, because they know that God's kingdom shall never end.

Nowhere in today's world, apart from the Christian creed, is such an alternative vision of the world and of humanity so clearly stated. Essential to an authentic creedal Christianity, however, is the conviction that the creed is not simply "an alternative view," as if it were another opinion offered for consideration, like social Darwinism. Christians offer what they believe to be the truth about the world in every respect. It is not only "true for them" that God is creator and Father, but true for all. It is not simply a Christian opinion that God entered humanity through Jesus Christ, but the truth about God and about humanity. It is not simply a bracing point of view to say that all humans face the judgment of God, but the soberest truth about every human who ever has or ever shall live.

That is the positive witness the creed makes to the world. Negatively, creedal Christians can, on the basis of the vision of reality given by their myth, prophetically challenge the dominant idolatries by which the world mainly runs. It is because Christians believe in a God who creates the world anew at every moment and whose gifts are therefore without end that they can challenge the age-old idolatry of a life centered on pleasure, which in contemporary culture is expressed in self-absorption and addiction. It is because Christians celebrate a God whose very being consists in sharing all things, and who calls humans created in the image of the triune God into a life of sharing all things, that they can challenge the age-old idolatry of a life centered on the accumulation of possessions, which in contemporary culture is expressed by treating all creatures (including the earth itself) as if they were commodities and giving them only the value the market assigns them.

It is because Christians worship as Lord the one who revealed the real nature of power when he emptied himself of divine status to take on our humanity, and then gave himself in utter weakness and foolishness and shame on the cross, that they can challenge the age-old idolatry of a life centered on visible and obvious power, which in contemporary culture is expressed above all in the subtle enslavement of minds and hearts through the manipulation of the other idolatries of addiction and avarice.

Finally, because Christians find their mythic vision of reality confirmed intellectually by its beauty and coherence, and confirmed experientially by its capacity to transform and heal the human heart, and confirmed experimentally by the existence of actual communities living by the logic of this myth, they are able to challenge the intellectual idolatry of the Enlightenment, which succeeded in domesticating religion by first reducing the range of human thought and imagination. The Christian myth is not a smaller version of the truth but a larger one. It does not, like the Enlightenment mind, demand the fearful contraction of the mind to what the mind can grasp and control, but encourages the mind to follow the lead of the imagination. It does not eliminate human freedom through appeal to mechanistic processes, but enhances human freedom by appeal to moral responsibility.

The critical function of the creed against the prevailing idolatries can only be exercised by Christians who say these words, not simply as an oddity or heirloom from Christianity's past, but as the proud and public profession of a living community. Here is the connection between the internal and external voices of the creed. The more the boundaries of Christian communities are shaped by the powerful yet flexible myth of the creed, the more confident Christians grow in their identity, and the greater grows their capacity to speak coherently a life-giving word to a confused and corrupt contemporary world.

THE CREED AS RULE OF FAITH: GUIDE TO CHRISTIAN EXISTENCE

For the actual life of Christians—as distinct from the need for ecclesial self-definition and a prophetic voice within the world—the creed's most important function is to serve as a Rule of Faith. It does this first by providing a story or myth for Christians and second by explicating the most fundamental convictions concerning God, the world, and humanity. The creed defines and professes. But as a Rule of Faith, it also guides Christians in the living out of their faith: as a guide to the reading of Scripture and as a way of discerning the genuinely Christian manner of life.

Of first importance here is the way in which it guides the reading of Scripture. On no point are contemporary Christians more in agreement than on the importance of basing Christian life in Scripture. And on no point are Christians today more divided than on how Scripture should be read. The Modernist-fundamentalist debate of the early twentieth century continues unabated in the early twenty-first century. There seems to be little middle ground between the position that demands the sacrifice of the intellect to save the inspiration and inerrancy of the text and the position that demands the sacrifice of inerrancy and inspiration to save the intellect.

If there is a middle ground, indeed, it is that both extremes agree on the supreme importance of history and on the minimal importance of the creed. The fundamentalist side proves inspiration and inerrancy by arguing that Scripture is accurate on every point, and the Modernist disproves inspiration and inerrancy by arguing that Scripture is inaccurate on most points. The fundamentalist, suspicious of any norm other than Scripture itself, minimizes the importance of the ancient Christian creeds, while the Modernist uses the critical reading of Scripture to argue for the creed's inaccuracy and irrelevance.

Creedal Christians offer a healthy alternative to these two extremes. In contrast to a commitment to history found in both opposing parties, creedal Christians insist on the superiority of myth to history. Yes, we must know history and know it well, to read Scripture responsibly. But the truths of which Scripture speaks can scarcely be contained within the framework of critical history. Creedal Christians are free to engage Scripture in all its richness and complexity, learning from all its varied ways of speaking truth, because they are not captive to a view that we cannot know more than the historian can tell us.

In contrast to the false opposition between Scripture and creed set up by each extreme, creedal Christians regard them both as instruments of the church's tradition that illuminate and inform each other. Our investigation has shown how the creed offers an amazingly subtle and thorough reading of Scripture, but without pretending to replace the greater richness of Scripture itself. In turn, we have seen how confusing and even contradictory the witnesses of Scripture can be.

The plain fact is that both fundamentalism and Modernism have their own "rules of reading" to which they give as full a dogmatic force as the classical Christian creed. Fundamentalists claim to base themselves on the literal sense of Scripture alone, but in truth, they prefer a handful of texts that support their chosen "fundamentals of faith" and then make the other texts harmonize with them. The Modernists who reject the church's creed have their own critical dogmas that dictate what is read and how it is read. The difference between these "rules of reading" and the church's traditional Rule of Faith is that the contemporary versions both arise out of an Enlightenment preoccupation with history that is totally foreign to Scripture, and that each therefore truncates the capacity of Scripture to speak in its own voice.

Thus, the creed guides the practice of reading Scripture in the church. It is also a Rule of Faith directing other practices in the life of Christians. Once more we touch on an issue of central importance in the church's present crisis of identity. The church is a genuine body—and can witness to God's power and presence in the world—to the degree that it actually embodies practices and patterns of life that express its convictions in a consistent and coherent manner.

By "practices" I mean the repeated actions that are carried out over time by the community as such, such as hospitality, worship, and the sharing of possessions. The word also includes the patterns of behavior that individual members of communities live out, precisely because they adhere to the group's convictions, such as fasting and prayer and almsgiving. Such practices, not the interior motivations or attitudes of individual Christians, constitute the church's witness to the world.

Many Christian communities today, however, are anything but consistent or coherent in their practices. So individualistic has Christianity become in the United States, indeed, that one could argue that there is no church in America. In some cases, Christianity is truly on the verge of becoming a club that people can join on their own terms. The terror of nonsurvival discourages community leaders from enunciating the community's standards to members, much less seeking to enforce them, lest the members leave to seek a more accommodating place.

Some do not even join an actual community, but call themselves Christian because they watch a worship service on television. Others sporadically attend a worship service in the denomination most convenient to their neighborhood without making any commitment to its community life. The cultural and economic pressures that demand hypermobility and multitasking of everyone, leaving little space even for genuine domestic life, also militate against churches creating and sustaining practices of local presence.

Even those "high-definition" Christians discussed above, who do state and demand group standards of behavior, often focus on the most private dimensions of morality and piety, enabling many of their members to live a life devoted to the acquisition of wealth or power, and enabling a congregation to call itself a community of reconciliation yet select its members to be totally homogeneous with respect to class, wealth, ethnicity, and sexual orientation. Still other churches select one or another relatively trivial practice to define authentic Christianity—baptizing in a certain fashion, speaking in tongues, preaching in a certain style, reading a specific translation of Scripture, recognizing a certain leader—and reject as not fully Christian those who do not consider that same practice essential.

The church in America (insofar as we can use that expression) is, in summary, either fearful of expecting of the faithful any standard of practice beyond good citizenship, or wildly erratic in its choice of the standard on which to insist. Small wonder that outsiders have little grasp of what Christians actually believe or what difference belief might make, when Christian communities are themselves unable either to articulate or to embody their convictions.

At the very least, the creed offers the church a clear frame-work for discerning the proper standard for Christian practices. It is a framework, moreover, that is publicly shared by the churches (is catholic), derives from its own earliest traditions (is apostolic), provides a common point of reference (is one), and stands in sharp contrast to other interpretations of the world (is holy).

The creed itself speaks explicitly of only two practices, which it connects closely: baptism and the forgiveness of sins. With their creedal status, they provide an excellent starting point for the church's discernment of how its faith is expressed in practice. How, for example, does this community's preparation for, celebra-tion of, and subsequent teaching about baptism enable the paschal mystery—the mystery of our moving from death to life, from slavery to freedom—to be embodied by the church? What prac-tices (e.g., the sign of the cross) ought to be more closely linked to the profession of a triune God and a crucified Messiah? What other practices (e.g., speaking in tongues) ought to be measured by the criterion of all being one in Christ Jesus?

Likewise with the forgiveness of sins: the church needs to ask what specific practices actually embody this essential dimension of its life. If the church offers no actual practices of public or pri-vate confession, of prayer, of fraternal correction, of penance, of restitution, of discernment, of mediation, of truth-speaking, of prophecy, of reconciliation, can the church actually claim that "forgiveness of sins" is an essential dimension of its life?

Having begun with the practices of baptism and forgiveness, the creed implicitly invites the church to reflect on how its con-victions are, or ought to be, embodied by consistent patterns of in-dividual and communal behavior. How, for example, should the confession of God as creator of all things visible and invisible shape the practice of the church? Should it think of stewardship, for example, primarily in terms of financial support for the ecclesiastical institution or primarily in terms of the church's call to serve creation? How should it, in this specific time and place, embody Scripture's consistent demand that faith be expressed not by the accumulation but by the sharing of possessions?

If God is the creator of all things, how should the church's practices with regard to the life and death of humans be evaluated, not only the borderline moral issues of abortion, euthanasia, and capital punishment, but the more quotidian practices concerning sexuality and marriage and childbirth and adoption and the creation of every form of family? And how should the church's own practices shape a politics that speaks prophetically for creation against the forces of idolatry?

A similar set of questions arises from the profession of "one Lord Jesus Christ." How ought the worship practices of the community express the conviction that Jesus is not merely a human figure of the past, but the powerful presence of God in the present? Of particular pertinence here is the practice of the Lord's Supper, or the Eucharist. How does the exchange of word and gesture cultivate the sense not merely of friendly communion among us gathered, but also our awesome communion with the transcendent power of the Living Jesus? How does the pattern of partaking in the meal imprint the pattern of "life for others" that is the "Law of Christ"?

The Lordship of Jesus ought to affect more than worship. How does the conviction that the Risen Lord identifies himself with the strangers and little ones affect the community's practices of hospitality, of outreach to the sick and imprisoned? How does the community life express a politics of resistance to the idolatries of the age? The observance of "the Lord's Day" as one of rest and worship and avoidance of commerce could actually make a difference for the liberation of the oppressed.

A classic example of how the creed can positively shape practices into a coherent political stance is in the German "Confessing Church" in its stand against National Socialism. There, the profession of "one Lord Jesus Christ" enabled resistance both to the idolatrous claims of Nazism and the all too eager impulse of German Christians to "get along by going along" (see the Barmen Declaration of 1934).

Other questions about practices arise from the creed's statements concerning the Holy Spirit. How do the community's practices of reading Scripture, for example, cohere with the statement that the Holy Spirit "spoke through the prophets"? What practices of the church enable it to hear the voice of prophets through whom the Holy Spirit continues to speak? Are the church's structures of discernment and decision-making open to the work of the Holy Spirit, or are they devoted only to maintaining precedent and the privileges of power?

How does the church in its internal life express the conviction that the Holy Spirit is truly "Lord and Giver of life"? Does the church risk speaking the truth in all circumstances, relying on the Spirit's guidance rather than mere human calculation? Does the church express its trust in the Spirit's capacity to "give life" more than in its own capacity to control outcomes? The creed also invites the church to reflect on how its practices enable the Holy Spirit to make the church more one, more holy, more catholic, and more apostolic.

If on each of these ideals the church's actual practice moves in the opposite direction, it may be asked whether the church believes what it says in the creed. Does this community have practices that express holiness but none that express catholicity? Or does this community's practices tilt its understanding of "apostolic" entirely in the direction of "staying traditional" rather than in the direction of "staying radical"?

Finally, the creed enables all Christians to understand the

process of their personal transformation in the Holy Spirit—or spirituality—in a manner consonant with the public profession and practices of the church. These are the patterns I mentioned earlier. The classic form of Christian spirituality rejects the premise of Gnosticism in which holiness demands withdrawal from the material world to cultivate the inner life of the spirit. It says that we are sanctified in and through the body and the life of the community. Classic spirituality also rejects the premise of liberationist ideologies that so focus on the changing of social structures that contemplation and silent prayer appear almost as counter-revolutionary.

Creedal Christianity allows the Christian to embrace both the body and the spirit, to pursue both internal transformation through prayer and the transformation of society through prophetic engagement. It does so because it grounds them in the work of the triune God, and understands sanctification as a process of participating ever more fully in the life of the triune God. Grounded in sound doctrine and healthy practice, creedal Christians are able to recognize and reject the many-headed heresies of personal development, self-cultivation, and ersatz spirituality that constantly proliferate among those of every age, gender, and circumstance, who, "overwhelmed by their sins and swayed by all kinds of desires, are always being instructed and can never arrive at a knowledge of the truth" (2 Tim 3:6–7).

THE BLESSED SIMPLICITY
OF PROFESSION

One of the qualities of the creed that most recommends it to contemporary Christians who find themselves confused about essentials and divided by nonessentials is its remarkable simplicity in profession. As with friends, so with beliefs: the fewer the better. The ancient philosophers well understood that in friendship there is an inverse proportion of number and quality. More is demanded of friends in trust, loyalty, and depth of commitment than can be asked from casual acquaintances. So also, faith demands selectivity. People who claim to believe many things equally cannot possibly be deeply committed to them all. They inadvertently identify themselves as superficial acquaintances of faith rather than friends with God (James 4:4).

Now, simply with respect to economy of expression and content, the Apostles' Creed is considerably superior to the Nicene-Constantinopolitan Creed that has been our text. It says everything that needs to be said, and nothing more, which probably accounts in part for its continuing use and influence. The Nicene-Constantinopolitan Creed, however, is far superior to every subsequent creed and confession elaborated by Christians.

It adds to the Apostles' Creed what is required to clarify the identity and work of the Son of God, and the work of the Spirit and the church. In this elaboration, it has shown itself faithful to the full range of scriptural testimony and the extraordinarily complex character of the Christian story. But it stops there. It retains the virtue of reticence. For this reason, and for its central place in the liturgical life of many Christians, this version of the creed deserves the close attention of the church today.

The simplicity of the creed is notable first in those matters on which it speaks. The creed consistently affirms *what* without trying to specify *how*, and thus liberates in two ways: the minds of believers are free to examine and investigate, without constraint, the gaps left within by the creed's propositions, and their minds are not imprisoned by extraneous and possibly unworthy explanations or elaborations. The creed thus provides a stable confession within which the faithful can find a variety of acceptable standpoints and interpretations. This is part of what I meant by saying earlier that the creed gives boundaries, not barriers.

The creed states, for example, that God is one and all-powerful. But it does not seek to explain or illustrate this power except through God's being "creator of heaven and earth." The creed does not attempt to pose or solve the intellectual problems presented by belief in God's omnipotence. It offers no theory of evil on one side or of the way humans and the divine can possibly work together on the other. The creed instead faithfully expresses convictions about God as found in Scripture and in prayer, without binding the faithful to a form of speculation that is at once inadequate and distracting.

When the creed states that God is "maker of heaven and earth, of all things visible and invisible," it says what is necessary for any true apprehension of God and for the full obedience of faith. This proposition also opens up, as we have seen, a vision of the world as constantly coming into being, a vision that is at once mysterious and profoundly satisfying and therefore deeply demanding of human attention. But the creed mercifully refrains from any explanation of how God creates all things.

It does not, for example, subscribe to any one of the biblical creation accounts, thereby requiring belief in a particular version of the story. Christian belief in God as creator is thereby liberated from any explanatory system, and is thereby also compatible with any number of scientific or philosophical explanations that respect the integrity of the belief.

Not only is the theory of evolution compatible with the creed, it actually does more honor to the best biblical understanding of creation as a continuing process sustained by the Living God than does a "creationist" version that treats Genesis as though it were a science textbook. Equally important, however, if the best contemporary scientific explanation for the origin and development of the material universe were to be discredited by a subsequent theory, the creed's statement that God is maker of heaven and earth, of all things visible and invisible, would be no less true, for it is not an explanation of the "how" in natural processes but a profession of faith in the "what" of existence itself.

Similarly, the creed included "things visible and invisible," as we saw, to reject the Marcionite position that the true God could not be responsible for material things. Ancient believers took for granted that part of the proposition that some contemporary believers now find most difficult, namely that there are "things invisible." The biblical world speaks often about Satan and demons and unclean spirits and a variety of angels and powers and principalities as real beings with real power over humans. Many contemporary Christians do not experience such beings in the manner described in the Bible—or, to be more accurate, do not perceive themselves as experiencing them.

But the creed does not identify the "things invisible," only states that God makes "all things visible and invisible." The creed does not demand that we think of angels and demons as part of our world. It does push us to realize that "things that appear" do not constitute all reality. Invisible things can refer, not only to demons and unclean spirits, but to processes and dynamics that are real but invisible, such as the machinations of power or even the movements of love. The creed leaves open a variety of interpretations of "things invisible," but it does not leave open the possibility of speaking as though "things visible" adequately comprehended reality.

The same liberating reticence marks the creed's statements about the Son. It does use language like *homoousion*, but only to reject an attack on the divinity of the Son—an attack that would have eviscerated Christian faith—and maintain the integrity of Scripture. The *filioque* is the single and noteworthy example of the creed's overstepping theological modesty, for there was really nothing essential to defend, and the scriptural testimony was sufficiently ambiguous to discourage definition in one direction or another.

These cases aside, the creed is wonderfully simple in its statements about the Son and salvation. It tells us enough about the particulars of Jesus' birth and death to confirm his full humanity and his place in a particular history, but it refrains from providing a full biographical or historical rendering. Not only would such a "filling in" require a narrowing of the complex witness of the New Testament to the human Jesus, it would lead believers to miss the essential point: salvation was accomplished by God entering fully into the fabric of our humanity "for us ... and for our salvation,"not by the particular words and deeds of the human Jesus.

The brief explanatory phrase "for us ... and for our salvation," furthermore, refrains from elaborating any theory of sin (original or otherwise) or any theory of atonement or election. In this respect, the Nicene-Constantinopolitan Creed is clearly superior to later confessions, which enter into elaborate discussions of such points (e.g., the Calvinist Westminster Confession of 1646, chaps. 6–10). Such reticence is liberating in at least two ways. First, it draws believers' attention away from themselves and toward the gracious act of God. Second, it allows the full complexity of Scripture on all these points to remain open for new meaning.

The creed tells us what is absolutely essential: God acts in the world for the sake of humans and to save them. The "how" and any further inquiry into the "why" remain unstated because they are both (ultimately) unknowable and unnecessary. Because the creed does not attach belief in God the savior to any specific theory of the "fall" of humans—indeed, refrains altogether from mentioning the fall—Christians are left free to engage in scientific inquiry into anthropology and the interpretation of Scripture, knowing that the essential point of the faith is not why humans get sick but that they are healed through God alone.

The creed likewise states only the essentials about the existence of God's people in the world. There is a church, and its ideal is to be one, holy, catholic, and apostolic. This is, to be sure, a great deal. It defines Christianity in terms of a public and historical people rather than as a loose assemblage of spiritual seekers. It locates specific ideals that, despite the tensions internal to each and the tensions that exist between them, nevertheless describe a community whose values and practices ought to be prophetic over against the ways of the world based upon idolatry.

But the creed's reticence on the church is even more remarkable. It does not, beyond baptism and the forgiveness of sins, say anything about the church's practices, even its sacramental ones. It says nothing about how the church should be organized. It does not even prescribe how the church is to be one, holy, catholic, and apostolic. It states these ideals and the basic defining practices of baptism and forgiveness, and then leaves the church free to invent itself in a variety of forms consonant with Scripture and the direction of the Holy Spirit. The creed does not exclude any specific form of ecclesiastical life, nor does it recommend any one as superior to others.

Finally, the creed liberates by its reticence concerning the end of the story. By declaring that Jesus will come to judge the living and the dead, and that his kingdom will have no end, and that there will be a resurrection and future life, the creed certainly says something definite. It excludes those who think the present order of things permanent, or who deny any end or goal to history, or who assume for themselves the role of judge, or who declare resurrection beyond the power of God. But what the creed says about the future is grounded in the human experience of God in the past and in the present. It is a conviction, a hope, an expectation. It is not a prediction.

The creed does not, in any fashion, subscribe to any particular scenario (biblical or otherwise) concerning the "how" of the future. Its language is biblical, to be sure, but it refrains entirely from using any of the scriptural imagery concerning the endtime. Creedal Christians are bound by their creed to hope and expect God's judgment and rule through Jesus, a blessed resurrection, and a world to come. But they are not bound by their creed to any specific theory of these things, any more than they are bound to any specific theory of the origins of the world. As for the beginning, so for the end: the creed states what is necessary for an authentic Christian existence, and refrains from going further.

There are also many aspects of Christian life that the creed does not address at all. It gives no account of Judaism or how Christianity relates to Judaism. (Its reticence on this point is the more remarkable when we remember how prominent supersessionist theology—the idea that the church completely replaces Israel as God's people—was in the patristic period.)

The creed likewise says nothing about the Lord's Supper or other sacraments. Did the shapers of the creed regard them as unimportant? Not at all, but they are not essential, and if they are not essential, then definition should be avoided and a plurality of observance should be allowed or even cultivated—as the earliest Christians did in their Eucharists. The creed says nothing about prayer or other forms of piety, not because prayer is unimportant but because defining it is not essential. The same can be said for the creed's total silence concerning the moral life and the relationship of the church to the state.

Thus, the creed, far from being a restriction on Christian thinking, actually liberates the Christian mind. The simple and thrifty creed defines a few essential points and opens reasoning faith to many others. In this way it proves a model of establishing boundaries that are not barriers.

How pleasant it would be to report that subsequent Christians had cultivated the same theological simplicity as the creed. But in fact, much of the history of the church can be read as a series of arguments and mutual exclusions over the points that the creed did not define. Christians in subsequent ages insisted on defining them, often enough acting as though such definitions were essential, when in fact they were not. The endless—and continuing— debates over the meaning of "the real presence" in the Eucharist are only one instance among many, in which the frenzy to define the indefinable has led to the crassest forms of theological immodesty—and the breaking of communion!

I will mention two examples from my own Roman Catholic tradition. First, the extraordinary amount of energy that has gone into defining and defending a specific form of ecclesiastical hierarchy, and above all the supreme (infallible) authority to be given the bishop of Rome. The elevation of that (defensible perhaps but surely not necessary) form of polity into the criterion of inclusion and exclusion, and then the further extension of the "necessary" elements to such accidentals as celibacy and a males-only priesthood, is breathtaking in its arrogance. Here is a case where the will to power has become so confused with theology that its practitioners actually think they are doing the latter when they are only exercising the former.

Second, the obsessive need to define the role of Mary. I am not attempting here either to attack or defend the theological legitimacy of such doctrines as the Immaculate Conception or the Assumption of the Blessed Virgin. I am addressing only the compulsion to push for the definition of such doctrines as required beliefs, as a condition of inclusion within the Roman Catholic tradition. No one who has any sense of proportion—or any knowledge of the Scripture and tradition—would pretend that the confession of the Immaculate Conception or the Assumption was essential. Their complete absence from the Nicene-Constantinopolitan Creed argues that they are not essential to a robust Christian faith.

Why then are these doctrines necessary to define? And why does the appetite for definition in this matter now extend even further, even to the desire to define Mary as co-redeemer? One cannot argue that the definitions are necessary because the doctrine has developed, for any aspect of faith can more deeply be appreciated without it needing to be defined. Nor can one argue that the doctrine must be defined because of a growth of popular piety. Even if such growth in piety could be demonstrated in the case of the Immaculate Conception or the Assumption, it can scarcely be claimed in the case of Mary as co-redeemer. But there is no necessary connection between growth in piety and official definition.

No, such definitions are acts of power, and when such power is employed where something essential is not being denied, it must be regarded as arbitrary and harmful. It erects the nonessential to the level of the essential, and seeks to create boundaries that truly are barriers. And these barriers not only keep out those who do not yet accept the Christian message, they needlessly divide Christians from each other.

Christians today can learn much about how to think and act as a church both from studying the contents of the creed and from imitating its example of theological reticence.

RECLAIMING THE CREED

I am not so foolish as to think that the Nicene-Constanti-nopolitan Creed is the prescription for all Christianity's contemporary ills. But I am firmly convinced that Christianity today would be healthier—and far more interesting—if it actually believed what the creed says, and acted in a manner that expressed that belief. I would suggest five steps in the process we might call "creedal renewal."

All Christian communities should examine their own practice with regard to the creed. Do they use it in worship? Do they ever preach on it? Does it play any role in their teaching of converts and the young? Does the congregation spend time studying it? Does the creed serve as a Rule of Faith to guide and direct the practices of the congregation? Such self-examination will reveal what the actual role of the creed is in the life of a church, and this is the first step toward recovering its significance.

A second step is devoting serious study to the creed. Christians should learn the origin and functions of the creed, so that they do not regard it as an instrument opposed to Scripture, or as a late imposition of ecclesiastical authority. They should come to grips with the creed's sometimes strange language and ask, "Do we actually know what we are saying when we say this?" Here the same exegetical skills demanded of the responsible reading of Scripture come into play. In fact, an essential dimension of such study is reading Scripture in light of the creed, and the creed in light of Scripture. Only this kind of reading will help Christians understand the reciprocal and mutually informing relationship between Scripture and the creed.

A third step is to move to the harder level of appropriation: "Now that we understand what we are saying, do we still want to say it, do we really believe what these words say?" Congregations must reflect together on the specific congregational practices and personal patterns they should follow to make the creed live in their lives. In this way, the creed becomes the basis for doing theology within the congregation.

A fourth step is using the creed, not only in the Eucharist and in the ritual of baptism, but as a common element in the life of the church. Within the congregation, the creed should become the common point of reference for the reading of Scripture, for the discernment of spirits, for the refining and reforming of practices, for the shaping of character. The creed should also become the rallying point for the church's prophetic voice within the world. Children should be required to memorize the creed as they do the Lord's Prayer and the Ten Commandments, and be given equally serious instruction both in its meaning and in its application, so that the creed becomes one of those living texts that, because they are imprinted early, remain powerfully alive and influential throughout life.

A fifth step is celebrating and defending the creed both within and outside the congregation of the faithful, as the powerful emblem of identity, a coherent statement of life as originating and returning to God, as rescued and enlivened by the Lord Jesus Christ, as empowered and directed by the Holy Spirit, and as lived within a public community of character called the church. To be a creedal Christian is to be a definite Christian. It is also to be a Christian who knows the difference between the nonessential and the essential, who is free to think and imagine boldly within the strong and flexible framework of faith, and who is open to wisdom from any source, confident that wherever there is truth, it is from God.

LUKE TIMOTHY JOHNSON, a former Bene-
dictine monk, is the Robert W. Woodruff Profes-
sor of New Testament at the Candler School of
Theology, Emory University. He is the author of
several books, including *The Real Jesus* and *Living Jesus*, as well as two Anchor Bible Commen-
taries, *The Letters of James* and *I & II Timothy*.